Life With Marian

AND OTHER TOPICS LESS LOVINGLY ADDRESSED

"Her name is Marian,
and she has blessed my life
these past 48 years..."

Life With Marian

AND OTHER TOPICS LESS LOVINGLY ADDRESSED

By Harold W. Andersen

Omaha, Nebraska

The first edition of LIFE WITH MARIAN
was published in 2008 in Omaha, Nebraska, USA.

ISBN 0-9748433-3-4

Published in 2008 by Harold W. Andersen, Omaha, Nebraska.

James. D. Fogarty, Fogarty Creative Group, editor, Omaha, Nebraska.

Wayne Kobza, Pencil to Press, publication design, Omaha, Nebraska.

Printed and bound in the USA.

Cover: April 19, 1952, wedding day of Marian Battey and Harold Andersen.

C O N T E N T S

MY THANKS

My thanks to those who helped make "Life with Marian" a reality.

Thanks first to The Omaha World-Herald for making 15 years' worth of my columns available for selected use in this book.

Then a heartfelt "Thank you!" to the readers, whether they agreed or disagreed with me. Certainly among the factors which encouraged me to keep writing was reader reaction, with special thanks to those who said things like, "Keep writing about Marian and the dogs and your family life."

Especially appreciated also were occasional comments like that from a widow who said that when I wrote about Marian and our family life, it brought back happy memories of the years she had enjoyed with her late husband.

Incidentally but importantly, I should not forget to express my appreciation to my multi-talented editor, Jim Fogarty, to my production designer Wayne Kobza and, of course, to my executive assistant, Jackie Wrieth, who was at her cheerful, competent best in helping us dip deeply into more than 1,300 columns to find the material included in this book.

And most important, my thanks to Marian Andersen. She is a born civic leader but a remarkable wife, mother, grandmother and friend. It is Marian's often humorous but frequently touching interaction with both people and dogs (and sometimes squirrels!) that contributes the most to the readability of this volume.

— **Harold W. Andersen (Andy)**

P R O L O G U E

The opening chapter in the story covered in this volume was written in 1950 when Marian Louise Battey of Lincoln, Neb., and Harold Wayne Andersen of Omaha (that's me) met on a blind double-date ... and she was with the other guy.

That guy was Charlie Thone, a Phi Gamma Delta fraternity brother of mine, a future Nebraska governor and, over the years, a good friend to Marian and me.

Our first official date came on Nov. 20 of that year. Having encountered Marian quite by chance, I mentioned I had two tickets to a Sadler Wells Ballet at the University of Nebraska-Lincoln Coliseum and wondered if she wanted to attend. She did.

I had worked at the World-Herald Lincoln Bureau nearly up to curtain time and didn't get a chance to eat. After the show, Marian took pity on her famished date, brought me to her home and served me a peanut butter sandwich.

Seventeen months later, April 19, 1952, Marian and I were married. But journalism, the University of Nebraska-Lincoln and late dinners remained staples of our lives together.

Nearly 57 years have gone by, and the old newspaperman in me believes it's time to deliver a full report on my "Life with Marian."

Much of what appears in this book already has been published in my twice-weekly column that has appeared in The Omaha World-Herald since 1992. I've devoted my entire column space, at times, to Marian, but more often I've included stories about her as segments of columns. Many of those have appeared at the end of my comments on one or another of the "heavier" news topics of the day.

Marian graduated from the University of Nebraska-Lincoln with a major in journalism. My majors were in English and history, with a minor in journalism.

On public occasions, Marian has more than once kidded me with this: "Imagine how far Andy could have gone in his career if he had majored in journalism."

Over the years, a great many readers have written or said to me: "I read the last item in your column first." As this volume demonstrates, the most likely subject of such final items is Marian.

This book is written for Marian, our children and grandchildren, and we welcome extended family and professional associates here for a look, too. But my mail over the course of 15 years of column writing strongly suggests there's considerable eavesdropping interest in our Andersen family story. Thus, this book is being made available to the public, as well.

In response to readers' stated desires, we have pulled together (and lightly edited) these "Marian" episodes in the first 16 chapters. But my editor, Jim Fogarty, and I felt that a proper mix for this book should also include some of my columns on weightier issues.

So we have devoted the last chapter – 17 – to several columns that don't relate to Marian. These offerings give readers a sampling of my perspective on the sometimes controversial issues of the day.

Life with Marian inevitably involved her active interest in support of my work. She has been the bright, widely-read advisor on column content, and columns were regularly reviewed by her before publication.

We thought it appropriate to include a sampling of columns which didn't include anecdotes about Marian, but were certainly much a part of "Life with Marian" during the 15 years the columns appeared twice weekly.

* * *

As many of my World-Herald column readers know, my weekly offerings now are available on an Internet site: www.haroldandersen.com. If you are not already receiving a weekly reminder of the column and each week's subject matter and would like such a reminder, let us know via the website.

— **Harold W. Andersen (Andy)**

Such a Remarkable Person

Among the tens of thousands of lines I have written these past 15 years, many describe the relationship I continue to enjoy with Marian, my wife of 56 years. Following in this chapter are columns and segments devoted to a favorite topic … life with Marian.

'Wife Tops List of Life's Greatest Blessings'

As I count the blessings that are special to me this Thanksgiving season, it's not hard to start my list: Her name is Marian, and she has blessed my life these past 48 years.

Today, her right arm suspended in a pillow-like sling following her eighth major orthopedic surgical procedure, she continues to radiate that warmth of personality and concern for others (thankfully including me!) that makes her such a remarkable person.

Marian's reaction to her long siege of surgery tells a good deal about the upbeat way she approaches life. With a medical record that includes four artificial hip joint implants (two in each hip, need I explain?), an artificial right knee joint, rotator cuff repair and the fusing of a cervical disc, I've never once heard her complain. Her attitude is consistently positive, grateful for the fact that her serious involvement with osteoarthritis can be surgically addressed.

Marian with Sister and Sugar.

She has become something of a counselor to acquaintances with joint problems. Her consistent advice, given diplomatically but clearly, is to stop limping painfully around and consult a doctor about the possibility of surgical relief.

Marian's resilience in the face of surgical adversity is noteworthy. She rebounds quickly, as evidenced by the fact that on her second day home after three recent days in the hospital following rotator cuff surgery, her right arm in a sling, she served me left-hand-scrambled eggs for breakfast while trying to take charge of the allocation of our tickets for the Colorado-Nebraska football game.

> "Marian's memory for names and dates – especially people-related dates like birthdays – continues to astound me after all these years."

(I know there are readers out there who have demonstrated – or who have loved ones who have demonstrated – courage and grace in the face of physical adversity over a period of years. In telling Marian's story, I would hope to indicate my admiration for all those individuals whose stories would make compelling reading if I were in a position to report them.)

* * *

Marian's friends and I could cite countless examples of her genuine interest in other people, their lives and their problems. A typical example:

Late one evening I heard Marian on the phone discussing an airline ticket reservation with a United Airlines employee in Denver. It seemed to me the conversation was taking longer than should be necessary to make a reservation. I figured out what had happened when I heard Marian say something like:

"Well, it's certainly been nice talking with you. And I hope your mother gets to feeling better real soon."

Marian's memory for names and dates – especially people-related dates like birthdays – continues to astound me after all these years. I can walk into a cocktail party and work hard to remember the names of two or three people I've met, while Marian can give you the name of everyone she's met, where everyone is from and, likely as not, how many children they have.

* * *

As for her memory of birth dates, a recent example: I was on a mid-November golfing trip with the Fairfield brothers, Terry, president of the University of Nebraska Foundation, and Bill, chief executive officer of Inacom.

Marian said to be sure to wish the Fairfields a happy birthday. She had remembered that they were born, two years apart, on the same day of the year, Nov. 30. (I'll leave it to Bill or Terry to tell you who is older.)

It is this genuine interest in others that, I believe, has led Marian to work so hard on behalf of so many civic causes dedicated to helping others – whether they be students at the University of Nebraska or recipients of the various services the American Red Cross and United Way of the Midlands provide to people in need.

Marian's civic service was well summarized by Loretta Carroll of KMTV when Marian was recognized as one of KMTV's Women of Mid-America. Carroll said of Marian:

"Marian Andersen … who has shown again and again that women of ability and determination can make great contributions to society.

"As chairman of the National Search Committee, Marian recruited Elizabeth Dole to serve as president of the American Red Cross, and she co-founded the Alexis de Tocqueville Society of United Way. Marian's numerous leadership roles have brought such events as Shakespeare on the Green to thousands in our community. If there was a glass ceiling standing in her way, Marian Andersen simply ignored it, or broke through it, becoming the first woman to head the University of Nebraska Foundation and the Heartland Chapter of the American Red Cross."

On the occasion of Marian's 60th birthday, I prepared a special card in the form of an "Honorary Degree of Doctor of Friendship and Concern for Others." Half lightheartedly and half seriously, I listed these among Marian's achievements worthy of special recognition:

"Exhibiting the good judgment to pursue and capture a Scandinavian-American for her husband.

"Adding immeasurably to the clinical experience – and the income – of a wide spectrum of members of the medical profession, including (but not limited to) three orthopedic surgeons, a plastic surgeon, two internal medicine specialists and anesthesiologists and radiologists beyond count.

"Educating countless listeners (some of them even interested listeners) in the strategic intricacies and the statistics, as well as the personalities involved, in a wide range of competitive athletics.

"Finding time in the midst of all her other activities (civic duties, visits to hospital emergency rooms and doctors offices and all the rest) to be a splendid wife and mother. (The fact that during her tenure as president of the Omaha Junior League, she temporarily forgot the names of her two children and on several occasions neglected to chill her husband's martini glass was considered by the family to be a forgivable departure from the norm.)

"Doing all of these things with an unfailing sense of good humor and a warmth of personality and friendship based on a genuine interest in the lives and welfare of others, thereby touching many lives in a most positive way."

Touching many lives in a most positive way, including especially, of course, my life and that of our children, Dave and Nancy.

What better words to suggest why my list of blessings this Thanksgiving season starts with the name Marian.

* * *

I should give credit to the late Jim Murray, superb sports columnist of the Los Angeles Times, and to the editors of the Times for prompting me to write today's column. After Murray's recent death, the Times republished several of his most memorable columns. One was a very moving tribute to his wife, written shortly after her death. The column ended with the thought of what Murray had intended to tell his wife on their 39th wedding anniversary, which they never reached. Murray wrote:

"I had my speech all ready. I was going to look into her brown eyes and tell her something I should have long ago. I was going to tell her, 'It was a privilege just to have known you.' I never got to say it."

I decided I would write the column you are reading today, making sure that Marian is here to read the sentiments I am proud to share with my readers.

* * *

Incidentally, Marian's favorite among the get-well messages that came her way this past week: The cover page of the card advises, "Sit back, relax, let people wait on you."

Turn the page and you read: "In other words, act like a man."

— **November 29, 1998**

Well-Merited Tribute

Hey, fellow husbands, no really hard feelings, I hope.

I refer to some of the reaction I received to my column last Sunday in which I said that heading my list of special blessings at the Thanksgiving season is my wife, Marian, who has blessed my life these past 48 years.

I went into considerable detail, and the result was the greatest response to any column that I have written.

Several friends and fellow husbands passed along comments like this from my brother-in-law, Charles Battey, Jr., of Kansas City, Kan., who said the column "makes it awfully hard on the rest of us." But like the other husbands who commented in this vein, Chuck added that he thought the column was a well-merited tribute to a wonderful wife.

The calls and letters included messages from four or five wives who said the column moved them to tears. One husband wrote that his wife had "started to read your column aloud to me, but could not finish it. She was crying."

Another friend said his wife had shown him the column, which he described as "a wonderful love song." Then he summarized my feelings about as well as I could have done: "She is a grand, brave, gracious woman, and you are a lucky man."

Three husbands wrote to express thanks for, as one of them said, "a great reminder to all the rest of us to tell our loved ones how much we care, as often as we possibly can."

If the column had produced no other result than this "great reminder," it was well worth the writing, I believe.

— December 13, 1998

Continuing Responses

Good news also – good news, at least, to me – are the continuing responses to my column describing Marian as the greatest of my blessings this holiday season and every other season.

I'm not thinking only of the positive things that many readers have said about Marian and about my having written about her. I'm thinking particularly of messages like the one that came this past week from an old friend who said his wife cut the column out "as a reminder to me, and I was happy for the needed nudge."

My friend also wrote something that I think implies good advice for all of us:

"It is very heartwarming and inspirational to read of your devotion to each other after 48 years of marriage. In fact, it would be encouraging if more couples felt that way about each other at any time during their marriage.

> *"The best gift you can give to your children is a solid marriage built on love and respect. You certainly have given that to Dave and Nancy."*

"The best gift you can give to your children is a solid marriage built on love and respect. You certainly have given that to Dave and Nancy."

Another reader called to say that he had recently lost his wife and my column prompted him to share a poem with me. He read the poem over the phone. It included these sentiments:

"The time is now. If you're ever going to love me, love me now while I can know the sweet and tender feelings which from true affection flow.

"Love me now while I am living. Do not wait until I'm gone and then have it chiseled in marble, sweet words on ice-cold stone.

"So if you love me even a little bit, let me know it while I'm living so I can know and treasure it."

The caller added: "And, you know, until you lose a wife, you really don't know how much that poem means."

As we concluded our pleasant conversation, the caller and I agreed on an important expansion of the thoughts we had been discussing: While we should tell our mates how much we love them, we should also tell our children and our parents, and tell them now.

— December 24, 1998

What Better Way?

A final word on the column in which I said I count Marian as my greatest blessing during the season of Thanksgiving and in every other season:

The continuing response to that column is by far the greatest I have received following anything I've written.

So to each of those who commented favorably – by letter, phone or in person – Marian joins me in a heartfelt "Thank you!" for your comments.

And please hold on to the thought suggested by what I wrote: If you love someone very much – husband or wife, child or parent – deliver the message, and deliver it now.

— February 14, 1999

Appreciating Blessings Begins With One's Family

An addition to those Thanksgiving Day sentiments of three years ago:

Certainly among the blessings to be recalled every Thanksgiving Day is the love that is shared throughout the year by the entire family, including son David and his wife, the former Leslie Roe of Bennington, and daughter Nancy Karger of Denver. And, of course, the six grandchildren: Lindsey, Robbie and Katie Andersen and Jack, James and Grant Karger.

As I've said in this space before, I know there are many proud parents and grandparents out there, and I'd like to think that I am, in a way, speaking for all of them when I speak of the love that Marian and I share for our children and our grandchildren. It's just that I have the advantage of being able to name them and write about them in a very public forum, the pages of The Omaha World-Herald.

— November 22, 2001

Old Family Photos Are Treasures to be Organized and Distributed

Advice for anyone (I know you're out there – lots and lots of you) who has a large collection of unorganized, unmounted family photographs:

Run, do not walk, to the room or rooms where those unorganized photos have accumulated. Get on promptly with the job of organizing and distributing them in whatever fashion best suits your family's needs. But don't put it off any longer.

I speak from experience. Even with the dedicated help of my efficient secretary, Jackie Wrieth, who probably worked more hours on the project than I did, I put in countless hours sifting through a 50-year accumulation of photographs and letters and other memorabilia, making copies in numerous cases and organizing them for mounting in albums which I gave to family members to commemorate Marian's and my 50th wedding anniversary.

I decided that rather than hinting for a gift involving gold (that is the 50th anniversary metal, isn't it?), I would do the gift presenting, with the result that two-volume sets of photographs, with handwritten comments alongside a good number of the pictures, were presented to a surprised daughter Nancy, son David and roommate Marian. The title embossed on each volume: The Andersen Family. A Love Story.

I'm certainly glad that Jackie and I did it, because the response was enthusiastic, as I had hoped.

I highly recommend that you or some other family member take on such a task, if you haven't already done so. It will ease your conscience, and your family members will be delighted, I predict.

I had set aside a desk drawer in which I collected notes and birthday cards and Mother's and Father's Day cards that Dave and Nancy had written Marian and me over the years. In the photo albums, I included some narrative material reporting some of the contents of that drawer.

For example:

A brief "I love you, Daddy," note from little Nancy. It had to be brief, since it was written on the back of a Doublemint gum wrapper.

And a note of the type that Nancy frequently wrote me when I was headed out of town on some business trip. The message typically said Nancy hoped I would have a good time and ended with symbols for lots of hugs and kisses. There were also enclosures with such messages. In one case, a 25-cent piece – Nancy wanted me to have a little spending money on the road – and a lime Lifesaver.

Dave, who showed a talent for drawing at an early age, presented Marian and me with a number of hand-drawn cards, including one that, along with a Father's Day greeting, made me an "honorary member of the Fairacres Volunteer Fire Department." This took note of the fact that real Fire Department firefighters had appeared on the scene when I accidentally set off our fire alarm system.

Among the cards Dave drew for Marian, one of my favorites showed her playing tennis and included this wording recognizing her 48th birthday: "Mrs. Andersen, don't you think you're a little over the hill for this?" Marian's reply, according to Dave's card: "Over the hill? Why, I haven't even started climbing yet!"

Among the family memories recalled in the narrative I wrote for the volumes, one of my favorites was this:

We were driving back from Lincoln from Marian's mother's funeral. Nancy, 10, said she wondered where Gram was now. Dave, 13, had a quick reply: "Gram's an apprentice angel now."

Marian and the children had suggested various ways to recognize our 50th anniversary. One proposal was that we take the whole family on a Disney World cruise in the Caribbean. I said I would be glad to pay for the cruise if I were allowed to stay home.

Dave and wife, Leslie, invited Marian and me to an anniversary dinner at Cafe de Paris. When Dave and Leslie stopped by to pick us up, the doorbell rang and there, to our delighted surprise, was daughter Nancy, who had come from Denver.

We had a delightful dinner. We talked, of course, about old family times and about new family times involving six grandchildren.

Marian and I could not have imagined a nicer anniversary celebration.

— June 23, 2002

Other Blessings I Share

Moving beyond family, let me speak of other blessings I share with so many of you: Gratitude for the opportunity to live in the heartland area of a nation that has brought freedom and opportunity to its citizens in ways unequaled anywhere else in the history of the world. America in a sense is still a work in progress, with its blessings not shared as widely as we hope and continue to work toward. But Thanksgiving Day, it seems to me, is a time to emphasize blessings. We surely hear enough about our continuing problems during the rest of the year.

And I know I'm dealing with a common theme when I say my Thanksgiving list of blessings emphatically includes the friendship of a good many people and a special friendship with those to whom we feel especially close.

Irish poet William Butler Yeats expressed the value of friendship as beautifully as I have ever seen it described when he wrote these lines:

> *Think where man's glory*
> *most begins and ends,*
> *and say my glory was*
> *I had such friends.*

A heartfelt "Amen!" to that.

— **November 27, 2003**

A Last-Minute Gift

Old work habits are hard to change, especially when you enjoy the work.

That truism crossed my mind on Christmas Eve when I left the office about 4:30 p.m., having finished a couple of columns that would be published in the following weeks.

My mind went back to a Christmas Eve day a half-century ago – sometime in the early 1950s, after Marian and I were married in 1952. It was about 3:30 p.m. when I finished teletyping my final story for the Christmas Day edition. From The World-Herald Lincoln Bureau in the Federal Securities Building, I headed north for a block or so to the Hovland-Swanson store on Lincoln's O Street, looking for my "big" (some of our gifts weren't all that big in those days) present for Marian.

Fortunately I found the present quickly – a red jacket that, as it happily turned out, Marian liked very much.

Last Christmas Eve day, I was happy that I didn't have to leave the office and come up with an 11th-hour Christmas gift for Marian. Her "big" gift had already been selected. It was considerably more expensive than that red casual jacket but was no more meaningful to me – and I hope to Marian – than that last-minute gift purchased a half-century ago.

— **January 4, 2004**

Parallel Lives

We are six years older, and we have six grandchildren instead of four. But those six years have only given me added reason to say again how my list of Thanksgiving season blessings begins.

I wrote this in 1998: "As I count the blessings that are special to me this Thanksgiving season, it's not hard to start my list: Her name is Marian, and she has blessed my life these past 48 years."

My decision to repeat those words this year was prompted by a very welcome communication from a valued longtime friend, Emil Reutzel, retired editor of the Norfolk Daily News.

From the Reutzels' home in Coronado, Calif., Emil a few weeks ago sent along a copy of that 1998 column. He said his wife, Chloe, had saved it these past six years.

Emil indicated that he wanted Marian and me to know how much he and Chloe had been impressed by that husband's tribute to his wife. And he indicated also that my words reflected the kinds of feelings he holds for Chloe.

* * *

I hope you won't think it presumptuous if I offer a few pieces of advice this Thanksgiving Day:

Take some time to reflect, preferably in rather specific terms, on the things you have reason to be thankful for.

Take time also to think about what you might be doing as an individual, or joining with others, to see that the good things in the American way of life are more broadly shared. Remember how much I appreciate your readership and your comments. And tell someone that you love him or her. (Telling several someones would be even better.)

— **November 25, 2004**

Grandkids, Hip Surgery and Sugar Magnolia

Grandchildren; Marian: sports fan and baseball expert; the NRA; Marian's hip surgery – with dedicated health providers at UNMC; the Navy chief's a flier, just like son, David; crutch-chasing lawyers; "Health Nazi" sets fat quotas; where's the phone?; memories of Sugar Magnolia; Sugar II moves in; reader feedback.

Gladness and Sadness

Let me deal today with some things that gladden or sadden one's life.

Grandchildren have all manner of ways to charm grandparents – who are, of course, eagerly available to be charmed.

Our granddaughter, Lindsey Andersen, has come up with a somewhat unusual but definitely direct route to Grandmother Marian's heart.

A bit of background: My wife, Marian, is a sports enthusiast. (She has told me I must stop calling her a sports nut.)

She has, as perhaps the most outstanding example, seen a baseball game in 26 of the 28 major league baseball parks. And the only reason she hasn't seen a game in the two newest major league parks – in Denver and Miami – is because the first games won't be played in those major league expansion cities until this spring.

On a not untypical summer evening, Marian may have three television sets going – family room, kitchen, garden room – so as she moves around she can watch the Braves, the Cubs or the Mets and whatever teams might be playing on ESPN that evening.

Like many another grandchild, Lindsey, who will be 3 next month, is nothing if not observant of what goes on in the adult world around her.

Still, it was something of a surprise – a very pleasant surprise to Marian, whom Lindsey calls Muz – when on a recent visit to our home, trailing along behind grandmother as she regularly does, Lindsey came upon the garden room television set and suggested:

"Hey, Muz, let's turn on a baseball game."

Now little Lindsey obviously doesn't know precisely when baseball season begins. But she clearly understands that her pal Muz is hooked on the game.

And she seems quite ready to share her grandmother's enthusiasm for America's national pastime. At least that's the way we read the signs, which include Lindsey's rendition of "Take Me Out to the Ball Game."

Believe me, Lindsey will be taken out to the ball game this summer. She and Muz are laying plans for an early-season visit to Rosenblatt Stadium to see the Omaha Royals play.

If you'll indulge a grandfather in another comment about the daughter of our son, David R. Andersen, and his wife, the former Leslie Roe of Bennington:

Lindsey was a premature baby. Her early arrival, of course, gave us some early concern.

But we now entertain the theory that this little bundle of energy and alertness perhaps was just eager to get started with growing up and enjoying life, so she opted for a two-month head start on those nine-month babies.

Lindsey and Muz.

— **February 28, 1993**

———————— • ◆ • ————————

Advisor Suggests a Respite

Followers of "Rumpole of Bailey," a delightful series that appeared on ETV a few years ago, will recall that when Rumpole, the British barrister, referred to his wife, it was frequently as "she who must be obeyed."

In our household, there is no wife "who must be obeyed." But Marian does frequently offer advice, usually very good advice. A recent example:

"Why don't you come home this afternoon instead of writing a weekly column? Your regular readers may miss you, but then they should enjoy your next column all the more."

This will serve as notice to those regular readers – bless your hearts – that occasionally I'm going to follow the advice of my best friend and take a week off from punditry.

So for those who have been kind enough to say they look forward to the column, please don't lose interest during the occasional absences. I'll be back.

For one thing, I will want to tell you of some of my recent mail. Included is a letter from a central Nebraska National Rifle Association member. He wrote the executive director of the NRA, suggesting that the NRA expel me as a disloyal member. The fellow even offered to contribute $25 more per year so the NRA wouldn't lose revenue if I am kicked out.

— April 11, 1993

Navy Chief is a Pilot

Our son, Dave, wants the world to know that the new chief of naval operations comes out of the Navy's air arm.

Nothing against those good Americans who serve on destroyers and cruisers and the like, nor those who go to sea submerged in submarines like the USS Nebraska.

It's just that news stories telling of Adm. Jay Johnson's appointment to the top job in the Navy have referred to his recent assignments – most

David flew as a radar intercept officer in F-14s.

recently as deputy chief of naval operations – but not to the fact that he started his career and advanced through the command structure as a naval aviator. And Dave, who served eight years in the naval air arm, is under-

David aboard the USS America.

standably proud of the fact that he sailed and flew with the new chief of naval operations, then a captain.

In the 1988-90 time span, Johnson was commander of the nine-squadron air wing on the USS America.

Johnson was an F-14 pilot. Dave, now a broker with Paine Webber here in Omaha, recalls fly-

ing several times as the "second-seater" (radar intercept officer) in F-14s piloted by Johnson while the America was cruising in the Mediterranean and later on winter maneuvers in the North Atlantic.

— June 16, 1993

And Now, 'Crutch-Chasers'

Last Sunday my column referred to an overabundance of attorneys and unnecessary litigation. An interesting coincidence:

On the same day that the column was published, my wife was grocery shopping when a friendly appearing man stopped her and said something like:

"Pardon me, but I noticed that you are on crutches. Have you been in an auto accident?" Marian replied no, she was recovering from surgery involving replacement of an arthritic hip joint.

The friendly stranger explained that if Marian had been involved in an auto accident, he was going to give her the name of an attorney friend of his who does a good job representing people injured in auto accidents.

We've all heard the expression "ambulance-chasing" in regard to zealous pursuit of legal business. But I had never before heard of an example of what might be called "crutch-chasing."

*   *   *

Marian has described herself as my "health Nazi." I love her for her good intentions, although sometimes those intentions produce a line of advice and questioning that seems to make her "health Nazi" self-description reasonably accurate.

The other day I sent out for a sandwich to eat at my desk.

"What did you have for lunch today?" Marian asked. Hesitantly, I replied, "An egg salad sandwich."

Marian's reaction: "I love egg salad sandwiches – now if they just didn't have eggs in them …"

Marian, you see, is very high – or should I say very low – on cholesterol as a food component to be watched. She is also very attentive to the fat level of certain foods.

Mention a food and the quantity involved, and Marian will instantly reply with something like:

"That's 20 grams of fat, and that's a third of your daily allowable quota."

I find that many of my male friends – the married ones – are subject to similar "advice" from their health fuehrer.

Marian recuperating after hip surgery.

Take an after-golf luncheon in the locker room, and chances are that three of the four fellows in your foursome will describe the things that they hadn't better have for lunch because their wives wouldn't approve.

— August 1, 1993

'There's the Phone'

Surely I can't be the only one to wish that television programs of any kind would never, never include ringing telephones.

Too often I find myself saying, "Marian, there's the phone," only to learn that the phone is ringing in the home of a family featured in a TV ad or sitcom.

Why do I say, "Marian, there's the phone?" Before being accused of male chauvinism, let me explain:

Long experience has proven that the overwhelming majority of telephone calls directed to our home are for Marian.

In a recent two-week test period, 89.9 percent of the calls directed to our home were for Marian. For outgoing calls, Marian's percentage rose to 98.3.

No, no, I didn't really run a test. But I would submit that an actual tally would produce something very close to those percentages.

It thus becomes simply a practical matter to let Marian answer the phone.

And before some feminist raises the question, let me say that I don't do windows either. But then, neither does Marian.

— **November 7, 1993**

Sugar's Eyes

A reader's letter about the loss of her dog brought to mind the last time I saw Sugar Magnolia, one of our cocker spaniels.

I still get a lump in my throat as I think of that final visit to the veterinarian's, where dear little Sugar was dying of liver failure.

When the nurse brought her into the receiving room, her head was drooping as she lay cradled in a blanket in the nurse's arms. She raised her head just a trifle and her eyes turned toward me, as if in recognition.

I scratched her ears and kissed her three times, put on my sunglasses (it was really not sunny as I left the reception room) and drove home.

Marian and I still have happy memories of Sugar bouncing down the stairs, her ears flying, with an exuberance that seemed to say, "Here I am! What can I do to make you happy today?"

But I also have that memory of the look in Sugar's eyes as she seemed to recognize me as she lay in the nurse's arms. I wonder what that little brain was thinking.

Perhaps: "Yes, I know you, and I know you would help me if you could."

And to this day, little Sugar, I do so wish I could have helped you.

* * *

A happier turn of events followed Sugar's departure from a home she had brightened for five years.

A very good friend, Mrs. Mark Kratina, whose children had voted cocker spaniels as the family dog after meeting our cockers, decided that the best medicine for Marian and me was to get another cocker spaniel.

We still had Sister, the other member of the pair of cockers who had been part of the family, but Sugar's departure left a void.

So Janet Kratina, bless her friendly heart, set out to find a cocker puppy for the Andersen family. She made long-distance calls without success and finally found a beguiling puppy close by at the Council Bluffs kennels of Paul Hadfield.

We could think of no greater tribute to the first Sugar than to name our new cocker Sugar II. In a way, a new dog can never truly replace one you have lost, but we have continued happily to be a two-cocker family (plus a few hunting dogs who live off premises). And we continue to be grateful to Janet Kratina for having found such a delightful new member of the family.

And speaking of being a two-dog family, I think of a conversation I had with the late Angie Skutt. She and husband, V. J., were two of the grandest people whom Marian and I have had the privilege to know.

It was at a dinner party one evening when we got to talking about dogs, and Angie said: "Andy, why in the world would you have two dogs living with you?" And I replied: "Because I absolutely refuse to allow Marian to have three dogs."

— November 21, 1993

No Last Tasty Bite

Readers of this column – bless their hearts – sometimes have clever ways of letting me know that they have been reading my weekly output.

At a dinner in Blair honoring major donors to Dana College's most recent major fund-raising effort, a smiling lady came up to me after dinner and said, "I was watching to see if your wife would let you eat all of your meat tonight." (The meal had featured several generous slices of chateaubriand.)

I was puzzled until Ruth Schaff, wife of the Rev. Robert Schaff, minister of the Lutheran Church of the Master in Omaha, reminded me that I had written recently about Marian's intense interest in my intake of calories in general and fatty calories in particular.

I told Mrs. Schaff that I had left some of the meat uneaten, despite the temptation to consume the last tasty bite. And I said, like a proud pupil, that I did so without any coaching from my calorie-counting teacher, who was sitting next to me.

On a Monday morning, after publication of a column in which I had discussed the nine-to-one odds against winning even one dollar in the Nebraska state lottery, another smiling lady, Sibby Wolfson of Omaha, volunteered this information:

"I want you to know that I didn't take the chance of betting $9 to win $1."

— December 5, 1993

CHAPTER 3 - 1994

Jungles of India to the Court of Ak-Sar-Ben

An elephant ride to see a mother tiger & four cubs; Brijendra Singh; Vinod Gupta; Andersen's Law of Home Maintenance; vehicular liberation after a 4th hip surgery; Sister's 9th birthday; Mike Walsh's splendid life; gun issues and Sarah Brady; Marian inducted into Ak-Sar-Ben's Court of Honor; preventative approaches to health; a Christmas gift.

In India, Trailing a Tigress and Her Cubs

So there we were, Marian and I, riding along on an elephant's back with the grandson of an Indian maharajah, looking for a mother tiger and her four cubs.

As we came out of the lush green tangle of the forest, the setting sun was painting a delicate pattern of bright purple and muted orange in the mists above the Himalayan foothills.

Although we saw the bones of a small deer she had killed to feed her family, we didn't see the tigress and her cubs, but we did meet one of the most interesting and impressive characters whom we have encountered in our 41 years of traveling.

His name is Brijendra Singh. His grandfather was a wealthy maharajah ruling one of the native states in the Punjab in the northwest area of India in the days of British rule before Indian independence.

Brijendra could have used his inheritance to finance a life of leisure. Instead, he chose a career of public service, concentrating on the preservation of wildlife, especially the Indian tiger.

Not that Brijendra hadn't killed tigers in his time. He shot his first at age 11. But with the alarming decline in the tiger population in recent decades, he does his shooting now with a camera and works as a member of the steering committee of Project Tiger.

We met Brijendra in Jim Corbett National Park, an 817-square-mile nature reserve in northern India. It is named for an Englishman who gained fame as a killer of man-eating tigers and as an articulate advocate of wildlife conservation.

In 1973, Project Tiger was inaugurated in Corbett National Park where Brijendra Singh is a regular visitor and conservation leader.

Project Tiger has been successful in the tiger reserve in and around Jim Corbett Park, where the tiger census has risen from 57 in 1976 to 90 in 1993. (There is some feeling that the official census figure of 90 may be somewhat low and that there could be closer to 120 tigers in the area now.)

In the 18 other tiger reserves in India, however, the story is not encour-

Marian, Brijendra, Andy and guide riding an elephant in India along the Himalayan foothills.

aging. A Nov. 20 report in The Times of India said that the official census will show fewer than 4,000 tigers – a further decline from the already alarming estimated total of 4,334 tigers in India in 1984.

Devastating poaching has resulted largely from the demand for tiger bones to be used in various medicines in China. The other serious pressure on the tiger population – disappearance of favorable habitat – was blamed in The Times of India article on "the land and timber mafia which includes local criminals and politicians."

Brijendra Singh paid a tribute to American hunters, contrasting them with many of the hunters in other parts of the world.

"In America, sportsmen are the best wildlife conservationists, realizing the importance of financial support for wildlife preservation and the necessity of closed seasons and reasonable bag limits during the open seasons," Brijendra said.

As Marian and I rode atop that elephant with Brijendra, I asked what would happen if we spotted the tigress and her cubs. Brijendra indicated that tigers, like many other wild animals, aren't looking for confrontation with humans and thus the tigress would be unlikely to charge us.

However, he said, the particular elephant on which we were riding "doesn't like tigers" and might charge the tigress.

Marian and I quickly agreed that, unlike our elephant, we had nothing against tigers and would settle for spotting the tigress and her cubs from a safe distance.

We were in India as a guest of Vinod Gupta, a native of India who earned two graduate degrees at the University of Nebraska-Lincoln and now lives in Omaha where he has built a successful company, American Business Information Inc.

Vin makes regular visits to be with family and friends in India, where he moves in influential circles. (We had tea at the presidential palace as guests of Vin's friend, A. D. Sharma, son of the president of India.)

Others among Vin's guests were Gary Schwendiman, dean of the College of Business Administration at the University of Nebraska-Lincoln, and Bill Kerrey and his wife, Terry. Bill Kerrey is a vice president of American Business Information.

While looking for a way to express our appreciation for the splendid hospitality which was extended to us at Jim Corbett Park, we learned that Brijendra Singh and his wife are patrons of a school for children of the staff at the park. We offered to contribute to a "Nebraska Fund" as an endowment to help finance the continuing operations of the school.

We were astounded to learn, from an enthusiastic and grateful Brijendra, that 3,000 American dollars would create an endowment whose income would "assure the life of this school for 20 years."

So in the years to come we will find satisfaction in knowing that a modest contribution on our part is helping finance the education of some children half a world away – children like the youngster who proudly recited the ABCs, to show that his class is learning English as well as Hindi.

— January 9, 1994

Andersen's Law

Marian said it was time for a minor face-lifting job in our kitchen and laundry area.

So the other morning, I counted five people in the kitchen (six if you include Marian) plotting strategy as to how to color-coordinate the new floor, the new cabinets, the new counter tops and the new sink. (Insofar as I know, the light fixtures will not be changed.)

Outside in the driveway, I counted five vehicles that had brought this small army of "minor face-lifters" to our home.

I told the assemblage in the kitchen that I was promulgating Andersen's Law of Home Maintenance (for future application, of course): If it takes more than three cars to bring the workmen to our job site, we can't afford the project and should scrub it.

If I were given to gambling, I'd bet that Andersen's Law will be violated – probably next year, when Marian and our friend and interior designer, Jan Buckingham, decide on another "minor face-lifting" in another part of the house.

— January 23, 1994

Vehicular Liberation

Recovering nicely from her fourth hip operation, Marian had been bugging her doctor for approval to start driving again.

Six weeks after the very complicated but very successful surgery, Dr. Kevin Garvin gave his cautious approval. I joined Dr. Garvin in admonitions as to the care Marian should exercise.

It was with these admonitions in mind that Marian informed me that she planned her first driving excursion but "only to a couple of small places."

It had not previously occurred to me that the hazards associated with driving bear some direct

> It had not previously occurred to me that the hazards associated with driving bear some direct relationship to the size of your destination.

relationship to the size of your destination. When I pointed this out to Marian, we both had a hearty laugh – and she returned safely from her driving excursion to those "small places."

Encouraged by her success on the first day of her vehicular liberation, Marian stepped up the pace a bit the next day, leaving me a note that she was going to drive to "several medium places."

She returned safe and sound from her "medium places" excursion. She has not yet informed me of her plans to take on some "big place" destinations.

— February 6, 1994

Sister's 9th Birthday

It was Apology Week on Prairie Avenue.

Not Marian apologizing to me or me apologizing to Marian. It was Marian apologizing to Sister, our 9-year-old cocker spaniel.

A few weeks ago we had thrown a birthday party for Sister on what Marian said was her 10th birthday. (You'll note I'm placing the blame on Marian, but that's because I can't remember anybody's birthday except my own, and Marian usually has a steel-trap memory for everybody's birthday.)

The other day it occurred to Marian that Sister, the elder of our two cocker spaniels, was really 9 years old. Sister, of course, is a female. And you just don't do any tampering with a female's age – unless, of course, the female herself decides to do a bit of creative birthday subtraction. (I must quickly add that males have been known to do this, too.)

So Marian apologized to Sister, saying something like, "We're so glad you're 9 instead of 10. That means you have even more time to spend being such a lovable part of our family."

Now to some readers, I suppose, that sounds pretty schmaltzy. But dog owners will understand.

— May 8, 1994

Mike Walsh's Life a Splendid History

When I heard of my friend Mike Walsh's death, somehow these lines from "The Rubaiyat of Omar Khayyam" came to mind:

"The moving finger writes, and, having writ, moves on. Nor all your piety nor wit shall lure it back to cancel half a line, nor all your tears wash out a word of it."

The moving finger has sadly written finis to the life of Mike Walsh, and neither prayers nor tears can change that final chapter.

But what a splendid history of a man's life – all too short a life, but a splendid history nonetheless – had been written before Mike Walsh died in Houston early this month, a victim of cancer at the age of 51.

Marian and I became close friends of Joan and Mike Walsh during the five years that Mike spent in Omaha as chairman and chief executive officer of the Union Pacific Railroad before moving to Houston to become chairman and CEO of Tenneco, Inc.

Marian and I knew Mike and Joan and their children – Kim, Jenny and Jeff – as around-the-corner neighbors.

When Marian stopped by on one of her neighborhood dog walks, our cocker spaniels, Sister and Sugar I, were free to roam the Walsh house as if it were their own. You have to like neighbors like that.

So Marian and I came to know Mike not just as a bright, charismatic, exceptional business leader but also as an exemplary husband and father and warmhearted and witty friend.

Mike and Joan liked nothing better than to entertain friends and children of friends at parties

Andy, Marian and Mike Walsh.

where beneath the laughter you could feel the warmth of deep affection.

Mike loved to ski and ride horseback, especially with son Jeff. He kept in trim physical shape, a fact he once demonstrated to us by doing a standing-start jump over a sofa.

Several hundred of Mike's friends and business associates from across the country, including a number of Omahans, gathered in Houston Thursday for what proved to be a very moving memorial service.

Father Val J. Peter, executive director of Boys Town, on whose board Mike Walsh served, brought a message of thanks for what Mike had contributed to the welfare of the 17,000 young people whom Boys Town serves in Omaha and a number of other cities.

Father Peter spoke of Mike Walsh as a man with a brilliant mind who "wanted to make a difference by helping."

The three Walsh children spoke, their remarks a mixture of love and laughter as they recalled memories of life with their remarkable father.

Another speaker was John W. Gardner, former secretary of Health, Education and Welfare, the founder of Common Cause and architect of the White House Fellowship Program. Informed of Mike's death, Gardner had said:

"Mike Walsh was one of the most gifted leaders of his generation … Many large organizations tend toward rigidity and lethargy. Mike Walsh knew how to make them jump."

Included in the memorial service was the reading of a letter from President Clinton, who wrote of Mike Walsh:

"The example he set and his guidance will live with us forever."

> "… if Mike were here today he would do precisely two things: the first would be to change every detail of this memorial service, and the second would be to either shake your hand, or hug you, and say, 'Thanks for being a player in my life, how lucky I've been.'"

The printed program from the memorial service included a "Dear Friends and Family" letter from Joan Walsh. Joan wrote:

"… if Mike were here today he would do precisely two things: the first would be to change every detail of this memorial service, and the second would be to either shake your hand, or hug you, and say, 'Thanks for being a player in my life, how lucky I've been.'"

The printed program included a number of quotes from Mike, including this advice for young people looking to rise to leadership positions in the business world:

"The main requirements of leadership are guts and judgment. To win trust, you have to make yourself vulnerable. You've got to be out there dealing with real problems, on the front line where people can watch you and personally size you up …

"You'll need to be strong enough to enjoy having other, strong people around you … You'll also need to like taking risks."

And this quote from Mike Walsh in regard to the illness that was to take his life:

"I know that only 15,000 out of 250 million Americans contract brain tumors … but for some reason I just don't have an ounce of 'why me?' in me. I've already had way more luck in life than I ever deserved."

Marian and I will remember Mike as a superb business leader who left his imprint on the Union Pacific Railroad as well as Tenneco.

We will also remember Mike as a former White House Fellow whose sense of public service led him to spend several years as a public defender and U.S. district attorney for Southern California and kept him on the Boys Town board after he had moved to Houston.

But the Andersen family's most heartwarming memories of Mike Walsh will be of a cherished friend whose family, we hope, is finding consolation in the splendid legacy that Mike Walsh left for them and all others whose lives he touched.

— May 15, 1994

'Both Sides Debate Gun Issue Emotionally'

Readers of these weekly musings will recall an occasional column criticizing the leadership of the National Rifle Association for what I consider its emotional and sometimes downright loony positions on gun control legislation.

Sarah Brady, "chair" of the NRA's detested enemy, Handgun Control Inc., now has my name on her mailing list, so I have fresh evidence that emotional, exaggerated arguments are not confined to the NRA leadership in the continuing battle over gun control.

Chair Brady does not make as frequent mailings in her efforts to raise money, and her language is somewhat more restrained. But some of the techniques are similar to those used by the NRA:

A "survey" form which asks a series of loaded questions ('Are you concerned about the growing menace...?') designed to produce the desired answers – answers that can be interpreted as "Yes, I'm with you. Carry on the good fight and here's my money to support you."

Fundraising letters that go on and on and on – four pages in the case of the latest Brady mailing to reach me.

The kind of language that, it seems to me, turns off open-minded people who believe controversial issues should be addressed by the brain, not the viscera. Some examples from Chair Brady's letter:

The lack of gun laws is so critical "that the lives of all Americans are seriously endangered."

"Until Handgun Control Inc., came on the scene, the NRA literally controlled Congress. I'm not exaggerating."

But you are exaggerating, Ms. Brady, and weakening your case in the process. Now as to the latest National Rifle Association mailing to come my way:

NRA makes an effort to personalize the letters to a greater extent than does Handgun Control Inc. But this is a tricky business, as evidenced by the fact that the latest NRA letter to me starts: "Dear Wayne."

Now Wayne is my middle name, but people like Wayne LaPierre, executive vice president of the NRA, who address me on a first-name basis per-haps should know that I don't go by that name. Next time, Mr. LaPierre, just call me Andy.

(In another NRA mailing that had reached me a few days earlier, LaPierre had addressed me as "Dear Harold" and said he was "writing you this letter Saturday evening." Get it? The issue is of such vital importance that LaPierre was hard at work on it on a Saturday evening.)

In addition to the "Dear Wayne" letter, LaPierre's latest mailing included a less personalized missive addressed "Dear Fellow American." The letter began:

"You told me you wanted me to stand up, stand tall, speak out, show our colors and defend the Second Amendment."

I don't recall giving any instructions to LaPierre as to his posture or his speech. As to defense of the Second Amendment ("the right of the peo-ple to keep and bear arms"), I certainly defend the NRA's right to argue before Congress – rationally and responsibly, I would hope – against legis-lation that the NRA believes to be unconstitutional.

I've said before that I own a number of shotguns and rifles – so many that I'm not going to put it in print, because Marian reads this column. And I'm a dues-paying NRA member because I believe in a number of NRA programs.

But I don't believe that I or others among the American public need emo-tional, exaggerated exhortations from Wayne LaPierre – or Sarah Brady – to help us make up our minds on the controversial issue of gun control.

— July 3, 1994

A New, Improved Ak-Sar-Ben Gala

Among that variety of reasons for my special enjoyment of this year's Ak-Sar-Ben gala: The recognition that came to Marian Battey Andersen, my wife for going on 43 years, who was one of four Nebraskans inducted into Ak-Sar-Ben's Court of Honor.

As to the recognition for Marian:

She could have been a success in any working career that she might have chosen. But she chose to concen-trate her attention on our family while still finding time to compile a remarkable record of leadership in a variety of worthy causes. Her genuine interest in and concern for others – including me, to my great good fortune – is truly remarkable.

Now as to the first picture accompanying this article:

While Marian was proceeding to the Ak-Sar-Ben stage the other evening, there was a big-screen projec-

Marian at age 5, holding a football.

tion of still pictures, illustrating various phases of her life. One of the pictures puzzled some viewers. One good friend said it looked to her like it was a

picture of Marian as a child "holding a bowling ball or something."

The picture is reproduced here, and I would agree that it's not all that clear as to what the 5-year-old Marian Louise Battey of Lincoln, Neb., was holding so tightly in her arms. Let me explain: That was a football. It illustrates that Marian's

Marian's father, the late C. Wheaton Battey, longtime Lincoln banker, business and civic leader.

The late Freda Battey, with grandchildren David and Nancy.

well-known reputation as a sports enthusiast (she doesn't like me to call her a sports junkie) started developing at an early age. She attended her first Cornhusker football game with her parents, the late Wheaton and Freda Battey of Lincoln, at age 3.

— October 23, 1994

⸻⸻◆⸻⸻

Fat-Gram Counters

Among the clippings in my file of "Subjects I Will Get Around To" is an Associated Press dispatch that said: "Better eating habits, including giving up just one-third of an ounce of saturated fat a day, could help Americans live longer and cut their medical bills by billions of dollars, nutrition and public health groups said Monday.

"Most of the major health-reform bills before Congress ignore the role that improved nutrition could play, according to a study sponsored by the Center for Science in the Public Interest, the American Cancer Society, the American Public Health Association and other groups."

I do think there is great merit in putting much more stress on a preventive approach to health problems, instead of concentrating so heavily on how to treat the problems after they have occurred.

I should add that I have had considerable encouragement from my roommate in reaching this conclusion. Marian started zeroing in on the fat factor a few years ago. She has me so convinced that, when food shopping for a weekend hunting trip to our farm in northwest Missouri, I'm studying the comparative grams of fat reported on the various labels.

I would say that if I can be convinced that I should be fat-gram counting when shopping for a hunting outing with the boys, any fat-gram-counting wife anywhere shouldn't hesitate to tackle this subject with her husband.

There is, of course, always the possibility that Marian is more persistent and thus more likely to succeed than your average fat-gram-counting wife. (You'll note, Marian, that I spoke of persistence, not nagging.)

My conversion to the ranks of fat-gram counters was strengthened during a recent week when Joan Walsh stayed with us while overseeing the start of remodeling of the condominium that she is purchasing in Omaha.

Joan is the widow of Mike Walsh and lived here for five years while Mike ran the Union Pacific Railroad before moving to Houston to become chief executive officer of Tenneco. She has decided to move back to Omaha.

Joan is a close friend and a delightful houseguest, and we are among a good many Omahans who are pleased that she has chosen to maintain a residence here. She's also an outspoken proponent of healthful nutrition, so for a week I got a one-two punch on the subject.

I put my foot down just once – when Joan tried to convert me to skim milk instead of half-and-half on my bran-enriched cereal.

— December 4, 1994

———◆———

A Giver Surprised ...

Lying on a bench in the front hall when I arrived home from a recent hunting trip was what appeared to be a rather large box in Christmas-gift wrapping.

"That's one of the presents you're giving me," Marian said. Understand, I had no idea what was in the box, except that it was probably expensive.

Don't you want to know what it is? Marian asked.

"No," I replied. "Let's play out this reverse twist on the usual Christmas gift pattern. Let me as the giver be the one who is surprised when we open our presents." Then I added:

"And I certainly hope that you'll like – and can afford – the present you're giving me. I'll tell you all about it Christmas morning."

— December 18, 1994

Houseguests, Lightning and a New Grandson

Gifts that fit; surgery on four toes; when can Marian drive? (15 days); of storage and fashion cycles; skim milk vs. half-and-half; houseguest Joan Walsh; when surgeons can't take 'no;' recipe for boiling water; catalog for your dog; lightning; Marian & Ken Burns talk baseball; anonymous column critics; Chester Arthur and Millard Fillmore; daughter Nancy and baby James Wheaton Karger; to Harold and 'Ma;' Other readers.

A Receiver Pleased

A couple of weeks ago I wrote that Marian had returned from a shopping excursion with a large, gift-wrapped package and informed me that it contained my Christmas present to her. She asked if I wanted to know the package's contents. I told her I would wait until Christmas Day to learn what her good taste and my financing were providing as my Christmas gift to her.

On Christmas Day, I was pleased to learn that I had purchased a hand-

The Andersen home on Prairie Avenue in Omaha's Fairacres neighborhood.

some light gray full-length winter coat made of a suede-like fabric of wool and silk and a brightly colored silk scarf to be worn with the coat.

My surprise for Marian was that she was giving me a forest green waxed-cotton waterproof hunting coat. Marian seemed very satisfied with the exchange, especially since the financing ran about 4 to 1 in her favor.

More seriously, we were both pleased with this year's approach to gift giving, since it assured that each of us got a desired gift – and, not unimportantly, a gift that fit. If more people used this technique, the nation's retail stores wouldn't be engulfed in post-Christmas gift-exchangers.

— January 1, 1995

How Soon Can She Drive … ?

Speaking of guessing games, there is a Prairie Avenue guessing game going on these days. The question:

How soon will Marian be able to convince the doctors that she can start driving again?

Marian has had one of her periodic sessions with orthopedic surgeons. She is currently getting around on crutches in those oversized post-surgery shoes while incisions on four of her toes heal. She has been sternly warned not to risk popping the stitches by having to hit a brake pedal hard. Her doctors have talked of a four-week period away from driving. Marian is talking in terms of two weeks.

I've learned never to bet against her.

— January 29, 1995

Tie-ing Up the Attic

Marian was complimenting me on the job I had done in cleaning out half of our attic storage space. My reply was something like, "We'll have it filled up again soon enough." (I was definitely including myself in the "we.")

Marian said she thought mine was a very downbeat reply. She said she expected that we would keep the space clutter-free, adding that she belongs to the always optimistic "the-glass-is-half-full" school of philosophy.

I rejected the implication that I have a "glass-is-half-empty" outlook. Rather, I am a follower of the let's-be-realistic cult. One of the tenets of our cult – there are many tenets – is that the storage of all kinds of items will inexorably expand to fill the storage space available.

This applies, of course, even if the storer hasn't the slightest idea how the particular item might be useful in the future.

Marian says I have added to the storage problem over the years by, for example, keeping all those very narrow neckties as well as those four-inch wide ties, both of which have been out of fashion for at least two decades.

But I believe that fashion moves in cycles – apparently a very slow cycle so far as neckties are concerned – so my very narrow ties and my very wide ties are still safely stored in a garment bag, waiting for their time to come again.

— February 10, 1995

15 Days

Regular readers of these Sunday pieces will recall that a couple of weeks ago I mentioned a Prairie Avenue guessing game as to how soon Marian would resume driving following orthopedic surgery on four of her toes.

One doctor had advised Marian to keep her foot off a brake pedal for perhaps four weeks. She said she would be back at the wheel of her station wagon in two weeks.

Marian resumed driving in 15 days. She said she would have made her two-week goal except that her stitches weren't removed until the evening of the 14th day and the streets were pretty slippery that evening.

— February 12, 1995

Cold Turkey on Skim Milk

I wrote earlier about my conversion to a fat-gram-counting philosophy of nutrition, under strong prodding by my roommate. I said that I have been converted to the point that even when buying provisions for a hunting trip with friends, I find myself studying the supermarket labels and choosing the foodstuffs with the lowest fat content.

I added that I had put my foot down when a houseguest, Joan Walsh, tried to convince me to use skim milk instead of half-and-half on my bran-enriched cereal.

A couple of letter writers, clearly with my best interests at heart, picked up on the skim milk vs. half-and-half issue. A Lincoln friend wrote:

"…please follow Marian's and Joan Walsh's advice: Stop using half-and-half on your cereal. I know it tastes wonderful, especially on Grape Nuts, but it's a killer. I found that skim milk, like saltless foods, is an acquired taste. But once acquired, it is tasty."

An Omaha attorney: "If you will go cold-turkey on skim milk for a couple of weeks, you will never miss your half-and-half on your cereal."

My attorney friend said his brother had a "complete physical" in 1993 and 23 days later was dead, an autopsy showing that his arteries were 95-100 percent blocked.

I thank my letter-writing friends for their advice. But gosh, friends, don't I get a little bit of credit for fat-gram-counting foodstuffs other than half-and-half?

— March 26, 1995

Recipe for Boiling Water

I ended a recent column with a couple of paragraphs in which I observed that a recent Gallup Poll reported that 4 percent of Americans would have trouble boiling water. I said I hadn't realized I was a member of such an elite minority.

Mrs. John F. Barr of Wayne, Neb., responded with a recipe from a cookbook she said she had purchased years ago at a garage sale. The recipe:

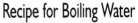

FAVORITE RECIPES

Take 2 qts. of water and put in a kettle. Put over a burner on electric stove and turn knob on high! As soon as water bubbles it is boiling and is ready to use. Can be used for cook-ing or washing dishes.

"Take 2 qts. of water and put in a kettle. Put over a burner on electric stove and turn knob on high! As soon as water bubbles it is boiling and is ready to use. Can be used for cooking or washing dishes."

I offer this for the education of any of my readers who have been want-ing to learn how to boil water – or whose spouses have been urging them to learn how to boil water.

Personally, I think I'll opt to stay in the elite minority. Once I learned to boil water, who knows what other kitchen chores Marian might wish to share with me? I can operate the microwave very well, thank you, and that meets very nicely a goodly share of my at-home cooking needs.

— April 2, 1995

'No' is a Lifesaver

It seems to me that a good many American hospitals have been slan-dered by the chairman of University Community Hospital in Tampa, Fla. You know, the hospital that was stripped of its accreditation when surgeons amputated the wrong leg of a patient and mistakenly removed another patient from a ventilator.

The hospital's chairman said that regulators were singling out the Tampa hospital in refusing to accept the fact that all – and I repeat all – hospitals have similar patient incidents.

I would suggest that the chairman does not have one shred of evidence to support his charge that all of America's 6,000-plus hospitals inflict on their patients major incidents comparable to the mistakes that cost his hospital its accreditation.

As we read of the problems of the Tampa hospital, Marian recalled the precautions that were taken to assure that surgeons operated on the correct hip when she was a patient in the University of Nebraska Medical Center in 1993.

Two days after the joint replacement operation on her right hip, Marian said, she noticed a rather large "NO" painted on her left hip. Too bad the surgeons at the Tampa hospital never thought of such a simple device for helping assure that its surgeons don't get involved in incidents like cutting off the wrong leg of a patient.

— April 23, 1995

---◆---

Sugar's Own Catalog

I know that many of you readers out there, like Marian and me, have been bombarded with catalogs from many directions. (Sometimes as many as 15 a day reach us either at home or at my office.) But how many of you have received a catalog addressed to your dog?

Such a catalog, offering illustrated and personalized mailing labels, came the other day addressed to Sugar.

Sugar is the younger of our two cocker spaniels. We speculate that a catalogue was addressed to her because a few years ago a young friend of ours, Courtney Kratina, thought it would be fun for cocker spaniels owned by the Kratina and the Andersen families to have mailing labels carrying their name and address and a picture of a cocker spaniel. Apparently that got Sugar onto a mailing list.

Marian and special friend.

So far, we have succeeded in keeping from our older cocker, Sister, the fact that Sugar is getting such attention.

Sugar, incidentally, will not be getting another supply of mailing labels. She doesn't write as many letters as she used to. She mostly uses the telephone now.

— April 23, 1995

Backing into a Twig

I've become accustomed to some examples of ingenuity when Marian responds to one or another of those questions that husbands and wives sometimes ask of each other. You know, the kind that go like, "Honey, could you please explain how …?" Or: "Could you tell me, dear, why …?

But I thought a couple of Marian's recent responses were even more ingenious than usual.

Question, after our insurance company informed me that Marian had reported that she lost a bracelet:

"Why didn't you tell me that you lost that bracelet?"

Answer: "Because I lost it while you were in the hospital recovering from surgery, and I didn't want to add to the stress you were under."

Question: "How do you suppose the tail light on your station wagon got cracked?"

Answer: "I must have backed into a twig."

— **April 30, 1995**

'When in Doubt, Take a Nap'

Followers of this column will know of efforts by my wife, Marian, and friend Joan Walsh to steer me toward a low-fat diet. As an indication of her broad-mindedness – or her sense of humor – Joan has sent along a clipping of a recent newspaper column written by a Seattle author, Robert Fulghum, who presents a quite different viewpoint.

"My wife has been trying to get me to read news stories about people who live long and healthy lives," Fulghum wrote.

"She's a doctor. And a vegetarian. She's excited about studies of isolated groups of people who dwell 12,000 feet up in the Andes or way out in the Russian boon-

> Let me make it perfectly clear that I'm not about to substitute napping (as much as I enjoy it) for a low-fat diet and occasional consultation with Mike Sorrell and other outstanding doctors.

docks. They eat chickpeas and gravy and walk six miles a day to get water – shriveled-up, old, prunish people whose life's secret is that they never change clothes or take baths."

Fulghum's formula for a long and happy life includes a number of simplistic rules, including his version of preventive medicine:

"… I read through my wife's medical school textbooks, and I noticed in just about every crisis, the book said to have the patient lie down in a comfortable place and make sure the patient could breathe, wasn't bleeding and was warm and dry.

"… No matter what you do, anywhere from 30 to 60 percent of what goes wrong with you heals itself if you just give it time and think good thoughts …

"It's elemental: When in doubt, get down. Take a nap."

Let me make it perfectly clear that I'm not about to substitute napping (as much as I enjoy it) for a low-fat diet and occasional consultation with Mike Sorrell and other outstanding doctors. I just wanted you to know that when it comes to the matter of "preventive" health practices, there are other points of view out there.

— May 14, 1995

Lightning Strikes Once

Marian and I last Tuesday morning got an unusual wake-up call – the sonic boom accompanying a lightning bolt that hit an elm tree about 30 feet from our bedroom.

A friend who lives more than a mile away helped us approximate the timing. "It was about 7 a.m. when I heard the boom," said Jan Buckingham.

It was one of those days when a driveway fills with service trucks – a total of six had stopped by before the day was over. Broken windows were repaired, as was most of the damage that resulted when the lightning, after shearing off a major tree branch, made contact with our underground electrical wiring system.

The charge that surged through the underground system and into the house knocked out the underground watering system, garage door openers, telephone and cable television circuits and electrical service in most of the house.

By noon the following day nearly all service had been restored except for the underground watering system, the control box for which exploded off the wall and shot across the garage.

Marian and I, of course, hope that we never have another such wake-up call. But we agreed we were lucky that the mighty surge of electricity hit the tree instead of the house.

In a sense, I suppose, you could say that that towering 60-year-old elm repaid us handsomely for our efforts to preserve its health during our nearly 30 years of residence on Prairie Avenue.

— June 11, 1995

Acclaimed Fans Talk Baseball and Nebraska

The most fun I've had in many a month came one recent evening listening to Marian talk baseball with Ken Burns.

Burns is widely known and acclaimed as the producer of two splendid public television series, "The Civil War" and "Baseball."

Marian is widely known and acclaimed – well, at least among our friends – as a knowledgeable baseball fanatic.

Burns was in Omaha at the invitation of the State Historical Society and the Nebraska Humanities Council. His visit started with a small dinner party at Gorat's Steak House, and Marian (I think she arranged it) wound up sitting at Burns' right.

The conversation ranged far beyond baseball. But when you get two baseball fanatics like Marian and Burns together, there was understandably a good deal of talk about America's national pastime.

I ventured to enter the conversation, observing that I thought Grover Cleveland Alexander was Nebraska's most noteworthy contribution to major league baseball. Burns quickly agreed and recalled the way in which his baseball documentary series focused on Alexander's most memorable performance.

The "Fourth Inning" in Burns' baseball film tells the story:

In 1926, Alexander (born in Elba, Neb., and later a resident of St. Paul, Neb., where he died in 1950 at age 63) was near the end of his career.

His career had seen him six times lead the National League in victories (including 33 wins in 1916) while with the Phillies and Cubs. It was a career that would put him in baseball's record book in second place with career shutouts (90) and third on the all-time list with total victories – tied with the great Christy Matthewson at 373 and trailing only such immortals as Cy Young (511) and Walter Johnson (416). In 1926, Alexander was nearly 40 years old, almost deaf, tortured by memories of his service on the Western Front in World War I, "sodden with drink." But Branch Rickey of the Cardinals bought Alexander from the Cubs in mid season because he thought Alexander had it in him "to be a hero one more time."

The Cardinals won the National League pennant, and Alexander won the second and sixth games of the World Series against the awesome New York Yankees of the Babe Ruth-Lou Gehrig era.

After the sixth-game victory, Alexander celebrated. On the day of the seventh and decisive game, Alexander sat in the bull pen "nursing his hangover." In the seventh inning, the Cardinals led 3-2, but the Yankees loaded the bases with two outs. Cardinal manager Rogers Hornsby called for Alexander, "hangover or no hangover."

The "lean old Nebraskan" walked slowly in from the left-field bull pen – and struck out a hard-hitting rookie named Tony Lazzeri (who went on to fame as a Yankee second-baseman) on three pitches.

Alexander retired the Yankees in the eighth and ninth innings and thus finished the 1926 World Series with a record of two wins and one save.

Baseball has known few more dramatic performances than that of "the lean old Nebraskan" in his bases-loaded, seventh game of the World Series, three-pitch strikeout of Lazzeri.

(Burns' "Baseball" film also spotlights another superb Nebraska-born pitcher, Omaha's Bob Gibson.)

— June 25, 1995

Too Much About Marian & the Dogs?

An anonymous critic has written to take me to task for writing too often about Marian and our dogs.

This fellow said he agrees with most of what I write but considers my column very unprofessional. He said other columnists don't write about such personal matters.

OK, let's hear the other side of the story.

Old friend Bernice Labedz, former state senator and now a Douglas County Board member, said to me the other day: "I love it when you write about Marian. Tell her that."

And this concluding paragraph in a very gracious letter from a Fremont woman who doesn't know either Marian or me:

> "How good it is that you like Marian so well! I'm sure the feeling must be mutual."

"How good it is that you like Marian so well! I'm sure the feeling must be mutual."

As to my critic's allegation that other columnists don't write about personal matters:

Some of the columnists, both national and local, whom I admire the most write very frequently about family and, yes, dogs.

Nationally syndicated columnist George Will, for example, writes occasionally about his son and the son's dog. Columnist James Kilpatrick has written movingly from his perspective as a grandfather.

On the local scene, World-Herald columnist Mike Kelly frequently writes interestingly about his family. Another World-Herald columnist, Robert Mc-Morris, also frequently gives us interesting family news.

Bob, as a matter of fact, has written more about the McMorris family dogs (including the late Fritzi and now Heidi II and Maggie) than I have written about our two smart, lovable, handsome cocker spaniels, the late Sugar I and now Sister and Sugar II.

(No offense, Bob. I'm not suggesting that you write too much about your dogs. I just wanted this uninformed anonymous critic to know that widely read veteran columnists like you write about dogs, too.)

— July 2, 1995

Jackie, Lucy and the Frisbee

Last week I told about an anonymous critic who says I write too much about Marian and her dogs. I was delighted to receive a variety of oral comments as well as letters saying, in effect, that the anonymous critic is all wet. Typical was this message from a woman reader in Lincoln:

"I enjoy your articles just the way they are, and I include the news about your wife and your dogs."

All of which encourages me to tell you today about my secretary, Jackie Wrieth, and one of the Wrieth family dogs.

Lucy is a very active black Labrador who loves to chase Frisbees. For some reason, Lucy has linked Jackie's lawn mowing with chasing a Frisbee.

I suspect that Jackie has spoiled Lucy in this regard. In any case, when Jackie fires up the lawn mower, Lucy runs for her Frisbee and then trots along beside Jackie for a few paces before moving ahead and dropping the Frisbee in front of the lawn mower.

This produces the desired result: Jackie stops the lawn mower and throws the Frisbee. Jackie starts the lawn mower and proceeds to cut a bit more grass until Lucy, Frisbee retrieved, drops it again in front of the lawn mower.

This obviously prolongs quite considerably the amount of time it takes for Jackie to mow the lawn. But when you and man's – or woman's – best friend are having fun together, that's a small price to pay.

— July 9, 1995

Chester Arthur & Millard Fillmore

In response to popular demand (well, a number of readers did say they enjoy reading about Marian and our dogs) I offer the following report:

There are some constants in Marian's running monologue directed at the dogs. (Marian says that it's really a dialogue in Sugar's case, because Sugar can talk, but it just sounds like growling to me.) There are also some variables.

Among the constants in Marian's canine-directed chatter:

"Do you girls want to run in the park?" And "Would you like to have dinner?"

So far as I know, neither of the dogs has ever indicated that she would not like to go run in the park or that she does not want dinner.

Among the variables in Marian's monologue are the names she calls the dogs. This past week, Sugar was known as Chester Arthur and Sister was called Millard Fillmore.

How come? I asked Marian. She said she had heard columnist George

Will expressing his opinion of past presidents and that he had described Chester Arthur and Millard Fillmore as among the least distinguished, "and the names just stuck in my mind."

Not that she considers our two cocker spaniels to be undistinguished, Marian hastened to add.

— July 30, 1995

Welcome, James Karger

Daughter Nancy Karger of Denver felt that her pregnancy had definitely come full term, and she wondered when the baby was going to agree.

Grandson John Andrew Karger had heard Nancy more than once say that she wished the baby would "come out."

Two-year-old John Andrew, eager to be of some help, aimed this message in the direction of Mommy's stomach:

"Baby, come out!"

The baby was finally induced to come out on Aug. 20 and turned out to be James Wheaton Karger, a robust 8 pounds, 13 ounces and 21 inches long.

Marian and I are thinking of him in terms of a Cornhusker offensive lineman or perhaps a Blackshirt middle guard.

— August 27, 1995

'A Family Like Ours'

A further dip into the mail bag:

An Omaha woman wrote to say "how much I look forward to your column each week," adding, "Please keep commenting from time to time on Marian's doings. It gives me the feeling that you're a real family, and in some ways a great deal like ours."

Marian and I both, of course, greatly appreciated those comments. But I did remind Marian that since a number of people have told us how much they enjoy reading about her doings, it's up to her to continue to do newsworthy things.

I fully expect that Marian will live up to the challenge.

— October 1 1995

To Harold and 'Ma'

Computerized methods of producing – supposedly personalizing – mass mailings may be more cost-efficient, but they frequently produce amusing inaccuracies. For example:

A recent letter soliciting funds on behalf of a Nebraska candidate in the 1996 elections was addressed to: Harold and Ma Andersen.

Now Marian is proud of our two children and certainly doesn't object to any reasonable reference to her motherhood – or grandmotherhood, for that matter.

Harold and Ma Andersen
Prairie Avenue
Omaha, NE

But Ma Andersen? Come on, Mr. Candidate. You and your mailing machine ought to be able to do better than that.

— **October 8, 1995**

4 Calls for Marian

If any of my readers should have occasion to call our home on Prairie Avenue and hear a male voice responding, "Marian Andersen's secretarial service," let me explain.

One evening last week, while Marian was out on some mission or other, the phone rang four times in 45 minutes. The tally: Four calls for Marian, none for Andy.

I decided that the next call would be answered, "Marian Andersen's secretarial service." The odds would have been strongly in favor of that being an accurate response.

But Marian returned home – just in time to take another call.

— **November 12, 1995**

Better Jeans

More than a few husbands out there will understand when I tell you what my dress code is: Try to find something that I like to wear and that will be greeted with a word of approval from Marian as I leave for the office.

The other morning I thought I had found success for one day at least when I headed out the door in casual attire and Marian said: "I like your jeans." But then she added: "But I like that other pair of jeans better."

— **December 17, 1995**

California, Fremont & Broken Bow

A doctor who lives in Omaha after 18 years in California wrote to thank me for my comments on Omaha drivers who run yellow and red lights.

"In California, red means stop (or risk death), yellow means stop and do not enter the intersection (or risk death). Both red and yellow violations mean $75 fines, plus (increased) insurance rates and driving school," the letter said.

This correspondent ended his letter on a certainly heartwarming note: "Keep up the good words."

A Fremont woman writes regularly. She indicates that she doesn't expect me to answer. She says she just enjoys writing, which I must say she does very well. Her latest letter ended with these words:

"Greetings to Marian. I'm glad she keeps you in line."

I'm glad, too. Marian is certainly one of the blessings I acknowledge this Christmas season or any other time of the year.

Particularly heartwarming, too, was a letter from a Broken Bow reader who said that he enjoys all of my columns "and have made a special file of the articles, which I cut out and save."

Whether you feel the articles are worth saving or worthy only of challenge and criticism, let me wish all of my readers joy at this holiday season and health and happiness in a productive new year.

And a final thought that seems appropriate at this season of good will to men:

What a better world this would be if each of us thought every day to take advantage of even a few of the countless opportunities we all have to reach out to someone in need of help, sometimes with our material support, sometimes with just a few words of sincere encouragement.

— **December 24, 1995**

Sister's Gone; Those Amazing Grandkids

An enlightened curmudgeon; so-long to top-dog Sister; sympathetic letters; wide open minds of grandkids James & John Karger; dog-lover Jackie Wrieth; siding with Kent Pavelka; when gas logs get in the way; Sugar's cataracts; Search for replacement for Sister; Sister Sarah arrives; cat comments; carry-on luggage; Clinton & Dick Morris; when Marian leaves town; Nebraska Arthritis Foundation's Woman of the Year; grandkids' vocabularies; visits to doctors & clinics; Tickle Me Elmo; being extra nice to Santa.

Crusty? Ill-Tempered?

An attorney friend of Marian and mine, commenting on my writings in this space, told Marian he considers me "an enlightened curmudgeon."

"Enlightened." I like that. But "curmudgeon"? I decided I'd better go to the dictionary to confirm or disprove my impression of what that description implies.

In the interest of full disclosure, I must report my dictionary's definition: "A crusty, ill-tempered or difficult and often elderly person."

The "or" would seem to leave room for choice among the various attributes. If forced to choose, I guess I'd settle for "difficult" – only occasionally, of course.

And "elderly"? I can't argue with that. But I would call attention to these lines from the poet Robert Browning's "Rabbi Ben Ezra":

> *Grow old along with me!*
> *The best is yet to be,*
> *The last of life,*
> *For which the first was made.*

The dictionary also said that an "archaic" meaning of curmudgeon was "miser." If I ever had any tendency in the direction of miserliness, Marian has helped me overcome it.

All of this reminds me of a story which may or may not be true, but I think it worth repeating. The story as I recall it:

"Cactus Jack" Gamer of Texas, vice president during Franklin D. Roosevelt's first two terms, once was described by an opponent as a "card-playing, whiskey-drinking, evil old man."

Cactus Jack is said to have replied that he rejected this description, explaining that he did not consider himself to be an old man.

— January 21, 1996

Sister Lived a Good Life

Today another Andersen family report, this a sad one. Sister, older of our two cockers, is no longer a part of the family. She was put to sleep to end her suffering after cancer was discovered throughout her body. She would have been 11 in March.

Sister was always ladylike – well, almost always – but definitely Top Dog, as evidenced, for example, by invariably taking her place in front of Sugar II when the two of them sat by my chair every morning, waiting for scraps from the breakfast table.

Sister showed her affection in many ways – jumping into laps or on the bed, following Marian closely and faithfully throughout the house, regularly seeking out a napping spot on the floor or sofa or chair close by Marian or me, volunteering face-licking affection whenever she got the chance.

It's too early to tell how Sugar II will adjust to being, temporarily, Only Dog and then Senior Dog. (The question isn't whether we will get another cocker spaniel but rather what we will name her. Granddaughter Lindsey Andersen suggests Sister II.)

While we very much miss Sister, Marian and I are buoyed by this thought:

We believe that loving much and being much loved contribute in large measure to the living of a good life. By that standard, Sister lived a good life indeed.

— January 28, 1996

A Thoughtful 'Consolation Kit'

Marian and I have received a heartwarming number of sympathetic letters and calls from readers who saw my report of the death of Sister, our almost-11-years-old cocker spaniel.

An Omaha woman wrote Marian to say she remembered a conversation with Marian when she (the reader) was looking for a buff cocker to replace her cocker who had died. She said that she had found a replacement, "a beautiful 9 $\frac{1}{2}$-month old female named D.G. (Dream Girl)."

She asked Marian to let me know that she cried when she read the last paragraph of my comments about Sister.

A longtime friend in Minneapolis sent us several pages of material, copies of which she said she sends to friends who have lost the companionship of a dog.

Most touching of the material in this very thoughtful "consolation kit" was a poem describing a dog reporting to master or mistress on what transpired when the departed pet arrived at the Pearly Gates:

I explained to St. Peter,
I'd rather stay here,
Outside the pearly gate.
I won't be a nuisance,
I won't even bark,
I'll be very patient and wait.
I'll be here, chewing on a celestial bone,
No matter how long you may be.
I'd miss you so much, If I went in alone,
It wouldn't be heaven for me.

* * *

Last week I wrote that we were considering what to name the new pup we will be seeking to join our surviving cocker, Sugar II. Brother-in-law Chuck Battey of Kansas City said he endorses granddaughter Lindsey Andersen's suggestion: Sister II.

I'm leaning in that direction myself, perhaps influenced by my family history.

Grandfather Andersen was named Andrew, my father was named Andrew and his first-born son, my oldest brother, was also named Andrew. Our two grandsons, John Andrew Karger and Robert Andrew Andersen, are carrying on the tradition.

In our family, we figure that when you've got a good name, stick with it.

— **February 4, 1996**

Bosnia, Tips and VCRs

A recent Washington-datelined news dispatch bewailed the fact that "test after test shows that too many Americans know too little," whether in history, science, geography or mathematics.

The story quoted a number of examples of American ignorance. I decided to test these examples against my own knowledge, with the following results:

"Science teachers say we confuse protons with parabolas." Guilty. I do this all the time.

"Geographers say we can't spot Bosnia on a map." Not guilty, I think. When I read that, I walked to the globe in my office and immediately found Yugoslavia, of which Bosnia used to be a part. Isn't that close enough?

"We can't calculate tips." I can calculate tips. It's Marian who can't calculate tips.

"We don't program our VCRs." That's me. My 5-year-old granddaughter can handle VCRs better than I can. But somehow I'm not the least bit ashamed.

It's the American way to want to have smart grandchildren.

"Geographers say we can't spot Bosnia on a map." Not guilty, I think. When I read that, I walked to the globe in my office and immediately found Yugoslavia, of which Bosnia used to be a part. Isn't that close enough?

— **February 18, 1996**

Not a Bummer

Like many a grandparent before me, I continue to be amused – and sometimes amazed – by the retention rate of the wide-open minds of wide-open-eared young children. The latest example in the Andersen family:

Marian had flown home from a brief visit to daughter Nancy and grandchildren John Andrew and James Wheaton Karger in Denver.

After taking Marian to the airport, daughter Nancy asked grandson John Andrew, who will be 3 in April: "Isn't it fun when Muzzy comes to visit?" John Andrew's reply:

"Yeah, it's not a bummer."

— **March 3, 1996**

An Obvious Truth About Stress

My secretary, Jackie Wrieth, a dog-lover like Marian and me and a number of readers who have communicated with us on the subject, called my attention to a news story reporting on a research project of the medical school of the State University of New York at Buffalo.

The study involved 240 couples, half of whom owned dogs. Researchers set up three stressful situations – giving a speech, performing math problems and dipping a hand in cold water.

The results, as reported by The Associated Press:

The test subjects experienced the least amount of tension when accompanied by their dog, while the "the stress levels were highest when the subjects were with their spouses."

Perhaps it's worthwhile to have such an obvious truth supported by research, but I could have told those researchers what they would find.

It does occur to me that there is perhaps one bit of information that I might be able to put to use as a result of the medical school's research:

Next time I have occasion to thrust my hand into cold water, I'll try to assure that our cocker spaniel, Sugar, is present but Marian isn't.

— **March 17, 1996**

Taking Marian's Advice

During a recent telephone conversation, an old friend said: "I'm glad you didn't take Marian's advice."

"What advice was that?" I asked. My old friend replied:

"The advice about taking an occasional week off from column writing. I think you've only missed one weekly column since then."

I was impressed with my friend's recollection of an item written many months ago and appreciative of the fact that he was glad I had only missed writing one weekly column since then.

All of which is a prelude to reporting that I'm going to take Marian's advice. I have a travel schedule that is pressing rather hard on hours available for column writing, so for the next few weeks, I'll be taking more Thursdays off than I have been, but I'll be continuing my Sunday offerings.

— **March 21, 1996**

Of Course Marian Knew

Like many another Cornhusker football fan, I've followed with keen interest "The Voice From the Grandstand" debate over whether Kent Pavelka should be continued as the radio voice of the Cornhuskers, now that his long-time employer, station KFAB, no longer holds Cornhuskers broadcast rights.

I'm on Kent's side. He has a pleasant broadcast personality and an enthusiastic style that I like. I'm glad the new holders of Cornhusker broadcast rights, Great Plains Media, Inc., want Kent to continue.

Now some friendly advice:

When setting the scene for your listeners, Kent, forget the "left to right" or "right to left" wording, as in "The Huskers in the first quarter will be moving north to south, left to right." Remember that for people sitting on the other side of the stadium, the Huskers will be moving right to left. And to your radio listeners, those "left to right" or "right to left" descriptions don't really mean anything.

Further friendly advice: Make sure that you don't use too much sports jargon that some of your listeners may not understand. For example, I follow basketball, but I wasn't sure what "in the paint" means until I asked Bob Williams of The World-Herald sports staff the other day.

Armed with my new knowledge, I asked Marian if she knew. Of course, she did. "It's the area between the free throw lines where you can't stay without the ball for more than three seconds," Marian quickly replied.

— April 7, 1996

Gas Log Gets in the Way

Now that warmer weather is on the way, perhaps the gas log will stop coming between Marian and me.

Let me hasten to explain how this unusual impediment to matrimonial togetherness has come into play in the Andersen household.

Marian included a gas log among our Christmas gifts in 1994. (I never quite understood how a gas log became a Christmas present. You'll have to ask Marian. One year my birthday present from her was our first color TV set.)

On any chilly evening the past couple of winters, the odds are strongly in favor of Marian's reading her newspapers (we subscribe to six daily newspapers) in the family room with the gas log burning. (Marian prefers that we not say the gas log is "turned on," on the grounds that makes it sound too much unlike a wood-burning fire.)

I continue to spend most evenings upstairs reading and working at my desk.

Before the gas log entered our life, most evenings at home found Marian upstairs relaxing and reading in the lounger in my room while I worked at the desk. The cocker spaniels were, of course, always near at hand sleeping on the carpet.

So it is that I say that warmer weather will encourage more togetherness, with Marian, I hope, moving back upstairs with me of an evening.

(Yes, I know, I could move downstairs with Marian during the winter. But I don't like a gas-log fire enough to abandon my upstairs desk and books and files.)

* * *

I've written in this space before about mass mailings that turn the recipient off instead of on. A single day's mail in a recent week brought five such letters. For example:

A supposedly personalized form letter from a candidate who is a friend of Marian's and mine came addressed to Mary J. Anderson. Marian and I assumed that it was intended for Marian B. Andersen – and tossed it aside as not even a near-miss.

Another letter was addressed to "Harold W. Andersen or Current Resident." Now there's a really personalized letter for you. I'm both Harold W. Andersen and the "Current Resident," but I threw the letter away anyhow.

— April 14, 1996

Tense Moments at the Animal Clinic

Sugar, the world's most lovable cocker spaniel, slept in the back seat, and Marian and I fretted in the front seat as we drove to Ames, Iowa, and the small-animals clinic at the College of Veterinary Medicine at Iowa State University.

Over the past several months, 6-year-old Sugar had been suffering from a noticeable loss of eyesight – occasionally bumping into furniture and staying safely within the sound of Marian's voice instead of ranging far and wide when the two of them took their regular walks in Memorial Park.

The question to be answered at Ames was whether Sugar had cataracts, which could be corrected by surgery, or was suffering from a degenerative eye disease that would leave her blind.

Marian and I figuratively held our breath while Dr. Dan Betts, specialist in eye surgery on dogs, clicked on his flashlight and peered intently into each of Sugar's eyes. Happy diagnosis: Cataracts, probably hereditary, not at all unusual in cocker spaniels (and other dogs, for that matter) and correctable by surgery.

Sugar was operated on the next day and is doing nicely, thank you.

I share this information with you because in the past, every time I have written something about Marian or our dogs, I have received a heartwarming response from readers who are dog lovers and those who say they just like to read about life in a happy family.

There was sad news for the owner of another dog brought to the small-animal clinic that day. Cody, a 4-year-old black cocker spaniel owned by a young woman from Oelwein, Iowa, was diagnosed as having a degenerative eye disease that would lead to blindness.

The friendly young woman from Oelwein congratulated us on our good news and said that she would, of course, continue to love and care for Cody as his eyesight faded into blindness.

* * *

Despite the complaint from one reader who said he likes my columns except when I write about my wife and our dogs, let me continue along the dog-family path with a couple more items.

First, a report on our search to find a replacement for Sister, our 11-year-old cocker spaniel who died in January:

Marian has been in frequent contact with a dog breeder in Minnesota, and next month we will be welcoming a new cocker spaniel to the family circle. Our name for the newcomer: Sister Sarah.

The "Sister" is in memory of our Sister, who died in January, and "Sarah" is just because we like the name. We will call her Sarah.

The fact that Sister Sarah is the name of the pretty evangelist female lead in the musical "Guys and Dolls" didn't influence us, although I can't resist the following observation:

The musical comedy Sister Sarah, some of you may recall, was an evangelist who reformed compulsive gamblers. She wouldn't have any trouble finding work in the Council Bluffs-Omaha area these days.

— April 14, 1996

Of 90 and 60

Waiting for Marian and me on our return home was the usual stack of mail, including a proxy statement for the shareholders' meeting of a company in which Marian holds stock.

I read with some interest – and perhaps a touch of envy – of the slate of directors to be voted on at the annual meeting of the company.

Having left the boards of four companies because of mandatory age retirement policies, I noted with interest that the chairman of the company seeking Marian's proxy was standing for re-election at age 90. I suppose the company's retirement age policy might be influenced by the fact that the 90-year-old chairman owns more than 60 percent of the voting stock.

— May 5, 1996

Senior Dog Outpoints Master in This House

If you're not interested in dogs, please come back next Sunday.

But if you agree with those numerous readers who have told Marian and me that they enjoy reading about dogs, including ours, read on.

A number of people have asked us about Sister Sarah, the 5-month-old buff-colored cocker spaniel who has come to live with us following the death of our 10-year-old cocker, Sister.

From one of Marian's comments, you can get an idea of how glad we have been to welcome the newcomer into our home. Marian was schmoozing with Sarah while our 6-year-old cocker, Sugar II, and I looked on. Said Marian:

"Sugar, you're a 10. And Andy, you're a 10. And Sarah, you're a 10½." Marian has never given me a 10½ rating, even on my very best days.

Sugar has moved from her brief tenure as Only Dog to Senior Dog status with commendable good grace. There were minor flare-ups in Sarah's first days with us, when Sugar indicated she was above playing with a puppy. But now she will occasionally romp with Sarah, who indicates her affection for her foster sister by vigorously licking Sugar's nose.

In contrast to Sugar, Sarah is a reacher, tending to pull from tables anything she can stretch up to. She also delights in running wildly through the house, for no apparent reason except that she is a puppy. She also engages in occasional noisy if one-sided confrontations with that buff-colored cocker in the full-length mirror.

The new arrival is quite teachable and is beginning to respond by searching me out when Marian says, "Where's Daddy?" She also likes to bite my toes while I'm shaving, which I'm not sure is a sign of affection.

Sarah might have wound up as a show dog, like other offspring of her father, Champion Krismyth's Says It All. Sarah has the face to be a show dog but not the coat, we were told.

So far as we are concerned, Sarah has a fine-looking coat, and she certainly does have a pretty face. Lucky for us and, we would like to believe, lucky for Sarah, her coat doesn't measure up to show-dog standards. We hope Sarah will be a lot happier living with us on Prairie Avenue than traveling around the country to dog shows.

* * *

My comments about cats in a recent column brought a good-natured letter from Arnie Ziels of Ralston, who wrote:

"As a cat lover, I would like to express my gratitude for last week's respite from your usual dog stories."

Ziels called attention to a TV show, "The Pet Department," airing daily at 2 p.m. on the Fox Network.

The show, co-hosted by former Iowa State veterinary student Steve Walker and his dog, Jack, has a daily feature titled "Pet Department Road Test." It spotlights a pet and concludes with a rundown as to make, model, maintenance, tune-ups and sticker price.

"Give the show a try," my Ralston reader wrote. "I think you'll like it." He kindly added:

"Oh, yeah – I like most of your other stuff, too."

* * *

Here's what may be the last word – at least it will be the last word for today – in terms of a man's or woman's devotion to a pet.

Marian, in Washington for a meeting of a Red Cross advisory committee, started talking about dogs with a fellow committee member – a woman who lives on a 1,000-acre farm near Louisville, Ky.

Marian's new friend said that when her two pet dachshunds ran off she launched a search that included the use of a helicopter for four days. No luck.

The dachshund owner said she next consulted a psychic in California who conjured up a vision of "a barn and overalls." (There's a real psychic for you. Dogs disappear in a rural area and the psychic "sees visions of a barn and overalls.") No luck.

Next, the dachshund owner said, she consulted a psychic from London. No luck.

Eventually one of the dachshunds was found by a resident of the area who apparently had seen one of the numerous ads and posters that had been widely circulated. I can't resist the observation that it pays to advertise.

— May 26, 1996

Credit Where It's Due

A thought that occurred while watching Marian moving from room to room, portable telephone in one hand with the other hand free to pick up dishes, turn on the microwave, feed the dogs, flip the TV set to a baseball game or whatever:

I wouldn't exalt them to parity with the 19th Amendment (women's suffrage) to the U.S. Constitution, but how about crediting microwave ovens and portable telephones with playing some part in the women's liberation movement?

— June 9, 1996

Stealing Marian?

Time for this column to go to the dogs again.

I wrote recently about the newest member of our household, a beautiful cocker spaniel puppy named Sarah. The first reader reaction to reach me was an anonymous note saying, "Andy, your ego is out of control," and deploring a report on the Andersen family dogs as unworthy of The World-Herald's opinion pages.

Happily, the favorable comments then started piling up, by letter, by phone calls as well as by comments from people whom Marian and I encountered. I stopped keeping count when the total passed 25. Typical was this note from an Omaha businessman:

Sugar has earned a 10½ rating from Marian, who has moved Sarah up to an 11. (No improvement in my rating yet.)

"You just keep writing about your dogs and Marian, too. We dog-lovers and wife-lovers like it!"

Thus encouraged, I report that Sarah, who observed her 6-month birthday June 6, is receiving increasingly higher popularity rankings from Marian. Some readers may recall that Sarah started out a few weeks ago with Marian rating her a 10½, compared with 10 ratings for me and our other cocker spaniel, Sugar.

Sugar, as Senior Dog, is adjusting nicely, allowing Sarah to share plate-licking opportunities and showing no objection at all when Sarah joins in back-to-back naps. She even occasionally plays with the frisky pup. In fact, Sugar has earned a 10 1/2 rating from Marian, who has moved Sarah up to an 11. (No improvement in my rating yet.)

Speaking of my occasional references to Marian in this space, an old friend now residing in Blair has written to say:

"You may be cutting your own throat, so to speak, when you keep bragging about this woman Marian. One of these days your readers are going to realize what they are missing and one of them may try to steal her away from you."

Need I say that this was one of Marian's favorite quotes among the various ones I have passed her way?

A Lincoln reader called to say "amen" to one of my columns about the Clintons and said she had recently learned that the Arkansas State motto is "Land of Opportunity." She indicated she thought Bill and Hillary had certainly tried to take advantage of their opportunities during their residence in Arkansas. And she asked that I keep readers informed on "how the puppy is doing."

— June 23, 1996

Only Two Carry-ons

For one reason or another, Marian and I have been doing a good deal of travel by commercial airlines in recent weeks.

This has given me opportunity to observe the massive array of what some people define as – and the airlines seem willing to accept as – "carry-on luggage."

In the gate area, there usually sits a metal-frame device designed to outline the maximum dimensions that the airline supposedly will allow for a piece of carry-on luggage. Not once have I ever seen anyone use one of these gizmos to test the dimensions of a piece of luggage.

Also in the gate area, the waiting passengers are frequently told that they are each allowed two pieces of carry-on luggage, each of which "must fit in the overhead bin or under the seat in front of you." A goodly number of the passengers, if not the majority, promptly proceed down the jetway with from three to five pieces of carry-on luggage, at least two of which could not possibly be jammed into that allowable-dimension measuring rack.

Please understand that I'm not crusading on this subject – just observing. The ignore-the-restriction system seems to work, although occasionally I am a little irritated when one of my carry-on items (never more than two, of course!) gets squeezed out of shape by another passenger jamming a small trunk into the overhead rack above our seats.

Besides, rigid enforcement of the two-carry-on-item rule would mean that Marian, who is the family clipping service, no longer could spend her air hours reading the bag full of newspapers and magazines that are invariably contained in her customary array of three carry-on items.

— August 4, 1996

Sister Sarah: The Complete Package

"Lighten up," my roommate advised me after reading my column last Sunday.

Marian said she agreed that it was appropriate for me to devote an entire column to the way the "people's right to petition" has been abused in Nebraska this year.

But, she said, people also like to read columns with more variety and some lighter touches. Yes, ma'am. And I'll start with a lighter touch about Marian herself.

I believe the bonding process between Marian and Sister Sarah, the newest family member, has ended. I mean, how much further can you bond than to give this lovable 8-month-old cocker spaniel the nickname "C.P." (for "The Complete Package") and occasionally walk around the house, Sister Sarah at your heels, singing to Sarah the Cole Porter classic, "You're the Tops?"

Sugar II, our 6-year-old cocker, is certainly not being neglected. But it's hard not to have the spotlight fall rather heavily on the newcomer as she exuberantly pushes her pretty face into everything in the house, in the yard, in Memorial Park or wherever.

— August 25, 1996

One Way to Keep a Lead

As to the other big story in Thursday's political news:

My roommate questions whether Clinton's candidacy will be damaged significantly, if at all, by the resignation of his closest political adviser, Dick Morris, after a news report that he had a relationship with a prostitute and allowed her to eavesdrop on calls to the White House.

(The story broke a day after Time magazine arrived at our house with pictures of President Clinton and Dick Morris on the cover and a story that quoted Morris as telling a Time correspondent: "It's very important for me to convey how deeply I care about this man, what an inspiration, even a guide he's been." Some guide!) Said Marian of our Teflon president, to whom the character issue never seems to stick:

"I think Clinton could have streaked through the convention crowd Thursday night and still had a double-digit lead in the polls."

— September 1, 1996

Food Revolutionary!

I guess I lead a sheltered life. The New York Times reports that there's been a revolution going on in the United States, and I'll admit that I hadn't heard a thing about it.

A front-page spread in the Living Arts section of The Times recently told a story of "Alice Waters, Food Revolutionary."

The story said that through her Chez Panisse restaurant in Berkeley, Calif., and as the author or co-author of six cookbooks, Ms. Waters "has single-handedly changed the American palate, inspiring a devotion to seasonal cooking emphasizing the importance of local organic ingredients."

I mentioned The Times story to Marian and asked her if she knew who Alice Waters is. I was not surprised by the reply from my omnivorous-reader roommate:

"Of course. She's the one who has that restaurant in Berkeley and has popularized cooking with organic foods."

The clear implication was that if I purported to be a columnist prepared to write on a variety of subjects, I, too, should have known about Alice Waters, food revolutionary.

The Times story said that Ms. Waters' restaurant would be celebrating its 25th birthday "with a week-long series of dinners, which are expected to draw people like Wolfgang Puck, Edna Lewis and Francis Ford Coppola."

Another confession: The only one of these three obviously famous people of whom I have heard is Francis Ford Coppola. I think he has something to do with movies.

Now before I get into trouble with Marian and Joan Walsh, my dietary advisers, I should add that I do like such local organic ingredients as sweet corn, tomatoes and cucumbers.

Ms. Waters recently prepared a fund-raising dinner for President Clinton and 30 of his top California contributors. The story didn't detail the menu for the presidential dinner, but as for me, Mr. President, I'm not going to give up Big Macs for "local organic ingredients." How about you?

Now before I get into trouble with Marian and Joan Walsh, my dietary advisers, I should add that I do like such local organic ingredients as sweet corn, tomatoes and cucumbers. Marian, does that earn me any points with you and Joan and Ms. Waters?

— September 8, 1996

Advice in Absentia

When Marian leaves town for more than a day, she makes sure that she continues, even in absentia, to play the role of active domestic partner.

Typical was her recent two-day trip to Denver for daughter Nancy Karger's 33rd birthday. (I had some civic assignments that kept me in Omaha but participated by sending along a check with instructions to Nancy to "shop till you drop" – completely unnecessary fatherly advice, I might add.)

Marian left me three hand written pages of suggestions (instructions?). Included were suggested breakfast, lunch and dinner menus and TV programs Marian thought I might enjoy. (Those who know my sports-junkie roommate will not be surprised that the suggested programs leaned heavily toward the kind of sporting events Marian watches.)

There was a reminder, too, as to which dog needs a certain pill with each meal. (It's Sugar.)

Carefully set out on the kitchen counter were two dishes, each with five pills. One of the pills is an aspirin prescribed by Dr. Mike Sorrell. The four others are vitamins and mineral supplements prescribed by Dr. Marian Andersen.

One of the dishes was labeled "Tuesday a.m."; the other, "Wednesday a.m."

Marian will be learning here for the first time that just to demonstrate to myself that I can show some independence in these matters, I took the Wednesday morning pills Tuesday and the Tuesday morning pills Wednesday.

I hope you won't be offended, Dr. Andersen.

— September 15, 1996

Woman of the Year

I don't know how long this sort of thing can go on before my roommate's innate sense of modesty gets bent out of shape.

I have in mind not only Marian's "Woman of the Year" recognition by the Nebraska Arthritis Foundation the other evening.

I'm thinking also of the fact that, in front of 50,000 fans at Coors Field in Denver, Marian threw out the first ball before a Colorado Rockies-St. Louis Cardinals baseball game last month.

On this particular evening, Marian was one step higher in the celebrity pecking order than Ken Burns, acclaimed producer of those splendid public television series, "The Civil War" and "Baseball." Burns, you see, threw out the second ball in the pre-game ceremony at Coors Field.

Marian is a sports fanatic, as evidenced by the fact that she has seen a ball game in each of the 28 major league ballparks. (People sometimes ask, "How come I never heard of any other woman doing that?" My standard reply: "I've never heard of another woman who was remotely interested in doing it.")

When Marian met Ken Burns over dinner in Omaha last spring, they agreed they would both enjoy a visit to major league baseball's newest park, Coors Field. Their joint attendance at a Rockies game was subsequently arranged for the evening of Aug. 25.

Somehow the Rockies management got word that Marian's attendance would enable her to update her record of having seen a game at each of the major league parks. (They keep building new parks, and Marian keeps going to see games in them, Coors Field being the latest example.)

Marian said she stood at the edge of the grass in front of the pitcher's mound. "And I threw a strike, too," she proudly reported.

— September 17, 1996

Go Ahead. Be Serious

The Papillion petition circulator wrote: "I believe in the process as much as (community promoter Ed Jaksha) does and think it should be a difficult and time-consuming undertaking, reflecting genuine concern on an issue. I've never taken pay, even the year I did the term-limits one twice."

My Papillion correspondent commented also on a column I wrote following the one dealing with the petition process. In the second column, I wrote that wife Marian had approved of the petition process column but advised me to "lighten up," saying readers like to read about less serious subjects, too.

The Papillion petition circulator said she didn't want to cause friction "between you and your roommate" but advised me: "Go ahead. Be serious," when there are serious subjects that need to be addressed.

— October 3, 1996

The Eyes Have It

My roommate's latest project (well, one of her latest projects; she has a lot of them) is to change the frames on one of my pairs of eyeglasses.

"Those gold frames have got to go," Marian said the other day. "They make you look like a grandfather."

I reminded Marian that I am a grandfather and proud of it. Her quick response: "Yes, but you don't have to look like an old grandfather."

How can you argue with logic like that? We (that's right; not I, but we) have an appointment next week with the eyeglass people.

— October 17, 1996

'Some of the Things She Do'

"No, no, no, no!" I heard Marian's firm voice as she padded down the hall toward my closed bathroom door.

I was reasonably certain that, since it was early in the day, I had not yet done anything to evoke such a stern reprimand from my roommate.

More seriously, I was quite sure that Marian's words were directed at one of our cocker spaniels, and I suspected that it was frisky 11-month-old Sarah and not 6-year-old Sugar.

After Marian returned upstairs, I learned that the problem was Sarah's running off with three pairs of freshly laundered pantyhose.

Marian said the incident reminded her of what a cleaning lady who had not yet quite fully mastered the English language once said about young Marian Battey of Lincoln, Neb.:

"We love her, but we don't like some of the things she do."

— November 17, 1996

Clots, Squirrels & Good News

Regular readers of this space will know that I both love and admire my roommate. So I hope the question I raise today will not be taken amiss by either Marian or those numerous readers who have told me how much they enjoy reading about her (and, of course, her two constant companions, the world's most lovable dogs, our cocker spaniels, Sugar and Sarah).

A letter arrived at our Prairie Avenue home the other day addressed to "Mr. & Mrs. Marian Andersen."

Have I perhaps been giving Marian a little too much attention in this space?

In any case, herewith another report involving Marian:

I was calling from the emergency room at the University of Nebraska Medical Center where I had gone to have a pain in my rib cage checked out. Having had a blood clot lodge in a lung following surgery a couple of years ago, I had been advised to be alert for any signs of recurrence. One sign of the first clot was pain in the rib cage.

I was informing Marian that I was in the emergency room when she interrupted with a cry, "Get out of there! Get out of there!"

I assumed that she wasn't suggesting that I get out of the emergency room. I figured that she was shouting at a squirrel that she had observed invading our bird feeder.

Marian indicated that she might put the phone down and go to the garden room door to scare the squirrel off. But, bless her heart, without any prompting from me, she stayed on the telephone to hear the rest of my medical report, a report that turned out to be quite favorable.

I choose to look at it this way: Marian and I both have been in and out of doctors' offices and clinics so often in recent years that while an emergency room visit certainly isn't routine, Marian manages to keep it in perspective.

— November 21, 1996

Special Reason to Be Thankful

I'm thankful that Marian and I continue to have opportunities to be involved in good causes that benefit fellow residents of a city and a state that we love and that have offered so many opportunities to us.

And, for a columnist, what better Thanksgiving week message than this:

A woman in Lincoln wrote to express thanks for "your down-to-Earth, very practical yet entertaining column." She said she saves my Thursday and Sunday columns until last when she reads her World-Herald, since she considers my column "the frosting on my cake." The letter added:

"Regards to you and your roommate."

For that reader in Lincoln and for all the other readers out there, including especially those who take the time to write or call with messages either supportive or critical, my best wishes and my thanks to you for giving this columnist a special reason to be thankful this Thanksgiving Day.

— November 28, 1996

Perfect Gifts

When Marian starts on a mission in any of her various roles – wife, grandmother, civic worker, baseball fanatic visiting all the major league ballparks – the question is when, not whether, she'll get the job done.

So it is that James Wheaton Karger, one of our two Denver-based grandsons, will be receiving a Tickle Me Elmo doll for Christmas. They tell me Elmo has become rather famous as a highly popular, hard-to-get toy this Yuletide season.

Marian says it really wasn't that big a deal. She just started her search early, got on a waiting list and reacted promptly when her name came up.

If the search had been left to me, I'd still be looking for a Tickle Me Elmo on Christmas Eve. Unless, of course, I had turned the job over to my always efficient secretary, Jackie Wrieth.

Speaking of grandchildren's Christmas gifts, if you promise not to tell Omaha-based grandson Robert Andrew Ander-

Marian and grandson Jack Karger.

sen, I'll tell you about one of his surprises. Robby's gift is a "mighty tractor-trailer with bulldozer" combination. To me, the most interesting feature of this particular gift is the fact that the box in which it comes carries this label:

"Guaranteed for Life."

I don't know whether the Tonka Toy manufacturers have a product promoter with a good sense of humor or whether they feel their toys have such longevity of appeal – and durability – that Robby will still be playing with his "mighty tractor-trailer with bulldozer" in retirement.

— December 8, 1996

Who Ordered It?

From time to time – as when the subject is acquisition of shotguns – Marian reminds me of this saying, "Sometimes, less is more."

I think that Marian – sometimes – has a point. For example, I haven't bought a new shotgun in all of 1996. (Although, I'm pleased to add, I did receive one as a gift.)

When the Yuletide season mood is upon me, I guess I believe that "more is more" when it comes to gift-giving. This year, I may have overdone the "more is more" approach to Christmas.

Twice in recent days, a package has arrived at the house simply addressed to Harold Andersen. The first package was a box of delicious Florida grapefruit. There was no indication who had ordered the box of grapefruit, so Marian called the Florida firm that produced and shipped the fruit. A somewhat incredulous employee at the Florida firm said something to the effect, "Why, Mr. Andersen ordered the grapefruit."

Another package without a Christmas greeting card arrived the other day. This contained one of those big cans of popcorn and a videotape of 1996 Olympic highlights – a combination that you would think would be remembered by whoever ordered it.

You're probably way ahead of me when I report that when I handed the shipping slip to Marian and said, "I wonder who this came from," Marian looked closely at the shipping slip and said, "You ordered it."

— December 12, 1996

Matching the Perfect Match

Another of those mass mailings addressed simply to "Resident" turned up the other day.

I normally toss these things away, but I couldn't resist opening an envelope that carried this wording:

"You're invited to meet your perfect match!"

It turned out that the mailing was from a nationwide organization that has an Omaha office and describes itself as a "personal introduction system."

Since I feel that I already have a "perfect match," I threw the solicitation away. But a troubling thought occurs: How many of my readers think I perhaps should have given Marian a shot at this solicitation from the "Perfect Match Personal Introduction System?" After all, the letter was simply addressed to "Resident," and Marian obviously also resides at our address.

Am I a closet male chauvinist or perhaps a never-in-the-closet male chauvinist?

Maybe I shouldn't have brought this whole thing up.

— **December 15, 1996**

Passing a Grin Test

I tested Marian's sense of humor with a comment on one of her Christmas presents.

The present was a cookbook, presented by The Readers Digest to members of the national board of directors of the Public Broadcasting System, which receives consistent generous support from The Readers Digest.

Informed of the cookbook gift, I sought – a bit facetiously – to determine the practical value to the Andersen household by asking Marian, "Is there anything in there about microwave cooking?"

Marian chuckled, passing the sense of humor test, as I expected she would.

— **December 26, 1996**

Santa and a 'Very Nice Lady'

A few years ago I wrote a special birthday card for Marian. It included a lighter touch, citing her for "educating countless listeners (some of them even interested listeners) in the strategic intricacies and the statistics, as well as the personalities involved, in a wide range of competitive athletics."

But after the light-hearted touch, there was this concluding paragraph on that special birthday card tribute to Marian:

"Doing all of these things with an unfailing sense of good humor and a warmth of personality and friendship based on a genuine interest in the lives and welfare of others, thereby touching many lives in a most positive way."

Those words came to mind last Sunday as Marian and I played host to our children, their spouses and their children in a pre-Christmas brunch at the Omaha Country Club.

I asked Santa how many people had asked him if he needed a refreshing drink. "Just one, a very nice lady," Santa replied.

More than 400 people were in attendance, and dozens of parents shepherded their children onto the lap of Santa Claus, there to be photographed and replaced in about 20 seconds by another child or two.

As the rest of the family went through the buffet line and gathered at our table, Marian was the last to arrive. She explained:

"I asked Santa Claus if he'd like a drink. I think he might have preferred a bourbon, but he said he'd appreciate a glass of water with a straw. I'll be back as soon as I take him a glass of water."

Later, as we were leaving, I asked Santa how many people had asked him if he needed a refreshing drink. "Just one, a very nice lady," Santa replied.

A minor example, perhaps, but I thought you would indulge me in giving you this Christmas season an example of what I had in mind when I wrote that Marian unfailingly displays "a genuine interest in the lives and welfare of others" – including, in this case, a hard working Santa Claus who later gave Marian an affectionate hug of appreciation for her act of kindness.

— December 29, 1996

Bird Feeder Battles and Peaches Marmalade

Waking up grouchy; word precision; plug the appliance in; the Battle at the Bird Feeder; 4MYK9S; making peace with squirrels; four amazing grandkids; movie credits; Phi Delta Theta & Phi Gamma Delta; welcome Peaches Marmalade; Cornhusker football euphoria; readers' preferences; presidential pup.

Pillow Talk

Marian and I were sitting in the family room the other evening while I read the paper and Marian leafed through a catalog. She came across an ad for one of those pillows embroidered with a humorous message, which she read to me:

"SOMETIMES I WAKE UP GROUCHY. SOMETIMES I LET HIM SLEEP."

I asked Marian if she had any reason to direct that particular message my way. Her reply:

"No, you wake up OK. You just get grouchy later in the day."

Another embroidered pillow message, this one recommended for your guest bedroom:

"DON'T CONFUSE ENDURANCE WITH HOSPITALITY."

— January 5, 1997

Whence Comes Affection?

Ever alert for news that shows man's – and woman's – best friend in a favorable light, Marian called my attention to a survey of 1,206 pet owners by the American Animal Hospital Association.

Forty-seven percent of those surveyed said they rely more on their pet than a spouse or a child for affection.

When asked if they were marooned on an island and could have only one companion, 42 percent of the pet owners picked a dog — a close second to the 46 percent who chose a human.

I didn't ask Marian how she would have responded if she had been one of those questioned in the survey.

— February 2, 1997

Word Precision

Having spent my adult life in a vocation in which a precise use of words is of fundamental importance, it may be that I am especially sensitive to imprecision in the words used by others. Others like my roommate, for example.

"If you're going to write about my being inarticulate, you have to write about your being so preoccupied that you forget to take your lunch unless I stick a reminder note on your Jeep's steering wheel."

Over the years I have gently remonstrated with Marian when she says things like this:

"The men came today and they couldn't fix it."

"The thing won't fit." And the latest:

"The box these go in is very snowy."

I tried some of this proposed column language on Marian and she said she didn't think "the box these go in is very snowy" was all that imprecise. I pointed out to her that I did not know what "these" are or what "box" she was talking about.

Later in the day after I had told Marian of my proposed comments about precision in the use of the words, she called the office to say:

"If you're going to write about my being inarticulate, you have to write about your being so preoccupied that you forget to take your lunch unless I stick a reminder note on your Jeep's steering wheel."

Yes, I've come full cycle, leaving home with — or, in some cases, without — my brown bag lunch. As a high schooler, I took a lunch from home out of necessity, because it was cheaper than eating in the high school cafeteria. Now (if I can remember) I take my lunch — tastily prepared by Marian, bless her heart — because I can save a lot of time by eating at my desk rather than going out for lunch.

— February 9, 1997

Plug it In

My advice to Marian over the years has included this friendly admonition:

Before you conclude that a household appliance won't work, consider the options. If it's an electrical appliance, for example, make sure that the cord is firmly plugged in. It's surprising how many "broken" electrical appliances this "repairs."

I had occasion to pursue the "consider the options" approach the other morning when Marian said, "The alarm didn't go off. The clock must be broken."

Quick examination revealed that the alarm was set for 8 p.m. instead of 8 a.m.

— **February 16, 1997**

Marian vs. the Squirrels

I was going to describe it as a battle, but it's more like a war: Marian vs. the squirrels.

The struggle, as you probably have already guessed, is over who controls the bird feeder outside the kitchen window.

Marian is willing to let the squirrels eat the sunflower seeds that fall to the ground from the feeder. But when one of those ingenious little rascals finds his or her (I wouldn't want to offend female squirrels by using politically incorrect language) way to the feeder itself, Marian goes into action.

Sometimes it is a noisy rapping on the kitchen window, accompanied by the cry, "Get out of there!" I surmise that the window-rapping is more effective than Marian's verbal exhortations.)

Sometimes she releases our two cocker spaniels, Sugar II and Sarah, with instruction to "go get those squirrels!" This tactic seems to work even though, as smart as they are, the cocker spaniels haven't yet learned to scale the feeder pole in a direct assault on the squirrels.

Ingenious little rascals or simply the enemy?

The dogs' pell-mell rush out the garden room door is enough to flush any squirrel that has somehow managed to prove that the feeder and its pole, despite claims to the contrary, are not really squirrel-proof.

Who is winning the war? Marian would claim that it's at least a draw when she is on picket duty. But, she says, "I can tell from the amount of bird seed that's been consumed, it's 10-zip for the squirrels when I'm out of town."

Marian's tactics include preventive action. The other morning, with no squirrel on the bird feeder, Marian ushered Sarah to the back door. I assumed that she was sending Sarah out with the usual encouragement to "be a good girl." Not so. "Sarah's on squirrel patrol," Marian explained.

Marian knows that in this squirrel-on-the-bird-feeder business, I'm on the squirrels' side. I admire their ingenuity. But so far I've not been able to win Marian over to my proposal for a peace settlement: Start calling it our "bird and squirrel feeder."

— **February 23, 1997**

'4MYK9S'

A recently rediscovered item that I somehow shuffled into the wrong file some weeks ago:

I had written about an Omahan and his beloved Beagle buddy – so beloved that the dog has his own celebrity license plates with the lettering: 1ST DAWG.

I invited other readers to let me know if any of them had a dog that had achieved such celebrity status.

Mary MacQuiddy, operator of Howl-Away Hounds kennel in Omaha, wrote that she has a dog celebrity license plate on the Dodge Caravan that she bought to travel with her dogs, Dr. Watson, an Otterhound, and Inspector Clouseau, a Petit Basset Griffon Venden, a rare French hunting breed.

The license reads: 4MYK9S.

I was flattered, incidentally, by the fact that Mary MacQuiddy started her letter by describing me as "dog person extraordinaire." I'll bask in that title for a while, but I think then I should pass it along to Marian, who is really the "dog person extraordinaire" in the family.

— March 9, 1997

Cease and Desist?

An attorney friend of mine the other evening said to me: "Please, no more columns about dogs. Cease and desist!" (Attorneys talk like that, you know.) He was smiling as he said this, so I don't know how serious he was.

But whether his plea was serious or in jest, I choose to ignore it. Let me tell you about a letter accompanied by a picture of two beautiful cocker spaniels, Buffy Sue and Lizbeth Too, owned by an Ashland reader.

I had written a column reporting that Marian had come across a poll in which 47 percent of those surveyed said they relied more on their pet than a spouse or child for affection.

"For 16 years my sweet and sassy cocker, Buffy Sue, has supplied love and affection," my Ashland reader wrote. "Now that she is getting older and a little slower moving about, her love is still abundant, as is mine."

And take this, my attorney friend who says I should stop writing about dogs: My Ashland reader ended her letter with these words: "I so enjoy your writings – especially about your life with Marian and, of course, the two 'loved ones,'" our cocker spaniels, Sugar and Sarah.

— March 23, 1997

Little Enthusiasm Greets the Idea of 'Peace Pact' With Squirrels

Recently I ended a column with a sort of combat correspondent's dispatch, a brief story of a backyard war: Marian vs. the squirrels.

Marian was losing. And, I must report, she still is losing, despite an outpouring of support and advice from readers from Kearney to Lincoln to Omaha.

I wouldn't say the callers and letter writers are necessarily anti-squirrel. They simply take the position that bird feeders are for the birds and squirrels should keep their itty-bitty paws and big furry tails out of there.

Now I hope readers won't think I'm wimping out when I say that I am both pro-bird and pro-squirrel. I enjoy watching the agile antics of the furry little critters. But Marian rejected my suggestion for a peace settlement: I said we should just start calling it our "bird and squirrel feeder."

I must report that my suggested peace pact was not endorsed by a single one of the numerous readers who responded to my report of Marian's losing battles. One reader sent along a book – "Outwitting Squirrels" by Bill Adler Jr. – that took a harsh view of my line of thinking. Adler wrote:

"I think that a lot of pro-squirrel people are actually quitters." These people, Adler wrote, are "tired of building barriers out of sharp metals, tired of transporting squirrels across state lines, tired of digging moats. A lot of former bird feeders turned pro-squirrel would rather take the afternoon off and nap." (I wouldn't take the whole afternoon off but a half-hour nap is attractive.)

A Lincoln woman called with a suggestion that Marian cover the feeder pole with vegetable oil. Not only does it keep the squirrels from climbing to the feeder, but it's fun to watch their efforts to climb the slick pole, my caller said.

An Omaha woman wrote to say she solved her problem by getting a pole shaped like a metal shepherd's crook. She also wrote, bless her heart, "Busy or not, don't stop your column."

A "constant reader" in Kearney said she has quit feeding the birds until at least next winter, after years of unsuccessfully "quarreling" with the squirrels. One of her unsuccessful efforts involved spreading "squirrel scram" on the feeder pole. One squirrel lost part of his tail, but "nothing deterred them."

An Omaha near-neighbor wrote to offer the services of his dog, Patch, described as "part Doberman and part breed-that's-obsessive-about-squirrels." The dog owner warned us that Patch's services would not be inexpensive since "she insists on Science Diet."

From Bellevue, "a faithful reader" wrote to tell us he has found a bird feed called "Squirrel-Free Pepper Treat." He said that, as he understands it, birds can't taste the chili-pepper-like ingredient in this bird feed mix, but squirrels can taste it and don't like it at all.

A Lincoln reader offered a similar suggestion and even sent along a sample of the package in which she has purchased "Squirrel Away," a bird seed supplement consisting of capsicum pepper. In this case, you mix the bird seed and the pepper yourself.

A reader in the Arcadia area in central Nebraska said that after some unsuccessful efforts to keep the squirrels off his bird feeder, he made a squirrel feeder "on which I stick an ear of corn for the bushy-tails to feed. It is just outside the kitchen window. I have taken pictures and videos of their antics."

From an Omaha reader came a similar report of what might be called bowing to the apparently inevitable – giving the squirrels their own source of food.

This Omaha correspondent said her husband has recently purchased a three-prong squirrel corn feeder, "a fancy one that spins." He did this after attending a bird-feeding seminar at which a visiting expert from Stillwater, Minn., said there is no getting rid of the squirrels. This Omaha correspondent quoted the visiting expert as saying that if you're successful in getting rid of three squirrels, for example, "you'll have three more move in and bring their buddies along."

But is it really a hopeless cause? Must the bird-feeder-for-the-birds army make peace with the squirrels, agreeing to joint tenancy of the backyard bird feeder or buying fancy three-pronged spinning corn feeders?

As I've said before, I favor a peaceful settlement, although some would call that surrender. But in his "Outwitting Squirrels" book, Bill Adler suggests tactics considerably more drastic than those that have come from my readers. For example:

"Rattlesnakes are a major predator of squirrels. Acquire some for your lawn. (They also help keep solicitors away.)"

"Practice hitting squirrels with golf balls. Your chances of making successful contact are about one in three billion, but your golf swing will improve."

Tongue still firmly in cheek, Adler ends his book on a hopeful note. He writes:

"We have survived world wars, the Cold War, devastating plagues. We have gone to the moon and sent probes past the outer-most edge of our solar system. We have eliminated major diseases, and we've invented 'Wheel of Fortune.'"

Surely, Adler suggests, if we can accomplish such things, there is hope that mankind (or should I say humankind?) can continue to progress "but only if we keep up our struggle to outwit squirrels."

Postscript:

Marian is now waging a two-front war.

"Now I'm having a terrible time with grackles, " she tells me. "If anybody has any advice as to how to get rid of grackles, I'd be grateful."

And did I detect a bit of softening in Marian's attitude toward squirrels? Here's what she said:

"Squirrels are kind of cute, but I hate the grackles."

The only anti-grackle weapon that we have tried so far is my owl hoot-call that sometimes rouses tom turkeys to reveal their whereabouts by gobbling. If you blow long enough and hard enough, grackles seem to become alarmed and fly off. (We try not to dwell on the fact that we have moved them and their irritating squawking into some neighbor's trees.

— May 4, 1997

When the Movie's Over

I've written before about how Marian and I enjoy staying until the very end of a movie, watching the credits, which sometimes seem to go on for about half as long as the film itself.

You know the kind of thing I'm referring to – who was the director, where was the film shot, who supplied the leading man's wardrobe, who dressed the leading lady's hair, who was the "best boy" (I still don't have the foggiest idea what that means) and on and on.

This habit of ours was responsible, for example, for our learning that in the film, "A River Runs Through It," directed by Robert Redford, all of the fish caught were released and not eaten, as might have happened if the film had been directed by someone less environmentally sensitive – or someone hungrier – than Redford.

Recently watching credits following a movie whose cast included three poodles, Marian and I chuckled when we saw a "poodle wrangler" named among the credits.

I asked Marian if she had ever thought of calling herself a "cocker spaniel wrangler." She indicated that she feels her relations with our cocker spaniels tend more toward mothering than wrangling.

— June 1, 1997

Long-Distance Duet

Considering the fact that Marian and I have four grandchildren, I don't think I've overburdened you with grandparenting stories. After all, we have more grandchildren than cocker spaniels, and I've written more about the cockers than the grandkids.

All of which is a prelude to a story about James Wheaton Karger, 22-month-old son of daughter Nancy, who lives in Denver.

In a daycare setting, James had picked up the first words of an old children's religious song, "Jesus Loves Me." Daughter Nancy told Marian that she would like to expand James' knowledge of the lyrics beyond "Jesus loves me," which James was singing over and over.

I volunteered to supply the rest of the words. (My long-term memory is still pretty good.) I called the Karger home and sang the lyrics into the voice message recorder.

Nancy saved the recording and now, when James asks to hear it, Nancy turns on the recorder and James and I sing a sort of long-distance duet.

Encouraged by James' willingness to engage in long-distance sing-alongs with me, I'm planning to introduce him to a song called "The Children's Train," a lullaby that has been sung in the Andersen family for several generations.

If my long-distance musical lessons continue to go well, I plan to introduce James also to a lively song dedicated to my college fraternity, Phi Gamma Delta, and its colors. (Purple and white, and thanks for asking.)

Both Nancy and our son, David, enjoyed "The Children's Train" and the Phi Gam song — although David inexplicably joined Phi Delta Theta when he enrolled at the University of Nebraska-Lincoln.

I want to get to James Wheaton Karger with a Phi Gam song before his Uncle Dave tries to teach him a Phi Delt tune.

— June 8, 1997

Of Peaches Marmalade & Mary Cornett

Let me introduce you to our newest dog. She is a cocker spaniel, of course, and her name is Peaches Getoutofthere.

Well, of course, her name really isn't Peaches Getoutofthere. It's Peaches Marmalade and she is a lovely, lively, get-into-everything, 9-month-old puppy whose perpetual-motion antics prompt a steady stream of "Peaches, get out of there," admonitions from Marian or me. (There are variations, of course, such as "Get down from there, Peaches" or "Peaches, put that down.")

Peaches is now a full-time Prairie Avenue resident, thanks to Sister Sarah, one of our two other cocker spaniels, and a mixed-breed female puppy named Itty Bear, owned by retiring longtime City Clerk Mary Galligan Cornett.

I'll explain all of this after informing non-dog lovers in the audience (like that attorney friend of mine who said, "Stop writing about dogs!") that this is not just a story about dogs and dog lovers. It's a story about government responding to the voice of the people.

Well, it was really the voices of Marian, Mary Cornett and Ron Hemingsen, executive director of the Nebraska Humane Society, but I believe they were speaking for a lot of people when they successfully advocated raising from two to three the number of dogs that can legally reside in an Omaha residence. The change brings Omaha into line with the dogs-per-household limits in other cities in the Midlands.

When one of our cockers, Sister, died a year ago, Sister Sarah came to live with us and our surviving cocker, Sugar II. Marian struck up a friendly relationship with the Minnesota dog breeder from whom we had purchased Sarah. After Sarah had worked her way into our hearts, the Minnesota dog breeder told Marian that she had another cocker spaniel who was just right for Marian.

I told Marian that there was a legal limit of two dogs per household. She was disappointed – for about 15 minutes. Then she said, "I'm going to try to get the law changed."

Marian went to work contacting members of the City Planning Board, Ron Hemingsen of the Humane Society and members of the City Council.

Came the day for the City Council to vote on the three-dog-limit ordinance change approved by the Planning Board. Council members indicated general approval but it was suggested that the vote be delayed so amendments could be considered.

Mary Cornett stepped to the microphone, a totally unexpected witness. The veteran city clerk said she thought the council members knew of her 7-year-old male golden lab named Gabriel and her 3-year-old female mixed-breed named Ginger. Now, she said, a third dog had entered her life – Itty Bear, a 6-

Cocker spaniel Daphne gets a squeeze from Andy.

month-old female whose mother was a dachshund with all the proper papers and whose father was, in Mary's words, "a traveling salesman."

So, Mary Cornett confessed, there were now three dogs residing in her home. "Please make me legal," she asked the City Council.

Council members promptly passed the ordinance, thereby making law-abiding citizens out of more than a few Omahans who have had three dogs living with them and opening the door for others who would like to add a third dog to the family circle.

— July 20, 1997

Motivatee?

Marian has come across a new variety of those "stick-it" notepads that you use as memory-joggers. The new stick-it note paper – which I'm sure I will see a good deal of in the weeks and months ahead – carries this heading:

"I'm not a nag – I'm a motivator!"

Let me ask my fellow recipients of spousal messages: Do you think you would notice any difference in being a "motivatee" instead of a "nagee"?

— August 17, 1997

What's in a Picture?

Marian had come across a 40-plus-year-old picture of a very slender me, snapped at an Arizona resort on an early-in-our-marriage vacation trip.

Marian showed the picture to daughter Nancy, who immediately said she wanted that picture of her daddy. Marian said she didn't want to give it up.

I, of course, was touched – both wife and daughter wanted possession of a picture of me.

A few days after Nancy had returned to Denver, I discovered Marian's true motive. The picture of slender me turned up on my dresser where it stares me in the eye every morning.

My roommate did not need to explain that this was a not-so-subtle way of encouraging me to return to a figure more like the slender me of 40-plus years ago.

No hypocrite she, Marian weighs about the same as she did when we took that long-ago vacation trip.

— **August 31, 1997**

Use It or Lose It

Danish researchers say that an examination of the brains of 94 cadavers indicated that men, on average, have about four billion more brain cells than women – an average of 23 billion cells in male brains compared to a female average of about 19 billion.

I read Marian the Associated Press dispatch from Copenhagen. Her response: "Men may have the extra brain cells, but they haven't figured out what to do with them."

— **October 19, 1997**

We'll Plant New Trees

As my roommate and I assessed the very substantial damage from last weekend's snowstorm, Marian's consistently upbeat spirit demonstrated itself again. "Look at the beautiful trees we have left," she said. "And we'll plant some new ones."

That upbeat spirit was tested twice again during the early days of the storm's aftermath. First Marian tripped and fell in our back hall and wound up with a bloody face and nose that took 23 stitches to repair. So once again she has to endure the healing process and I have to endure jokes about wife beating.

Then our power went out – two days after we had congratulated ourselves on being lucky enough to have escaped the power outage that affected so many Omahans.

— November 2, 1997

Favorable: 20 to 1

One anonymous critical comment came in a note that said:

"The articles about Princess Diana are far more interesting and newsworthy than your stories about your wife and her dogs!"

My secretary, Jackie Wrieth, and I have not kept a tally over the years, but we estimate that in regard to the subject of Marian or our dogs, favorable comment from readers runs about 20 to 1 in comparison with critical comment.

The most recent favorable comment – quite typical of those we have received over the years – came from a woman who said she liked my column about books I had enjoyed reading. She ended our brief but pleasant telephone conversation with these words: "And don't forget your wife and the pets."

— November 6, 1997

And from Blair ...

A correspondent in Blair said she agreed with all of a recent column, including my roommate's reaction to a Danish researchers' report. The report indicated that men on average have about four billion more brain cells than women. Marian's reaction: "Men have the extra brain cells, but they haven't figured out what to do with them."

My Blair correspondent said she hopes that there are some exceptions to Marian's judgment on male use of extra brain cells. Her letter concluded: "I always enjoy hearing of the pets. Keep writing!"

Another correspondent with a fondness for dogs wrote: "I feel genuine sorrow for anyone who has never felt the love and complete loyalty of a good dog. The complete devotion they show is an experience in life that you cannot describe (columnist's note: I try, I try) and that none should miss."

> *"Above all, keep telling us about those pets and, most important, your good wife."*

This reader, Fred H. Kohler Sr. of Omaha, said he would be proud if I used some of his letter in my column. He indicated that he and his "wonderful wife of 57 years," Dorothy, surely approve of my comments about both Marian and our dogs. His letter concluded:

"Above all, keep telling us about those pets and, most important, your good wife."

Fred Kohler, I'm delighted that the image of my "good wife" has come through in some of the columns I've written.

I can think of no more appropriate way to end a Thanksgiving Day column than to say that I have a great many things to be thankful for, including readers who are so free to share their opinions with me, but alone at the pinnacle of my thankfulness this day is the fact that the former Marian Battey of Lincoln, Neb., has shared her life with me these past 47 years.

— November 27, 1997

U-turns and Sweeping Studies

Medical researchers should, of course, pursue the truth wherever the search leads them.

But I wonder if some of the researchers realize how frustrating it can be to some of us diet-watchers when their research produces a sharp U-turn in what we are told is good for us.

Take the recent announcement that "a sweeping study" indicates that stick margarine increases a person's risk of heart disease by a much as one-third. This finding comes 30 years or so after Marian and I started using margarine instead of butter because we were told that margarine was good for us and butter was potentially bad.

Marian has been buying margarine in little round containers instead of sticks, so perhaps we won't have to switch nutritional gears again. But to be on the absolutely safe side, research people, is it OK if I eat bread without anything on it? Oh, perhaps with a little bit of grape jelly – unless, of course, there has been research that says grapes are bad for you, too.

Now before people think I am against medical research in regard to healthful diets, let me say I appreciate the work of the researchers. I'm confident that many of their findings have helped people live longer and healthier lives. It's just that I wish there weren't so many U-turns on the research road to good health.

— November 30, 1997

Intra-Household Communication

I was thinking that Marian had mellowed out, squirrel-wise. I based this on the fact that I have not recently heard her pounding on the breakfast room window and shouting, "Get out of there!" to a squirrel that had found its way to the top of the supposedly squirrel-proof bird feeder.

When I asked her about this, Marian said there had been no mellowing on her part. It's just that she is not seeing squirrels on the bird feeder as often as in the past. They seem to be finding enough to eat in the seeds that have fallen to the ground.

"So perhaps you should report that the squirrels have mellowed out," Marian said.

This, of course, is more consistent with the attitude of the roommate that I know and love. Marian doesn't mellow out in a battle in which she thinks she's in the right.

Another example of Marian's consistency:

She has an unshakable belief in the carrying power of the human voice. I'll bet there are other husbands or wives out there who will recognize what I'm talking about – oral messages directed your way under circumstances that you – but definitely not your mate – believe make clear communication virtually impossible. For example:

I'm in an upstairs bathroom, door closed with the water running. Marian comes to the foot of the stairs, and in a tone a bit more than conversational but definitely less than a shout, directs a question my way. I turn off the water, open the door and go to the head of the stairs, perhaps showing a bit of irritation, which in turn irritates Marian. Sound familiar?

Adding to the occasional difficulty of intra-household communication is the fact that Marian spends a good deal of time conversing with our three cocker spaniels. Well, not exactly conversing, although sometimes the dogs do respond with body language.

I will hear a question like "Are you ready for breakfast?" And I will reply, "Yes, I'll be down in a minute." To which Marian replies, "No, no, not you. I was talking to the dogs."

Long experience, however, has taught me how to handle this sort of thing on most occasions. I can frequently detect the difference in the tone of voice in which Marian addresses the dogs and in which she addresses me. Need I say more?

— **December 14, 1997**

Slow Reaction Time

I have discovered that I live with a coach, at least by her definition.

Marian over the years has used various descriptions for her advice, suggestions and critiques, never admitting to the slightest hint of nagging. (She totally rejects my suggestion that the only fair judge of what constitutes nagging is the naggee, not the nagger, since a nagger never pleads guilty.) But back to Marian as a coach:

The other morning, as I was preparing to head out for my annual physical, Marian suggested a couple of questions I should ask the estimable Dr. Craig Taylor. Perhaps a little testy because I hadn't had anything to eat or drink since 6 the evening before (and I'm not a cheerful early-morning person anyhow), I asked Marian if she would like to come along and ask the questions herself. "You're not very coachable" was Marian's reply.

I reported to Coach Marian that evening that I had asked the questions that she suggested. The result: I'm now going into a regular physical training program – as Marian had suggested two years ago. So I'm coachable, Marian. I just have a slow reaction time.

— **December 19, 1997**

Presidential Pup

I've been accused of being a "Clinton basher," to which I reply that I only bash when justified – justified in my opinion, of course.

But today my compliments to the president for his decision to take a Labrador puppy into the White House family.

I can't think of a better choice if a family is to have only one dog. Now before Marian comes down on me, let me say I love our cocker spaniels, too. I have my hunting dogs, including a Lab, down on the farm. But for a single, all-purpose dog – one that can hunt with you all day, then come home and lie by the fire while the grandchildren crawl all over him or her – you can't beat a Labrador.

So have fun with your chocolate Lab, Mr. President. I'm glad you decided not to send Buddy away for extensive training before you took him into the family circle. That particularly enjoyable puppy stage passes all too quickly.

— **December 25, 1997**

Losing Weight Like the President

My roommate the other day reported receiving her "all-time favorite birthday card." Message:

"It's not polite to ask your age, so how much do you weigh?"

Speaking of weight, Marian the other evening served me a mouthwatering dessert – blueberry pie a la mode – with a comment something like this: "I shouldn't be serving you this. I want to help you lose some weight."

I decided that I would forgo a rich dessert the next time it was offered, thus rising perhaps a bit belatedly to the challenge that Marian presented when she said, "Bill Clinton is losing weight, you know."

— **December 28, 1997**

Disneyland, Danes, Deer and Dogs

A zillion cardinals; 'my roommate'; sleep habits and annoying cheerfulness; skiing and falling; a puzzling dream; Danish origins; our three cocker spaniels; Marian's photo; high-energy wife; California and Mickey Mouse; time for retirement?; Lindsey Andersen, fax machines and computers; Caregiving 1.

Have Toothbrush, Will Travel

My mailbag was so full at year's end that I plan to use next Sunday's column to continue telling you what some readers have been telling me. But as I end today's column, please indulge me in a story about one of our grandchildren and his reaction to one of his Christmas presents.

John Andrew Karger of Denver, 4-year-old son of our daughter Nancy, was told Christmas Eve that one of his presents would be a trip to Disneyland next summer along with our three other grandchildren, their parents and his Omaha grandparents.

John Andrew promptly went to work packing his suitcase for the trip seven months away – shorts, T-shirts and his toothbrush.

At bedtime, he retrieved the toothbrush, used it and put it back in his suitcase, saying that he would continue to do that until time to depart for Disneyland. Daughter Nancy doubts that this routine will be continued for seven months, but she does feel that those are going to be a long seven months.

My roommate not only conceived the idea for the trip but is paying for it, bless her generous heart. For reasons best known to her, she chose for the California Disneyland visit a time frame that includes my birthday.

Do you suppose that if I'm a good boy, Mickey Mouse will come to my birthday party?

— January 4, 1998

Of Poets and Soup Ladies

Marian and I continue to stay to the end of each movie we see, partly in a search for identification of cast members, partly to see where the movie was filmed and partly to enjoy facts such as this: The First Production Unit involved in making the film "The Rainmaker" had a "poet in residence" and a "soup lady."

The staff of the Second Production Unit, we noticed, included neither a poet nor a soup lady. Looks to me as if there might be grounds for a lawsuit here. Surely in our litigious society there must be a lawyer somewhere who would be willing to take the film studio to court for discriminating against the staff of the Second Production Unit.

— January 22, 1998

————◆————

Cardinals and Another Critter

Some weeks ago, I quoted Willa Cather's description of autumn in rural Nebraska. I said then that I would return to the writings of Nebraska's most distinguished author and share with you her description of the season's first snowfall as she remembered it from her childhood years in Red Cloud, Neb.

We are certainly well past our first snow this season, but I hope you will still enjoy reading these words from what I believe was Willa Cather's finest work, "My Antonia":

"The first snowfall came early in December. I remember how the world looked from our sitting-room window as I dressed behind the stove that morning: the low sky was like a sheet of metal; the blond cornfields had faded out into ghostliness at last; the little pond was frozen under its stiff willow bushes. Big white flakes were whirling over everything and disappearing in the red grass."

Backyard bulletin from Marian, telephoned to my office during a recent snowfall: "There's a zillion cardinals at the bird feeder. I counted seven bright red ones."

* * *

Backyard bulletin from Marian, telephoned to my office during a recent snowfall:

"There's a zillion cardinals at the bird feeder. I counted seven bright red ones."

Now Marian and I both enjoy all the cardinals that come to our bird feeder, so I hope that gender-equity activists won't fault her for not reporting on the number of non-red cardinals that she saw. I would hope that they would be willing to concede that those bright red male cardinals are more likely to catch your eye.

And speaking of the backyard bird feeder, another guest has invited himself (or herself) to dinner. In addition to the squirrels that keep climbing the squirrel-proof feeder pole, a very small mouse has started to enjoy the sunflower seeds.

Marian has seen the squirrels climb the pole, but she doesn't know how the small mouse has managed to get aboard. Since arrival by parachute or one gigantic leap from ground level seems unlikely, we have to assume that this little critter has, like some squirrels, found a way to climb the pole.

Considering her "Get out of there!" window-rapping reaction to squirrels in the bird feeder, I find it interesting that Marian reacts differently to the presence of the mouse. Her comment: "I guess it's better than a rat."

— January 25, 1998

'Roommate' or Not?

In reader reaction to date, the vote is tied at 1-to-1 in the question of whether I should refer to Marian as "my roommate."

One reader said he likes my use of the term because it indicates that I consider Marian an equal partner in our marriage. Now comes another reader who writes anonymously because, he or she says, "I am a coward and do not want my name in the paper." This reader said it is bothersome when I use the term "roommate" when speaking of my wife.

"It sounds just too cutesy, or silly, for someone such as you who comes across as an urbane, rather conservative man."

She says she doesn't mind my calling her my roommate as well as my wife, but I had better never describe her as my "better half," "the little woman" or "the boss."

Now I was pretty sure I come across as conservative in my writings, but how about that "urbane"? My dictionary defines urbane as, among other things, "evincing the polish and suavity characteristic of social life in large cities" or "notably polite or finished in manner."

I always try to be polite. But suave? If calling Marian my roommate would make me seem impolite, that's one thing. But I don't think I'd mind being called non-suave.

In any case, Marian gets to cast the tie-breaking vote. She says she doesn't mind my calling her my roommate as well as my wife, but I had better never describe her as my "better half," "the little woman" or "the boss."

— January 29, 1998

Sleep Deprived?

Let's talk about sleep – or the lack thereof. The subject comes to mind as a result of two articles that Marian called to my attention. One dealt with "sleep deprivation" and the other talked of "the snoozing you're losing."

I don't know how the medical fraternity looks at this subject, but common experience tells us that different people need – or think they need – different amounts of sleep.

Marian and I try to get seven hours of sleep each night but frequently come closer to six hours.

Two of the hardest things I do each day is go to bed at night and get up in the morning, which means that I frequently stay up until 1 a.m. or so and don't get up until 8 a.m. or so. This also means that from time to time I get to become a television critic as I watch some of the morning shows while dressing. One of my critiques:

The NBC "Today" show should stop, immediately, that mob-on-the-street feature that has publicity-hungry travelers pushing their faces into camera range and waving and calling for attention.

But I digress. Back to the subject of sleep: My sleep habits make quite appropriate the embroidered sampler that Marian has hung in our bathroom for my benefit. The message:

"If God had intended us to see the sunrise, he would have made it later in the day."

Marian gets up a half-hour or so earlier than I do, and is, dare I say it, annoyingly cheerful. (She greets our three cocker spaniels each morning as though she hadn't seen them for months. "Superdogs!" is a typical morning greeting from their mistress.)

By "annoyingly cheerful," I think some readers will know what I mean. When you wake up reluctantly, there is a period of time when you really just want to be left alone.

Marian came across a joke that captures the spirit of what I'm saying here. The joke: "Sometimes I wake up grouchy. Sometimes I just let him sleep."

Now to a practical test of whether Marian is getting enough sleep:

Sitting comfortably in a leather chair by the fireplace, Marian was reading a Time magazine article on sleep deprivation. You guessed it. She fell asleep while reading the article.

— **February 8, 1998**

From the Book of Proverbs

The other day I wrote that Marian wakes up annoyingly cheerful – annoying in the sense that some among us wake up slowly and reluctantly and find it hard to understand how others can be so cheerful on arising.

An Omaha reader, a pastor, passed along a message that made me feel a bit better about my feelings in this matter. He referred me to the "Good News Bible" version of Proverbs, chapter 27, verse 14:

"You might as well curse your friend as wake him up early in the morning with a loud greeting."

Now I would prefer a loud greeting to a curse, but I would prefer even more just to be left alone while I adjust to the necessity of rising and trying not to sound too grouchy.

Incidentally, as I looked up Proverbs 27:14 in the King James version of the Bible ("He that blesseth his friends with a loud voice, rising early in the morning, it should be counted a curse to him") my eyes fell on verse 15, which reads thus in the King James version:

"A continual dropping in a very rainy day and a contentious woman are alike." Or, in The New Living Translation version: "A nagging wife is as annoying as the constant dripping on a rainy day."

Marian says that when she advises me on a given subject, she is acting as a "motivator," not a nag.

I may have to spend more time with the Book of Proverbs. I confess I hadn't realized there is so much wisdom therein.

Very Important Postscript: My quoting the "constant dripping on a rainy day" language should not be interpreted as a personal comment on my relationship with my roommate. As readers of this space may recall from an earlier column, Marian says that when she advises me on a given subject, she is acting as a "motivator," not a nag.

— **February 15, 1998**

Knowing Enough to Fall Down

Watching the Olympic downhill skiers brought to mind – by way of contrast – my one and only experience on a ski slope.

It was on a beginners' slope at Aspen in the Colorado Rockies. Good friends Paul and June Schorr of Lincoln were playing host to Marian and me. Marian had the good sense to spend her time reading a book or sitting in the sunshine or whatever, but Paul convinced me that a 60-ish type like me ought to be able to take up skiing, at least in a modest way.

Paul didn't just enroll me in a beginners' class; he arranged for me to have my own instructress.

First, I spent some time off to the side of the beginners' slope, presumably learning the fundamentals. I remember watching kids who could almost have skied between my legs zipping down the slope. I went out onto the slope rather timorously and quickly discovered that it was more like ice than snow and that I had to be careful that one of those cute kids didn't knock me flat.

After a couple of very tentative efforts, my instructress encouraged me to strike out on my own – for a short distance, that is. I quickly discovered that there was no way I could assure that I could ski only a short distance, having no idea how to stop.

At the bottom of the slope there was a line of skiers waiting to take their turn on the ski lift. For a scary few seconds, I was clearly out of control, heading straight for that unsuspecting crowd at the bottom of the lift.

My instructress tried to catch up, meanwhile shouting, "Fall down! Fall down!"

I fell down. And as my instructress came up, I struggled to retain just a bit of composure and pride by telling her, "You didn't have to tell me to fall down. I knew enough to do that on my own."

> *My instructress tried to catch up, meanwhile shouting, "Fall down! Fall down!"*

With that, I asked the instructress to help me off the slope and went in and had a drink. Thus ended my skiing career. But I still enjoy going back to Aspen – in the summer.

— **February 22, 1998**

Charles Woodson & Peyton Manning

My roommate's steel-trap mind trapped me again the other day.

We had read a news item that carried the headline "Bad Impression" and told of the performance of former Michigan cornerback Charles Woodson, Heisman Trophy winner, in connection with the Walter Camp Football Foundation banquet in New Haven, Conn. The USA Today report said Woodson "left an image of a spoiled athlete" by demanding first-class airfare for his mother, girlfriend and nephew and, while protected by two bodyguards, refused interview requests.

Marian and I agreed that this was indeed the image of a spoiled athlete. Marian then reminded me that I had said, before the Heisman Trophy balloting, that I was for Woodson, on the grounds it would be a welcome recognition of a defensive player instead of the customary honoring of an offensive star.

"I was for Peyton Manning," the Tennessee quarterback, Marian reminded me.

Here I am suffering from occasional "senior moments," and Marian's steel-trap memory is still working like, well, a steel trap.

— **February 26, 1998**

Brave Dreams

I know I have a lot of company in the matter of inexplicable dreams. (Inexplicable to the dreamer at least. Maybe a psychiatrist could figure some of them out.)

I don't intend to start telling you about all of my dreams or even a substantial portion thereof, but I had one the other night that was even more puzzling than the average and amusing enough (to me at least) that I thought I might share it with you.

In this dream I turned down an offer to join the board of directors of the Atlanta Braves baseball team. The offer was made to me by the manager of a drugstore in Atlanta who asked me, as I paid my bill for whatever I had purchased there, whether I would like to be a Braves director. He indicated he could arrange it if I were interested.

I declined, for reasons that were and are not clear to me. Perhaps it was my dream-sublimated way of expressing the fact that I am hardly a fan of either the Braves or their owner, Ted Turner.

The real baseball enthusiast in the Andersen household doesn't particularly like the Braves, either. But I'll bet if that Atlanta druggist had offered her the job, Marian would have accepted it faster than you can say "Take me out to the ball game."

— March 1, 1998

AKA John Elway

Now I know a lot of you out there have grandchildren who say unusual things that provoke laughter or, sometimes, amazement on the part of parents and grandparents.

Where I have the advantage over you is that I get to write about some of those sayings. Recent example, relayed by daughter Nancy Karger, who lives in Denver:

Nancy was trying to get the attention of 2½-year-old James Wheaton Karger (who these days will respond only if addressed by the name of the Denver Broncos' superstar quarterback John Elway). James Wheaton, AKA John Elway, gave this response:

"Don't bug me. I'm thinking."

P.S. — Latest development: I understand Jaymo will now respond only when called "Batman."

He calls his mother "Robin."

— March 29, 1998

'– sen' Names

Speaking of names of Danish origin:

The Wall Street Journal had a recent story that started like this:

"Copenhagen — Ever since Danish peasants started moving from the countryside to the city a century ago Denmark has been grappling with a tricky issue: What to do about all the people named Jensen, Hansen and Nielsen?"

Together, The Journal reported, those three names account for more than one-fifth of Denmark's five million population. If you include the Pedersens, Andersens and the Larsens and other '– sen' names, the proportion rises to three-fifths.

Among the ways the Danes are coping:

- The Copenhagen phone book lists not only address and phone number but also a person's middle name and occupation.

- Surgeons are extra careful about whom they operate on.

(This reminds me of the time, after one of her various hip operations, Marian noticed as she was recuperating that on her left hip the word "No" had been prominently painted. She was pleased to know of the hospital's care in assuring that the operation concentrated on her right hip, which was the one that was ailing.)

Some Danes go farther than others and file for a change of name, as in the case of a man named Fleming Larsen who changed his name to Fleming Axmark. But he's complaining about the fact that the government charges $425 for a name change.

I've touched on the subject of Danish names before, pointing out that my paternal grandfather was named Andrew Andersen, my father was named Andrew B. Andersen and my eldest brother was named Andrew R. Andersen.

Additionally, one of our grandchildren is named Robert Andrew Andersen and another is named John Andrew Karger. And Marian and a few of my friends often call me Andrew.

— April 9, 1998

News of Cocker Spaniels, Cats and a Raccoon

Fair warning to that sourpuss attorney friend of mine – and any others who don't like to read about our dogs:

Today we're going to deal again in some dog news, but before any reader turns away, I should tell you that we're also going to talk about cats and a pet raccoon.

First, the cats. Several factors influence me to address the subject:

Two or three of my friends had asked when I'm going to write about cats as lovable pets.

Then I received a Christmas card from friends Janyce and Richard Hunt of Blair. Richard is vice chairman of Huntel Systems, and the Hunts are active and generous supporters of good causes in the Omaha metropolitan area. The Hunts' card included a charming picture of their four white cats asleep on a bed. (A people bed, not a cat bed, that is.)

Finally, Marian called my attention to the results of a survey that purported to find that there are 71.8 million cats in 29.1 million U.S. households, compared to 59 million dogs and 41.3 million dog owners. (I wonder if they counted my five hunting dogs down on the farm.)

Marian and I, as readers of this space know, are dog lovers and like the way our three cocker spaniels go affectionately crazy when either one of us comes home. A good friend says cats also greet their owners but in the more cat-like way, purring and rubbing their way around their owner's legs, for example.

So maybe it's all a myth, this feeling of dog owners, reflected in a bit of humor Marian passes along:

"If you call a dog, he comes running and jumping and joyfully responding. If you call a cat, he says, 'Leave your number, and I'll get back to you'."

The great author, T. S. Eliot, whose book, "Old Possum's Book of Practical Cats," provided many of the lyrics for the musical "Cats," wrote this in the closing pages of his book:

> "The usual Dog about the Town
> Is much inclined to play the clown
> Slap his back or shake his paw,
> And he will gambol and guffaw.
> He's such an easygoing lout,
> He'll answer any hail or shout."

Turning to cats, Eliot wrote:

> "With cats, some say, one rule is true:
> Don't speak until you are spoken to...
> Before a cat will condescend
> To treat you as a trusted friend,
> Some little token of esteem
> Is needed, like a dish of cream
> A cat's entitled to expect
> These evidences of respect.
> And so in time you reach your aim,
> And finally call him by his name."

And now about that raccoon pet:

A very welcome letter came my way from a Council Bluffs veterinarian with whose family we have been friends for a good many years. He and his wife, he wrote, live in the rolling loess hills north of Council Bluffs, where they are surrounded by a delightful abundance of wildlife, "residing quite happily in the company of horses, a small sheep flock, much-loved dogs (three Irish setters), worthless cats and, until last summer, Lily the raccoon."

Lily was raised from a tiny baby and "amused and delighted us for 16 months until, as we knew she some day would, she threw in her lot with a smooth-talking boy raccoon," our family friend wrote. Enclosed were pictures of the now-departed Lily, including one with Lily lying on a bed schmoozing with her mistress.

The letter ended on a delightful note: "Please convey to your lovely wife my best regards and give each of your spaniel girls a long scratch behind each ear for me."

Speaking of those spaniel girls, I continue to get messages from people who say they enjoy reading about our family life, especially about Marian and the dogs. One caller, for example, said: "I love your column, your wife and your dogs in that order."

So herewith, in response to what some readers say they enjoy – and, even more importantly, in response to Marian's repeated suggestions – a report on the athletic ability of our youngest cocker spaniel, the irrepressible Peaches.

Marian says she believes Peaches is capable of a vertical jump that, if measured by Cornhusker strength coach Boyd Epley, might not qualify her for a scholarship but should get her an invitation to walk on.

In any case, I have determined that with her rear paws on the floor, Peaches can leap and stretch to a height of at least $27^1/_2$ inches – not bad for a 1-year-old who stands no more than 12 inches high at the shoulder.

Peaches' vertical jump doesn't enable her to climb onto any of the kitchen counters but makes it quite easy for her to pull down any food that Marian or I leave too close to the edge of a counter. This has led to a three-dog assault (Peaches shares) on a loaf of bread, several sandwiches and several bags of popcorn. It has also led us to try to remember to push things farther back from counter edges.

As to the other dogs, 2-year-old Sarah is getting a little better about not barking at strangers when they enter the house. Within the family circle, Sarah shines as the best mannered of the trio. The batting order at snack time is invariably this: Aggressive little Sugar, oldest but smallest, insisting on being fed first, with Peaches close behind. Sarah stands quietly, waiting her turn.

Eight-year-old Sugar, incidentally, continues to look thin. But she continues to enjoy life and regularly gladdens my heart by seeking me out and stretching full length at my feet, waiting for the customary ear-scratching and tummy-rubbing.

— April 12, 1998

Responding to Readers' Requests

I try to respond as well as I can to reader requests, but sometimes there isn't much I can do about them. (For example, the reader who wanted me to do something about what he considered the malfunctioning of doors at the Harney Street entrance to the Douglas County Hall of Justice.)

Marian Battey Andersen.

But if you look at the picture that appears with this column today, you will see an example of my responding positively to a reader's request. The picture, as some readers will know and others may have guessed, is of my roommate, Marian Battey Andersen. It replaces my picture today (now don't be writing or calling with suggestions that the change be made permanent) because of a suggestion from a reader in Blue Hill, Neb. Her letter concluded:

"My love to Marian and pooches. Why don't you put her picture where yours always is? We need to know what she looks like."

This friendly reader chided me for chiding frequent candidate Geraldine Ferraro for having "politicitis" and asked if I'm not affected with a form of "itis" – "editoritis." Her letter continued:

"Although I read your column faithfully, I sometimes wonder at your bias and your judgmental remarks. (Judge not, lest you be judged.)"

There were further comments, including this view of President Clinton: "He has done a good job as president. If only his morals were as good as his performance. Too bad he doesn't just resign. But I'm sure you would all start harassing (Al) Gore."

I was very pleased to hear from my 82-year-old faithful reader in Blue Hill and to accept her suggestion that we publish a picture of Marian. But I do feel I must reject the admonition, "Judge not, lest you be judged." Good heavens, dear Blue Hill reader and advisor, do you want to put newspaper columnists and editorial writers out of business?

Now in the interest of full disclosure and balanced comment, I must add something that may appeal to my Blue Hill reader, i.e., the time-honored description of editorial writers and columnists as people who "watch the battle from the hills and then come down and shoot the wounded."

— **April 26, 1998**

Marian in Action

Marian in Action, Chapter MCXIII:

At the recent dinner honoring Connie Claussen on her retirement after a splendid career as associate athletic director at the University of Nebraska at Omaha, Marian and I were hosts for a group that included two young Lady Mavericks, members of UNO's fine volleyball team – Erin Shafer of Colorado Springs, Colo., and Christyn Malone of Palisade, Neb.

My roommate was her usual ebullient self, talking animatedly with our various guests and jumping up from time to time to greet a friend at a nearby table.

All of which prompted vigorous young athlete Christyn Malone to turn to me and say: "Your wife certainly has a high energy level."

Couldn't have said it better myself, Christyn.

— May 24, 1998

Columns 'Ring of the Truth'

My thanks to those readers who responded so kindly to last Sunday's announcement that I will be taking a "semi-sabbatical" this summer, writing columns only for Sunday publication rather than both Thursday and Sunday each week.

An Omaha reader called to say that she will miss me on Thursdays. She loves to read about Marian and the dogs. (She also said – bless her heart – that the columns "ring of the truth and really sing.")

Another caller said she hopes that I'll have a good summer and "we'll miss you on Thursdays."

What a pleasant note on which to start my three-month "semi-sabbatical." See you next Sunday.

— July 7, 1998

Lovely, Renowned Marian

I wrote recently that Marian and I will be taking our children and grandchildren to Disneyland in late July on a trip that will coincide with my birthday. I raised the question whether, assuming I had been a good boy, Mickey Mouse might come to my birthday party.

This prompted someone to write me two letters, both signed "Mickey (Everybody's Favorite) Mouse" and both purportedly written in California.

The first letter said it had come to the writer's attention, through reading one of the "finest newspapers in the country," that I would be in California at the time of my birthday and continued:

"Since, by all reports, you have been such a good boy in years past, I would consider it a privilege if I could be invited to your birthday party."

A few days later came a letter saying the writer had been "talking with Minnie," who would also like to come to the birthday party. This letter continued: "She has heard a great deal about the lovely, renowned Marian Andersen and is quite anxious to meet her."

Whether or not Mickey and Minnie come to my birthday party, I'm pleased that some reader out there with a good sense of humor would write me letters including The World-Herald among "the finest newspapers in the country" and referring to my roommate as "the lovely, renowned Marian Andersen."

— July 19, 1998

'At Disneyland for 3,112 Years'

No, Mickey and Minnie Mouse didn't show up when Marian and I, our children and grandchildren celebrated (I guess that's still the right word) my birthday during our recent visit to Disneyland.

But we had a jolly good time nonetheless, and Minnie did join us – and a couple hundred other Disneyland visitors – at breakfast one morning.

I spent about 45 minutes on the Disneyland grounds, long enough to observe the length of the lines and to conclude that the Pirates of the Caribbean probably wouldn't miss me if I didn't watch them in action for a third time. Marian spent one morning on the grounds with children and grandchildren, having figured out a way to get the family group to the head of the lines for three of the attractions.

All of the adults, of course, vicariously shared in the delight with which the youngsters (Lindsey Andersen, 8, Robby Andersen and John Andrew Karger, both 5, and James Karger, 3) rode the rides, viewed the exhibits and gave wide-eyed accounts of how much fun they were having.

Perhaps the strongest testimonial to the fact the children were having the time of their young lives was this assertion by one of the 5-year-olds: "I'd like to stay at Disneyland for 3,112 years!"

— August 9, 1998

'Andy has Flunked Retirement'

People ask me if I'm enjoying retirement. My reply is that I've learned this lesson:

Before you take on retirement, make sure you have time for it. (Marian puts it this way: "Andy has flunked retirement.")

But I'm thoroughly enjoying keeping much busier in retirement than I had expected – busy doing things, both personal and civic-related, that I enjoy.

All of which brings to mind a retirement story that I heard more than once in my days at World-Herald Square. It went like this:

The late Henry Doorly, longtime publisher of The World-Herald and spokesman for the majority shareholders at the time, enjoyed retirement.

In fact, he enjoyed it so much that he retired several times.

— August 30, 1998

'Better Than Perfect' Dogs

Marian and I had the pleasure of sitting with Stephen E. Ambrose, the historian and widely acclaimed author, at a recent University of Nebraska President's Club dinner.

We talked about one of Ambrose's current best sellers, "Undaunted Courage," the story of the Lewis and Clark expedition, and of his next work, which will find Ambrose spending some time in Omaha working with Union Pacific historian Don Snoddy, preparing to tell the story of the building of the transcontinental railroad.

The conversation turned to dogs, and we learned that Ambrose has a 4-year-old yellow Lab. When I offered the opinion that Labs are "great dogs," Ambrose replied: "They're perfect dogs. Even better than perfect."

Marian and I decided that we wouldn't share Stephen Ambrose's dog opinions with our three cocker spaniels. Sugar, Sarah and Peaches think they're the perfect dogs, you see.

— September 27, 1998

Black Squirrels, Deer and a Fox

It isn't exactly the Lee G. Simmons Conservation Park and Wildlife Safari, but for an urban neighborhood in what could now be called east central Omaha, it's a pretty good show:

Recently spotted by Fairacres residents: Black squirrels, a couple of deer near the intersection of Fairacres Road and Prairie Avenue and a red fox in front of the John Lauritzen home on Underwood Avenue.

Marian thinks the black squirrels are handsome critters "as squirrels go." But she thoroughly disapproves of their joining their red-squirrel cousins in collecting acorns from our oak trees with the resultant littering of the front lawn.

— October 15, 1998

Edward VII's Hunting Parties

A splendid PBS program on English historic places included a visit to the royal residence called Sandringham, where during the era of Edward VII, hunting parties were often held.

Sandringham clocks were set forward by half an hour to assure an earlier start and a longer hunting day. Good idea for my hunting lodge.

Guests stepped on a set of scales on their arrival at Sandringham and again on their departure, the thought being that you should have gained weight as evidence that you had enjoyed the bounteous hospitality. Bad idea for my hunting lodge. I could never get that one past Marian and my platoon of doctors. (Well, it's not exactly a platoon – only eight at last count.)

— October 18, 1998

On a Sunny Autumn Afternoon

I'm about to go to the dogs again, encouraged by the number of readers who have said they read my last item first because that's where they find news about Marian or the dogs. (I don't press them as to whether they read the rest of the column. I don't want to put anyone in a position of disappointing me or telling a white lie.)

As househusband while Marian was attending a wedding of the daughter of good friends in Augusta, Ga., my conscience got to bothering me on a beautiful autumn afternoon. It was the kind of afternoon, I knew, on which Marian would have taken our three cocker spaniels for a romp in the park.

But I had to do some packing for a hunting trip, dictate a few column items and go out to Guns Unlimited to exchange a pair of hunting boots. As a sort of compromise with my conscience, I bought a quart of Dairy Queen soft-serve and took it out into the backyard sunshine, where the dogs and I had a grand time consuming it.

I may be rationalizing to ease my conscience, but I do believe that Sugar, Sarah and Peaches, if given the choice, would quickly and voraciously have voted for househusband's Dairy Queen party in the back yard over housewife's romp in the park.

— October 25, 1998

Random Jottings

Let's finish today with some random jottings from a columnist's notebook.

(Yes, I still use a notebook. It's my 8-year-old granddaughter, Lindsey Andersen, who types messages and notes into a personal computer.)

— October 29, 1998

Space-age Senior

At my age, perhaps I should be among those applauding 77-year-old Sen. John Glenn's demonstration of – to use The New York Times' words – "what a growing cohort of energetic seniors can achieve." (Can achieve, perhaps, if they have the political clout of John Glenn.)

But I must confess that I regard Glenn's second ride into space as something of an ego trip for an authentic space-age hero and a calculated effort to encourage public and congressional support for appropriations for the nation's space exploration program.

If the object was to generate favorable public attention for the space program, the mission has been a spectacular success, as witness the massive news media attention given to a mission that has been described as of limited scientific value.

The reaction of my roommate, who is neither anti-John Glenn nor anti-space exploration: "John Glenn hadn't even taken off yet, and I was already sick of the story."

— **November 5, 1998**

Catching Up With Technology

I've moved into the fax generation. Under persistent persuasion by my secretary, Jackie Wrieth, we have installed a fax machine in my workroom at home. (Marian won't let me call it my "home office." I don't understand why, but I've learned not to argue with her about such things.)

I know there will be some readers out there who will say that Rip Van Andersen has been asleep, technologically speaking, for a good many years, and that by the time he woke up, the fax generation had been overtaken by the personal computer and the Internet.

OK, OK, but don't rush me. I'll look next to the personal computer, sometime after the start of the new millennium. I want to wait for a computer that can tell the difference between the years 1900 and 2000.

My next catching-up-with-technology objective is not to master a personal computer. It's to figure out how to program my VCR.

— **November 22, 1998**

Caregiving I

I have passed my first test in Caregiving I, having helped my recuperating roommate out of her arm sling and nightgown into a warm-up suit for a visit to the beauty parlor.

Some of my friends have good-naturedly suggested that I might need to take Caregiving 101, in response to the fact that Marian will be recuperating for several weeks, mostly at home, after surgery for a torn rotator cuff in her right shoulder. But Caregiving 101 would be far too advanced a course at this stage of my schooling.

I'm just trying to pass Caregiving 1. Stay tuned.

— **December 3, 1998**

Peaches the 'Perp'

One of the delights of living with a wife who has boundless affection for three cocker spaniels is listening to the way she talks to her three furry darlings.

I've commented before on the fact that when I'm in another room, I can unerringly determine, from the tone of her voice, whether she is talking to me or to the dogs.

Sometimes I have a little trouble figuring out which dog Marian is addressing, since she frequently comes up with new nicknames for them.

Peaches is now "Perp." It sounded to me like "Perf" as in "Perfect." But Marian explained that "Perp" is short for "Perpetrator," since the energetic 2-year-old is consistently the ringleader in getting the furry trio into some kind of mischief.

Mischief like jumping and pulling a frozen smoked turkey – a Christmas gift from friends – off the kitchen counter the other day. Marian came upon the three dogs trying to eat a solidly frozen turkey – a sight that, she observed, was more amusing than irritating.

"Perp" may have paid the price for her mischief in this case, since she had an upset stomach for the next 36 hours, although the frozen turkey was largely undamaged.

— **December 17, 1998**

Thirty Big-League Ballparks

Prairie Avenue 'work room;' Life With Marian; grandkids' Super Bowl review; rotator cuff surgery; upping the cardinal-count; mouse-on-a-leash; new colors for street signs; formal dress shirts; a game in every ballpark; Sugar, Sarah & Peaches; stop this volunteer!

Feeder 'For the Birds'

From my second-floor Prairie Avenue "work room" (for some reason Marian doesn't like me to call it an office), I'm looking down on our two bird/squirrel feeders.

This is the scene at Bird Feeder No. 2 – the new, guaranteed squirrel-proof one: A squirrel – the typically acrobatic type – is hanging upside down and picking away at the supposedly forbidden sunflower seeds, some of which fall to other squirrels working the ground around the base of the feeder.

In a nearby tree, three beautiful red cardinals sit, apparently waiting for the furry invader to finish his meal from the "squirrel-proof" bird feeder.

As I've written before, all of this tends to disturb Marian, who thinks that bird feeders are for birds. She doesn't understand that nobody has ever explained that to squirrels.

— January 3, 1999

Heard From: Shorter-sleeping Night Owls

OK, you early-risers who insist that you need your eight hours of sleep every night. Now hear this:

A British study suggests that early to bed and early to rise does not make a man – or woman – healthy, wealthy and wise. Researchers from the University of Southampton studied questionnaires filled out by 1,229 people 65 or older. The researchers found that the early-to-bed, early-to-rise eight-hour sleepers scored no better than shorter-sleeping night owls on tests of thinking ability or general state of health. And as for wealth, night owls typically had a higher weekly income.

The lead author of the report that summarized the survey had this comment:

"We were struck with the fact that people who get up early and go to bed early tend to adopt an attitude of moral superiority. We think this isn't really justified."

I report the results of the British survey with considerable satisfaction because Marian and I are both late-to-bed, less-than-eight-hour sleepers. (It had never occurred to us that some of our early-to-bed friends might be looking down their moral noses at us.)

— January 10, 1999

Friend 'Scared to Death'

One of the funnier accounts of a housewife's encounter with a mouse came Marian's way following my report that we finally ended our battle with a kitchen-counter-invading mouse with a type of mouse trap of which Marian thoroughly approved.

The device, you see, caught the mouse inside the trap and all you had to see was the protruding tail when you checked the kitchen counter in the morning.

This report prompted a friend to write about her first post-marriage encounter with a mouse.

She spotted the mouse in a drawer and was "scared to death." A mouse trap was placed in the drawer. Weeks passed without incident until one night when her husband was out of town. Then, "in the middle of the night, the trap snapped, the mouse squealed!

"In my robe, I went to the neighbor's and introduced myself and asked for help." The man of the house "told me he realized right then that he knew he was living next door to a crazy lady."

— January 22, 1999

'Life With Marian'

Excerpts from my favorite book, Life With Marian:

- At the family farm in northwest Missouri, I get a call from Marian, informing me that she has found a mouse caught in a trap. I tell her that is fine because that is the reason we set out mouse traps.

What should she do with the mouse and the trap, Marian asks. I tell her that I cannot be of much help, since I am 120 miles away. I suggest that picking up the trap and dropping it and the mouse in the garbage can might be one solution. Marian says she doesn't want to pick up the trap.

Solution: Marian calls one of our nice neighbors, Dave Hubbard, who comes over and disposes of the mouse.

- Addressing a roof leak that threatened a portion of the ceiling in our upstairs sitting room, I was telling Marian the directions she should give when help arrived – how to get into the attic, where the ladder is stored, that sort of thing.

  Marian's response: "OK, OK. Now let me tell you that you've got to do something about those new pants you're wearing. They're too long."

- From one of Marian's one-way conversations with one or more of our three cocker spaniels:

  "How do you spell 'pest'? P-e-a-c-h-e-s. And how do you spell 'adorable'? P-e-a-c-h-e-s."

  I think it's well that the other cockers, Sugar and Sarah, bright as they are, haven't learned to spell yet.

  — January 31, 1999

Hard Knocks & Entertainment

Super Bowl debriefing:

Marian and I were delighted with the Denver Broncos' victory for a variety of reasons. Not the least of the reasons is the fact that our 5-year-old grandson in Denver, John Andrew Karger, had sent us hand-lettered "Go Broncos!" pennants the week before the game and our 3-year-old grandson, James Wheaton Karger, regularly runs around his Denver home in a red junior-size football helmet passed down by his uncle Dave Andersen of Omaha, shouting "I'm John Elway!"

My misgivings about the invitation to Cher to sing the "Star-Spangled Banner" before the game proved unfounded. Such invitations to pop-singing stars have sometimes produced grotesque results before other big-time athletic events. But I thought Cher showed good taste in foregoing her frequently provocative attire and singing the National Anthem with power and obvious enthusiasm and, as she had promised, a few "rock" touches, which, I thought, added to her performance.

Does a football game in Miami simply have to be accompanied by the kind of pointless halftime "entertainment" that marred the Super Bowl proceedings? A cast of thousands, a zillion electronic effects and featured singers shouting unintelligible lyrics – in short, something that looked as if it might have been left over from one of those awful Orange Bowl half-time spectacles.

— February 7, 1999

Giving a Lift

From time to time a critic ridicules my frequent reports on life with Marian and our dogs and squirrels and mice and other Prairie Avenue fauna.

So it's heartwarming to receive comments like the following, which are much more typical of those which come my way than are the jibes of some readers:

"Please write more about your wife and your little dogs," wrote a Bellevue woman.

"I find it such enjoyable reading. There is so much sadness in the world. I feel reading about your family gives a person a lift."

— February 25, 1999

Caregiving Expertise Available

My remarks about becoming a "caregiver" to Marian following her rotator cuff surgery brought a prompt response from a representative of Alegent Health Home Care & Hospice.

Cindi Leo-Gofta, clinical coordinator of resource and referral, wrote to tell me of the availability of care giving help from Alegent Health.

I had said that I was trying to pass Caregiving 1. Leo-Gofta wrote that if I decided to take on Caregiving 101 – from which she said she believed I would graduate with honors, bless her heart – she offered me the opportnity either to have a home visit from an occupational therapist or to be her guest at "Caregiving 101" classes that Alegent's University of Healthy Living is offering.

Marian's remarkable ability to rebound from surgery (she has had a lot of experience) and my untutored caregiving efforts obviated the need for outside assistance, but it is comforting to know that expert help is available for those families for whom, in Cindi Leo-Gofta's words, "caregiving is an enormous undertaking."

— February 28, 1999

Thwarted Again

An Omahan who has noticed my references to Marian's losing battle with the squirrels who invade our bird feeders wrote to suggest that squirrels in his neighborhood may be somewhat brighter than those that invade bird feeders along Prairie Avenue. His letter included several amusing squirrel-defeats-homeowner stories, including this one:

The homeowner finally installed an expensive, foolproof padlock on the backyard chest in which he stored various kinds of bird feed. The next morning, the same squirrel that had thwarted him before "was hanging by his hind feet upside down off the chest, with a hacksaw in one of his paws. Case-hardened to boot."

My Omaha correspondent concluded his letter thus: "Would I lie to a journalist?"

— February 28, 1999

Cards Miss Spring Training

I suppose only a baseball fan like Marian would have put it this way during a recent heavy snowstorm:

The Cardinals obviously aren't in spring training yet. They're all here eating at our bird (editor's note: and squirrel) feeders."

One of the pleasures of retirement – or semi-retirement or whatever status it is that I'm in – is the freedom to stay at home during challenging weather and feel no pang of conscience.

Instead of taking on the snow-clogged streets, I thoroughly enjoyed watching the snowstorm and playing "cardinal count" with Marian. Our maximum count: 15 at the feeders and in the nearby trees and bushes at one time, most of them the bright red male variety whose colors stand out so attractively against a snowy background.

— March 4, 1999

A Survey for Pet Owners

For pet owners out there who may have missed a brief story reporting the results of a survey conducted by the American Animal Hospital Association, here's a chance to compare your responses to those of the 1,252 pet owners who were surveyed:

- Have you ever ended a personal or romantic relationship because of your pet? Eleven percent of the pet owners surveyed answered yes.

- Have you sent or received a greeting card from your dog or cat? Fifty-six percent said yes. (Marian serves a birthday cake to the dogs on each of our three cocker spaniels' birthdays, and she sends me a birthday card signed with the dogs' names, so we clearly would be in the 56 percent category.)

- Have you ever dressed your dog in clothing? Twenty-eight percent said yes. (Marian puts Cornhusker red scarves on our cocker spaniels every game day. Does that count?)

- Do you use a special voice to speak to your pets? Seventy-six percent said yes. (Marian does indeed have a special voice for the pets. I sometimes wish she would direct that tone of voice my way more often.)

- Do you consider yourself to be emotionally dependent on your pet? Forty-eight percent said yes. (It's a matter of degree of emotional dependence, of course, but I would say both Marian and I would answer yes. I know I certainly get an emotional lift from the yelping, tail-wagging, leaping greeting that Sugar, Sarah and Peaches invariably give me when I open the back door.)

- Do you think your pet understands all or some of what you say? Eighty-nine percent said yes to this softball question. What I don't understand is how 11 percent of the responding pet owners could possibly say their pets don't understand all or some of what they say.

— March 14, 1999

T-shirt Chuckle

Add to T-shirt wording that either Marian or I have seen (Marian in this case) that made us chuckle:

"I can only be nice to one person a day, and today's not your day.

"And tomorrow doesn't look so good for you either."

— April 11, 1999

Mouse Leashes?

Herewith the story of a dream both amusing and, as so many of them are, inexplicable (inexplicable at least to Marian and me):

The fact that we have been having problems with a mouse – or mice – making nocturnal visits to our kitchen countertop must have something to do with it, but whatever the cause, this is what Marian dreamed the other night:

Marian discovers a close friend, a member of one of her bridge foursomes, leading Marian's pet mouse on a leash. Marian doesn't know how this came about, and before she can ask her friend for an explanation, the mouse slips out of the leash and runs away, much to Marian's dismay. (This was in a dream, remember.) Marian wakes up.

Earlier on, we caught seven mice with peanut-butter-baited traps but have had no success the past couple of weeks. I'm considering asking my always-resourceful secretary, Jackie Wrieth, to start searching the classified ads and the Internet for mouse-size leashes.

— April 18, 1999

For Reptiles, Too?

Some readers may remember that a week ago I recounted the story of Marian's dream about putting a pet mouse on a leash. I said that her dream undoubtedly stemmed from the trouble we have been having with mice and suggested that perhaps I should have my always-resourceful secretary, Jackie Wrieth, start searching the classified ads or the Internet for mouse-size leashes.

Jackie went along with the gag to the extent of searching Internet Web sites for references to either mice or leashes. She found a Web site advertising an establishment that sells mice to be used as food for reptiles.

I'm not even considering suggesting to Marian that we introduce a snake into our household as a mouse catcher, even though Jackie's Internet search also revealed that reptile leashes are available.

— April 25, 1999

Signs of the Times

For an investigative reporter (yes, I join the ranks of investigative reporters from time to time, even though I don't go to their annual conventions), no assignment is insignificant if it involves a subject that may be of interest to what is hoped to be a significant number of readers.

Such an assignment came to me recently from my executive editor, Marian Battey Andersen. (Well, actually, Marian is more a consultant or, in her words, "a motivator.")

"Why don't you tell your readers why they are changing those signs along the streets from black-on-yellow to black-on-chartreuse or whatever that color is?" my motivator asked me the other day.

So I called the traffic department at City Hall and got this answer:

The new black-on-"yellow/green" signs are replacing the black-on-yellow signs because they have a fluorescent quality that makes them more visible, especially in foggy or snowy conditions. Eventually the yellow signs will be largely replaced in states across the country. In Omaha, the traffic department is concentrating first on school-zone signs, which would have to be replaced in any case as they deteriorate.

The new signs are more expensive, but they promote safety and will last longer because of a tough vinyl coating.

— August 1, 1999

For Formal Occasions

I made the mistake, all on my own, of buying a formal dress shirt – one of those where your black tie goes on the outside of the collar, which has two little tabs which stand up behind the tie. Marian doesn't like such shirts, as I quickly found out.

So the shirt stayed in the drawer until a formal occasion which I attended while Marian was out of town. I wore the shirt I like instead of the more conventional shirt (black tie band under the fold-down collar) Marian had recently bought me.

When Marian discovered which shirt I had worn to the formal affair, she made even clearer to me why she feels the type of tux shirt which I like (it's easier to get your black tie hooked up) is not appropriate for men of my generation. (Note that I avoided saying "men of my age." We wordsmiths employ little techniques like that when we are writing about ourselves.)

Guess which shirt I'll wear next time Marian and I go to a formal affair together.

— August 15, 1999

Moderation and Dilution

My "Bartlett's Familiar Quotations" tells me that it was the Roman playwright known as Terence (more properly Publius Terentius Afer) who, more than 2,100 years ago, gave voice to this still-quoted sage advice: Moderation in all things.

Now I'm pretty sure that my roommate has read no more of the words of Publius Terentius Afer than I have, but she surely believes in his "moderation in all things" philosophy. A recent example:

I was comfortably situated in the family room, reading my World-Herald, single-malt scotch in hand, when Marian rose to go to the kitchen. "When you come back," I asked, "would you please bring a few ice cubes for my drink?"

Marian's reply: "I'm always glad to dilute your drinks."

— August 22, 1999

Drink Fluids; Eat Bananas

My sports-fanatic wife has now gone into sports medicine – well, sort of. Here's the story:

For some years now we have been friends of the Lula and John McPherson family, whose members include a son named Lornell who has developed into an outstanding athlete and has accepted a scholarship offer from the Nebraska Cornhuskers.

Marian attended the season-opening high school football game between Lornell and his Central High teammates and Lincoln East the other evening. After scoring three touchdowns, Lornell left the game with what turned out to be mild leg cramps.

Marian called the McPherson home later that evening, complimented Lornell and asked about his physical condition. She said that in this hot weather it was especially important to drink lots of fluids. Lornell said he had been doing that. Marian then advised that in addition he should be eating fruit, including bananas, for the anti-cramping potassium content.

I don't know whether Lornell is now eating bananas, but I had occasion to tell the story to someone knowledgeable in these matters, and she said that Dr. Andersen's advice was quite sound.

Incidentally, the Andersens believe that the Cornhuskers have a real winner in Lornell McPherson – and not just because of his "athleticism," the description so much in vogue these days.

— September 5, 1999

Nebraska's Open Spaces

My clipping service – her name is Marian – provided me with an item, gleaned from the travel section of the Sunday New York Times, offering fresh evidence that persons from other parts of this great land find beauty, as we do, in Nebraska's great open spaces.

Pam Houston, short-story writer, essayist and traveler, author of "Waltzing the Cat," who lives in the mountains in southwestern Colorado, was quoted as saying:

"In America, everything has been discovered in a way, and places seem to be more and more the same. I look for places that have maintained their character, like southwestern Nebraska. I spent a few days there once. I was on my way to Colorado from Provincetown.

"Near Scottsbluff, I saw little farmhouses on huge amounts of acreage. There were big white bluffs with rivers running through them, huge thunderclouds and that late afternoon, prairie light. It was magical. I was only three hours from Denver, but I stayed for a few days."

— September 9, 1999

30 Big League Ballparks

My roommate, as readers of this column know, has a record of having seen a game in every major league baseball park, currently 30 in number.

Thus she notes with special interest stories of persons driven by a similar "I want to do them all" goal.

One such story came to Marian's attention this past week in a news report of a 53-year-old man who, from his home base in Warrenton, Va., is pursuing a goal of eating in every McDonald's in North America. As of Aug. 19, Peter Holden, manager at a data-imaging company, said he had eaten at 10,894 of the more than 13,600 McDonald's restaurants in North America.

People magazine's account quoted Holden as saying he does this "because it's there. Any collector will appreciate the concept."

Marian throws the ceremonial pitch at Coors Field in Denver before a Rockies game.

Holden's one-day record: Burgers at 45 McDonald's restaurants in Detroit. His usual meal? Two sandwiches and no fries for the 6-feet-2-inch, 195-pounder with a low cholesterol reading of 169. "Fries put on the weight," Holden said. Marian agrees, so she sticks to hot dogs on her baseball park visits.

— September 26, 1999

'A Good Night'

Doing my best the other night to follow Marian's advice to "get a good night's sleep for a change," I was awakened by her occasional gentle snoring – gentle but nonetheless distracting for a husband trying to "get a good night's sleep."

First I tried sleeping with my right ear on the pillow, since it's the ear in which I have the better hearing. Even the less-sensitive left ear continued to hear those snores.

In the past, Marian and I both have utilized the approach of gently shaking the other awake and saying something like, "Why don't you roll over on your other side? You're snoring."

On this particular night, I tried a new technique, taking my bedside flashlight (usually used for other kinds of nocturnal journeys) and walking down the hall to get a set of earplugs I had just brought home with me from back-to-back hunting trips. Earplugs in place, I slept the rest of the night away without interruption. From that night forward, the earplugs will be close at hand in a drawer in my bedside table.

This leaves unresolved, of course, the question of whether I should buy Marian a set of earplugs. What do you say, roommate?

— October 17, 1999

From Elmer in Elmwood

My remarks in this space last Sunday about using earplugs to offset Marian's occasional gentle snoring drew more than a few comments from readers. Most meaningful to me were these words from my most loyal correspondent, Elmer Pinkerton of Elmwood:

"So your beautiful, happy, loyal, faithful roommate snores! I knew all along she was not perfect! However, you have the wrong attitude. The next time she snores and wakes you, stop and think of the terrible dead silence you will have to endure if she is not there at all. Then get in tune with the music and relax and go back to sleep."

Good advice, Elmer.

— October 24, 1999

Peaches' Star-Spangled 4th

Marian kicked off the Fourth of July weekend (I hinted to you that there were some oldies on today's menu) by tying a star-spangled red, white and blue bandanna around the neck of our youngest cocker spaniel, Peaches.

How come no bandannas around the necks of Sugar and Sarah, I asked.

Because Peaches would chew at the knots until the bandannas were removed, Marian explained.

We really don't hold this kind of behavior against the ebullient Peaches. It's just another facet of her personality, which Marian explained this way: "Peaches has never encountered a situation which she thinks could not be improved by her being in the middle of it."

— November 4, 1999

Joan's Cardinal Advice

Houseguest Joan Walsh is still giving mealtime advice, but with a different spin: Now she is advising us how to feed – or not feed – the cardinals that flock to our backyard feeder.

Stopping with us on her way to her home in Sonoma, Calif., Joan, who lived in Omaha while her late husband, Mike Walsh, was CEO of the Union Pacific Railroad, was looking out our garden room window at a plump cardinal sitting on a branch. She heard Marian say that cardinals and a variety of other birds were chowing down at a rate that made it hard to keep the bird feeder supplied.

"Only feed them every other day," was the prompt advice from our houseguest.

I replied that we liked to see the cardinals in action at or near the feeder every day, thank you very much.

And despite Joan's use-skim-milk advice of several years ago, I still use half-and-half on my cereal.

But the cardinals and I appreciate Joan's concern for our well-being.

* * *

A heartfelt wish to conclude this Christmas-season column:

For you and all those dear to you, Marian and I hope that you are finding joy in the true spirit of the holiday season ("good will toward men" sums it up as well as anything, I believe) and that the joys of the year ahead include the satisfaction that comes from helping others.

— December 23, 1999

Half-a-hundred Visitors

Now if those birds would just hold still for more than a few seconds, I could give you a precisely accurate count of the number that have been flocking to our two backyard feeders these cold, snowy mornings.

The best quick count/estimate that I could make of the maximum sunflower-seed assault force one recent morning: Between 45 and 50 birds, at least half of them cardinals, at the feeders, on the ground near the feeders or in nearby trees and shrubs.

And, of course, three or four fat and sassy squirrels enjoying the seeds that spill from the feeders.

Predictably, one or two of the squirrels have figured out how to get to one of the feeders, so Marian and I have begun our annual friendly disagreement, with Marian rapping indignantly on the window or sending the cocker spaniels out to flush the squirrels and me arguing that I admire the ingenuity of the clever little critters.

— December 26, 1999

Stop This Volunteer

My favorite among the Christmas presents I gave to Marian: a T-shirt on which these words were lettered: "Stop Me Before I Volunteer Again!"

Particularly appropriate for Marian at any time during her adult life, but especially so these days, when she shuttles so frequently between Omaha and New York and Omaha and Washington in her volunteer work for the Public Broadcasting System and the American Red Cross.

— December 30, 1999

CHAPTER 9 – 2000

New Grandkids, New Ballparks, New Hip

Get the car washed; lovable, quotable grandchildren; Jaymo's breadth of love; 'Dear Tooth Fairy'; Three new ballparks to visit; new left-hip joint; 10 surgeries in 14 years; Republican finance reform; Sister Veronica's services; Welcome Katherine Roe Andersen; dog's-eye-view of DC.

Exceedingly Well Treated

A Yuletide gift was one of those messages – this one painted on a small wooden plaque – you are supposed to hang somewhere around the house. The message:

"Spoiled rotten dogs live here."

As Marian showed the gift to me, she added: "And a spoiled rotten husband, too."

"Spoiled rotten" seems a little strong. I prefer simply "spoiled" or perhaps "exceedingly well treated," which I certainly am.

— January 20, 2000

Friendly Reminders

My roommate believes in taking good care of me even when she's on the road. For example:

When I got into my Jeep to head for the office one recent morning, I discovered two notes Marian had left before she flew off to Washington on another one of her American Red Cross assignments.

One note was stuck to the glass on the instrument panel in front of the speedometer. It read: "Go back to fridge and pick up Arby's sandwich."

In the matter of lunches, I have come something of a full circle – from taking my lunch as a matter of economic necessity while in high school to taking my lunch now as a matter of convenience, saving time by usually eating at my desk.

Marian speaking at an American Red Cross event.

The second note left by Marian read: "Get car washed so it will remember what it represents – you."

Yes, ma'am. I drove to the car wash that afternoon.

Incidentally, I had remembered to get my lunch from the fridge. But Marian's reminder was appreciated nonetheless.

— January 30, 2000

Silly, Silly, Silly

Marian and I both got a scolding from an Omaha reader who said she enjoys my column very much but thought it was "silly, silly, silly" for Marian to urge me – and for me to comply – that I get my Jeep washed "so it will remember what it represents – you."

Our friendly critic asked that "of all your accomplishments, you depend on your transportation to speak for you?" She added that "most of us who live in this sometimes slushy, dirty winter climate will cut you some slack if you don't wash your car every day, which," she added, "could get expensive for some of us."

We appreciate the offer to cut us some slack, but we reserve the right to keep our cars reasonably clean, even during the slushy winter months and even if some people – or at least one reader – think it is "silly, silly, silly."

Perhaps I should add that both Marian and I deny any implication that I want to be known mostly for the cleanliness of my Jeep.

— February 3, 2000

Love 'Bigger Than the Whole City'

Now I know that a great many grandparents out there have lovable and quotable grandchildren. And I hope you don't think I'm taking unfair advantage of you by sharing with (inflicting on?) you an occasional grandchild story like this one:

Four-year-old James Wheaton Karger, better known as Jaymo, youngest son of daughter Nancy of Denver, recently told his mother:

"I love you bigger than the whole city, and I'll love you forever, even when you're in heaven," then continuing without pause, "What do you think Tenzing is doing in heaven now?" Tenzing being the beloved family dog, mostly black Labrador, who died last year.

Nancy didn't have to respond to Jaymo's question, Jaymo being a sort of stream-of-consciousness talker who didn't wait for an answer.

But Nancy and I agreed it was nice that Jaymo, before moving quickly on to a variety of other subjects, had assured his mom that he loves her "bigger than the whole city" and that he hadn't forgotten his pal Tenzing.

—March 5, 2000

'... and All the Way to Canada'

Grandson James Wheaton Karger has broadened his definition of how much he loves his mother, our daughter Nancy.

I reported recently that 4-year-old Jaymo had told Nancy that he loved her "bigger than the whole city." His most recent affirmation of affection: "I love you all the way to Canada."

— March 26, 2000

Golf's Gender Gap

I'll share with you the results of a survey which points up a golfing problem that, happily, I don't have.

I do have golf problems, but not this particular one, which arises from playing golf – or not playing golf – with your wife. Marian, you see, doesn't play golf. She says she's not old enough.

The survey, reported in USA Today, based on figures from Golf Digest Woman magazine: A number (unspecified) of "recreational golfers" were asked about their favorite playing partners. Among males, 74 percent said they preferred to play with a friend, with 6 percent preferring to play with a family member other than their wife and 6 percent saying that they enjoyed playing golf with "anyone." Four percent said their wife was the favorite playing companion.

Among female golfers, first choice for a playing companion was a friend (60 percent). And the spouse as a favorite playing partner finished in second place (24 percent).

Six times as many women expressing preference for their spouse as a playing partner than men expressing a spousal preference. I'm glad I'm not a husband trying to deal with that kind of a gender gap.

— **April 6, 2000**

Tooth Fairy Cooperates

Herewith another grandchild story, with another acknowledgement that a lot of you readers out there also have grandchildren who do amusing things, but I simply have the advantage of this forum to tell you my stories:

John Andrew Karger, 7, son of our daughter Nancy of Denver, believes in him (or her) to the extent of opening negotiations with said fairy after his latest tooth loss. Along with the tooth, young Karger left this note:

"Dear Tooth Fairy: Please can you leave this tooth and bring back the other tooth I lost and still give me money. Thank you, Jack."

Jack's polite note resulted in total victory. The still-available first tooth was returned, the second tooth was left as Jack requested and the tooth fairy honored his request to "still give me money."

At this rate, I don't see why Jack Karger should ever stop believing in his cooperative friend, the tooth fairy.

— **May 7, 2000**

A Fourth Morning Award?

Marian frequently leaves the television in our upstairs sitting room tuned to one of the morning talk shows when she goes down to start preparing breakfast for the dogs and for me.

Thus as I move through the painful (to me) process of bringing my metabolism up to daytime levels, I am exposed to talk-show talk and Marian talk, Marian's being directed to our three cocker spaniels.

It will not surprise you to learn that I much prefer listening to Marian rather than Katie Couric or Willard Scott. A recent example of Marian talk directed to Peaches, Sarah and Sugar:

"You deserve an award, you deserve an award and you deserve an award, just because of who you are."

When I dictated this, my secretary, Jackie Wrieth, asked if Marian had suggested a fourth award that morning. I said no, perhaps because I don't spend as much time dancing affectionate attention on Marian as the dogs do.

— **May 14, 2000**

New Ballparks and Splash Landings

The running box score on my roommate's annual effort to keep intact her record of having seen a game in each of the current major league baseball parks: One down and two to go.

There are 30 major league parks, including three which are new this year, in Houston, Detroit and San Francisco. Marian has now seen a game in 28 of them.

We watched the San Francisco Giants beat the hapless Philadelphia Phillies in the Giants' new home, Pacific Bell Park, late last month. Marian's appraisal of the park, which is built with a generous portion of red brick and other features of the new style popularized by Camden Yards, home of the Baltimore Orioles: "Pac Bell Park is as good as any of the other new ones. The setting is fabulous. But I don't like any of the new ones better than the old ones – Wrigley Field (home of the Chicago Cubs) and Fenway Park (home of the Boston Red Sox)."

> "Pac Bell Park is as good as any of the other new ones. The setting is fabulous. But I don't like any of the new ones better than the old ones ..."

As for Pac Bell Park's setting: You can see San Francisco Bay in the near background behind the left and center-field bleachers. And the water is so close behind the right-field fence that the Old Navy retail store chain has a sign offering $500 to any Giant who creates a "splash landing" with a home run over the right-field fence.

At the time of our visit, Old Navy had paid for four "splash landings," all of them initiated by Giants' left fielder Barry Bonds.

Marian plans trips to Detroit and Houston later this summer. Then there are the new parks to come on line next summer in Milwaukee and Pittsburgh, the prospect of new parks in Montreal and San Diego in 2002 and plans for new parks in Philadelphia, Cincinnati and Boston in 2003.

It seems that my happily obsessed, ballpark-visiting roommate just can't get a season off.

— June 11, 2000

Friendly Farmers, Grill Covers & a Hairdo

If there are any dream analysts among my readers today, try your hand on this one:

Marian dreamed she is driving some of our family members to Kansas City in her convertible (apparently I had been left at home) where her brother and his family live. Somehow she has chosen a two-lane country road instead of Interstate 29.

She stops because a small calf ("a darling little calf," as she recalled the dream) has wandered onto the road and is in danger because of heavy traffic. Marian shoos the calf to safety, then discovers that others in her convertible have left without her. In a roadside farmyard, Marian notices a plastic cover on a barbecue grill. She puts the cover over her head to protect what she calls her "high maintenance" hairdo.

A farmer comes up and asks what has happened to the plastic cover for his barbecue grill. Marian explains that she has borrowed it to protect her hairdo from the rain, since she is on her way to a wedding and wants to look her best. The friendly farmer says that's quite all right, so long as she replaces the plastic cover when she's finished with it.

The other family members notice Marian's absence and return to retrieve her. Marian wakes up.

If any dream analysts are going to go to work on this, here are two obvious clues: The day after Marian's dream in our San Francisco hotel room, we were scheduled to attend a wedding in Sonoma, Calif., where, Marian had been told, there would be no hairdresser available for eleventh-hour rehabilitative work on her high-maintenance hair. And there will be a family wedding involving one of our nephews, Chuck Battey, in Kansas City in October.

Now you tell me how the "darling little calf" and the friendly farmer and his barbecue grill cover got into the act.

— June 25, 2000

A Patient Who Makes the Doctor Look Good

My roommate and I haven't been rooming together for the past several weeks. First there was the golfing outing that took me to Scotland. Then came more than nine hours of major surgery, which is still keeping Marian in the hospital as the healing process proceeds.

Marian now has a completely new artificial left-hip joint, replacing one that was put in place 14 years ago. (She also has an artificial right-hip joint that required additional surgery five years after installation.)

The latest surgery brought to 10 the total of major surgical procedures

Crutches don't keep Marian away from her speaking duties. Gov. Kay Orr, right, among the listeners.

Marian has undergone in the past 14 years — six hip operations, two knee operations (including the installation of an artificial right-knee joint), the fusing of a cervical disc and a rotator-cuff operation on her right shoulder. Plus assorted other surgeries on fingers and toes. All of this to deal with an obviously major case of chronic osteoarthritis.

Through all this, I have never heard Marian utter a word of complaint about the necessity for the surgery. Her attitude, rather, has been that she feels fortunate that treatment techniques developed and applied by skilled surgeons have enabled her to keep moving at a speed that outpaces, in my judgment, the great bulk of the surgery-free population.

One of Marian's doctors told me, "She's the kind of patient that makes a doctor look good." She is also definitely the kind of wife that makes a husband look good – or, at least, makes a husband look better than he otherwise would.

— July 16, 2000

Grand Old Postage

I have a brand new idea for campaign finance reform.

The Republican National Committee and Chairman Jim Nicholson could introduce this reform unilaterally, save a great deal of money in printing and mailing expenses and – perhaps most important of all – stop treating party members as if they were attention-starved dolts.

I didn't jump to this conclusion. I reached it after Marian and I received no fewer than 20 Republican fund-raising mailings from Washington in the first six months of this year.

I can't remember the exact sequence, but I know that Marian was the first in the family to receive an invitation to accept a "President's Club Inaugural Platinum Card."

Nicholson's letter (which didn't reveal until the 16th paragraph that Marian had to pay $1,000 if she wanted membership in that platinum-card club) started with this idiotic serving of goo: "It is the greatest privilege of my tenure as Chairman of our Party to inform you that you've been selected to receive the Republican National Committee's highest honor." Marian wrote "Stupid" on the envelope before passing it to me.

I'll admit that I was a little puzzled – perhaps even a little hurt – when the Republican National Committee's mail-order barrage to me didn't start with Nicholson's "greatest privilege" letter. I was simply asked to join the President's Club with a $1,000 contribution.

Now I think the world of my roommate, but if offering her a chance to contribute $1,000 to the Republican Party is "the greatest privilege" of Jim Nicholson's tenure as GOP national chairman, Nicholson must have had a privilege-deprived tenure.

I'll admit that I was a little puzzled – perhaps even a little hurt – when the Republican National Committee's mail-order barrage to me didn't start with Nicholson's "greatest privilege" letter. I was simply asked to join the President's Club with a $1,000 contribution. But I was told that my member profile would go into Nicholson's confidential file "so I will know when to contact you for insider knowledge and strategic advice."

Finally I received the "greatest privilege" invitation to become an "inaugural platinum member" of the President's Club. At first blush, I felt pleased that Chairman Nicholson had decided that there were two members of the Andersen family worthy of being objects of his "greatest privilege."

Then I realized that the "platinum-member" membership fee had been reduced from the thousand dollars asked of Marian to a minimum of $25 asked of me. An indication that Jim valued Marian's affiliation 40 times more highly than mine? More likely, I concluded, it was an indication that the $1,000 "greatest privilege" membership invitation was also regarded as "stupid" by a good many people other than Marian.

The Republican assault on common sense continued with another Jim Nicholson mailing asking my opinion on "critical issues" and seeking a contribution of $25 to $1,000.

Then there was a letter with the return address, "Voting Information Office." This letter turned out to be from the National Republican Senatorial Committee and combined a pitch for an "emergency contribution" of $25 to $200 with an absolutely irresponsible suggestion of Republican campaign strategy. Enclosed was a simulated license plate with this wording: "Just Say NO to TAXES. VOTE REPUBLICAN."

If Republican party leadership thinks a "Just Say NO to TAXES" campaign theme is a responsible route to the White House, the National Republican Party needs new leadership.

Perhaps the funniest aspect of all this business, I might add, is the fact that all of the business reply envelopes in which you are supposed to send a check or make a pledge – in one case a pledge of $4,000 – carry this suggestion: "By using your own first class stamp to return this envelope, you will be helping us to save much-needed funds. Thank you."

I'd suggest the GOP National Committee could save much-needed funds by ending the mailing of such stupid letters.

— July 30, 2000

More Than One Guest

Herewith another dog story, but this time not about the world's most lovable cocker spaniels – Sugar, Sarah and Peaches – and their lovable mistress, Marian Andersen, who is recovering nicely but understandably slowly from surgery replacing her first artificial left-hip joint with a new model.

The story today comes from my estimable secretary and one-person In-Depth Research Department, Jackie Wrieth. The story involves Jackie's beloved canine companion, Bud, a 90-pound yellow Labrador, and Jackie's sister, Judy Perry, who was known as Judy Dietz during her days at Omaha's South High School 40 years ago.

Judy decided to return for a South High class reunion and stayed, of course, with Jackie and her husband, Don. Judy was to sleep in a guest bedroom adjoining a recreation room where Bud regularly sleeps on the sofa.

Jackie admonished big sister Judy to make sure that the door was closed between the bedroom and the recreation room, lest a 90-pound Lab decide to share the bed with Judy. You can see this coming, I suppose. Judy failed to close the door, and 90 pounds of yellow Lab landed partly on the bed and partly on Judy.

After unsuccessful efforts to dislodge Bud, Judy yielded the bed to Bud and spent the night on the sofa, warmed by Bud's blanket.

The next night she closed the door.

— **August 31, 2000**

Sparing the Plumber

Marian has me under pretty consistent pressure to "clean up the mess" in my "home workroom." (For reasons I have never fully understood, Marian doesn't want me to call it my "home office.")

The few people who have seen my home office can testify that I have pretty successfully resisted Marian's pressure. But Marian concentrates on smaller targets, too, as evidenced by the suggestion she delivered to me one recent morning: "Why don't you pick up some of those things around your bathroom sink? The plumber's coming this afternoon to fix your toilet."

I was glad to comply. It took about 20 seconds, not too high a price to pay to spare the plumber the sight of a messy bathroom.

— **September 14, 2000**

Such Friends

If you can judge the quality of a person's character by the number and quality of friends he attracts (and I think you can), I'd say my roommate scores close to 15 on a scale of 1 to 10. Yes, I know, I've said a number of nice things about Marian in past columns. But a number of you said you enjoy reading about Marian and the dogs, so I don't hesitate to offer fresh comment when some new occasion seems to suggest it. For example:

Marian has been going to a west Omaha medical center for physical therapy several times a week, working to restore to something approaching normalcy her left knee and recently implanted artificial left-hip joint. A number of volunteers – yes, including me – have been taking turns providing transportation.

One recent day, the volunteer was a nurse, Sister Veronica of the Sisters of Notre Dame, whom Marian met while a patient at the University of Nebraska Medical Center. Marian and Sister Veronica, simply one of the nicest people we have ever had the privilege of knowing, have become fast friends. One result: Sister Veronica became one of Marian's volunteer transportation-providers.

I know I have used these lines before, but it seems appropriate to quote them again, in tribute to the friends new and old who have been so supportive of Marian in her more than two months of hospitalization and recuperation. So in the words of Irish poet W. B. Yeats:

> *"Think where man's glory most*
> *begins and ends,*
> *And say my glory was I had*
> *Such friends."*

I know that many of you also feel this kind of appreciation for friends, so I hope that as you reflect on those words from Yeats, they mean as much to you as they do to Marian and me.

— September 17, 2000

'Just One More Ballpark'

My roommate has again caught up with her version of the Holy Grail.

Marian can again report that she has seen a game in each of the current major league baseball parks, now 30 in number. She put the figurative 30th notch in her figurative Louisville Slugger bat (they still make them, don't they?) Aug. 27, when she watched the Pittsburgh Pirates lose to the Atlanta Braves 5-4 in the Pirates' new PNC Park. (Marian said she thinks "PNC" stands for a bank holding company.)

Marian had first grasped the grail in August 1991, when we attended a game in Veterans Stadium in Philadelphia. That marked her 26th and final visit to all of the major league parks then in existence.

But in the 11 years since that memorable evening in Philadelphia, when the Phillie Phanatic came down to our field-level box and kissed Marian and danced with her while the message board in right field told of Marian's achievement, 11 of the 26 major league teams moved into new ballparks, and franchises were awarded to four more cities – Tampa Bay, Phoenix, Denver and Miami. That meant that to be able to say this year that she has seen a game in each current major league park, Marian had to have visited 15 new ballparks in the past 11 years.

She would have reached her goal sooner except for some major summertime surgery. She plans, of course, to attend games when new ballparks open in Cincinnati and San Diego in the next two years.

Marian's companions for her trip to Pittsburgh – I was on a hunting trip – were long-time friends Joan and Pete

Andy and The Phillie Phanatic helped Marian celebrate her 'first' all-ballpark goal.

Elliott, whom we have known since 1956, when Pete spent a year as head football coach of the Nebraska Cornhuskers. He later coached at California, Illinois and Miami and retired after serving as head of the Professional Football Hall of Fame in Canton, Ohio, where the Elliotts still live.

Marian's comment on reaching her 30-ballpark goal and her plans for the future:

"I've told you I'm going out feet first saying, 'Just one more ballpark.'"

— **October 3, 2000**

Unquestioning Love and Loyalty

Among the "get well" messages that came Marian's way during her recovery from artificial hip-joint surgery was a card that included a picture of a cocker spaniel and a reminder of the unquestioning love and loyalty that dogs lavish on their masters and mistresses.

The reminder – and good advice it is: "May I always be the kind of person my dog thinks I am."

— **October 15, 2000**

Cosmetic Surgery?

Another dream for you amateur analysts to interpret – interpretation which, I hope, won't be too rough on this columnist:

My roommate, who is recovering slowly but surely from her latest major surgery, reports that she dreamed recently that I said I thought she should go under the surgeon's scalpel one more time.

"Why?" asked Marian, who has been hopeful that her new artificial left-hip joint would at the very least buy her a reasonable period of relief from further surgery.

My reply was that this time I was thinking of cosmetic surgery. Marian's somewhat startled response was, again, "Why?" My response to her question (remember, this was her dream) was another question: "Have you looked in the mirror lately?"

Yes, yes, I know; not a very nice way to treat your wife, even in a dream.

— October 22, 2000

Katherine Roe Andersen

Let me introduce you to Katherine Roe Andersen, who arrived Sept. 11 weighing 5 pounds, 9 ounces and measuring 18³/₄ inches long (or tall, I guess you would say if she could stand up). Like Lindsey and Robby, her older sister and brother, Katie couldn't wait to get started on the job of pleasing parents and grandparents – a job which she is performing admirably well. She was born seven weeks ahead of the normal delivery time.

"I think I'll get married someday, but first I'm going to get a Harley."

The newest child of our son David and the former Leslie Roe is doing nicely, thank you, so well behaved (she sleeps most of the time) that she has been accompanying Leslie to her job as president of the Bank of Bennington. She also attended a Federal Reserve meeting with mother, who is president-elect of the Nebraska Bankers Association.

Katie's other proud grandparents are Jerry and Mimi Roe, now of Omaha, formerly of Bennington, where Jerry continues as chairman of the Bank of Bennington, which has been owned by the Roe family for 73 years.

Elsewhere on the grandchild front, we have news that James Wheaton Karger, 5, of Denver, son of our daughter Nancy, recently told his mother a portion of his life plan:

"I think I'll get married someday, but first I'm going to get a Harley."

* * *

Still on the grandparent/grandchild news scene: Neighbor Sue Conine keeps us posted on the latest fascinating fantasizing of Allie and Kate, her 5-year-old grandchildren, twin daughters of Nick and Anne Baxter.

It seems that Allie and Kate have the advantage of both real grandparents and fantasy grandparents. Each of the twins has her own set of fantasy grandparents, but the two different sets of grandparents have the same names, Patty and George.

Allie's Patty and George grandparents live most of the time in Alaska and have lots of dogs, possibly a fantasy compensation for the fact that because of allergies, the Baxter family doesn't have real-life dogs.

Kate's Patty and George grandparents travel a lot. George died of breast cancer in Argentina, but recovered and he and Patty went on to visit the Sudan.

— December 3, 2000

Follow the Leader

I'm sure it wouldn't go to their lovable furry heads even if they understood the part they played in a very special Christmas gift coming to our house, but our three cocker spaniels did play leading roles. Here's the story:

The mailman delivered a book titled "Follow the Leader, a Dog's-Eye-View of Washington, D.C."

The book is represented to be a story by the miniature schnauzer so loved by former Senate Majority Leader Bob Dole of Kansas and Elizabeth Dole, former Secretary of Labor and former head of the American Red Cross. Here's how our cocker spaniels got into the act: The copy coming to our house is inscribed with these words:

"Sarah, Sugar II and Peaches — I do hope you'll enjoy this book written by my grandfather, Leader, and that I'll have the chance to meet your wonderful Marian and Andy in the near future. With much love (and lots of kisses!) to all. Leader II."

The handwriting of Leader II, who was adopted after his famous grandfather, Leader, died in March 1999, looks very similar to that of Elizabeth Dole, with whom Marian has had a close friendship since Marian, as chairman of an American Red Cross Board of Governors search committee, played a major role in recruiting Elizabeth to head the Red Cross.

The delightful volume, published by Eastbank Publishing Co., of Washington, recounts how Leader was rescued from the Washington Humane Society Animal Shelter 24 hours before he was to be put to sleep. (He had been found along a Washington street with, in the words of his book, "no ID tags, no collar, no future.") The book, full of appealing color photographs, goes on to tell, as if in Leader's words, the story of his rise to prominence over the next 15 years. For example:

> He is crowned "Chair Dog of the Bark Ball." He meets Larry King, Willard Scott, Jay Leno and David Letterman on national TV. He defeats the Clinton White House cat Socks, 55 percent to 44 percent, in an election via the World Wide Web. (The Leader/ Socks contest is described as the "1996 Presidential Paw Poll.")

At the end of the book, proceeds from which go to the Washington Humane Society, there appears an appealing picture of Leader II at nine months with a message that ends with these words: "I will never be able to fill Leader's paw prints, but as the years go on, I hope to someday go into politics. Follow me."

Marian and I, of course, are properly grateful to Peaches, Sugar and Sarah for allowing us to bask in the reflected warmth of their new friendship with a rising Washington celebrity, Elizabeth and Bob Dole's Leader II. After all, it isn't often that someone in Washington sends "much love and lots of kisses to all" to the Andersen family. I'm not used to this kind of treatment, especially when it comes from Washington.

— **December 24, 2000**

CHAPTER 10 – 2001

Golf with the President and a New Grandson

I'd like to …?; 'killing doesn't stop;' when the market slides; Sarah's shrink; loyal correspondents; Grant Andersen Karger arrives; golf in Great Britain with President Clinton; Marian's new shoulder; grandson Jack Karger's career plan; nagging vs. nurturing; World Series in Phoenix; the son of 'Dear God.'

Sure, I'd Like to …

I'll bet a great many of you out there have examples of amusing – or sometimes not so amusing – questions put by one spouse to another. Here are two of my offerings:

I was climbing the stairs from our first-floor hallway to the second floor. I was four steps up and still moving when Marian came on the scene and asked, "Are you going upstairs?" My reply: "No, I'm exercising. I'm going to go up a couple more steps and come back down." We both laughed and I continued my climb.

Andy, Marian and "fuzzy-eared kids" enjoy an evening at home.

My roommate has one way of question-asking that I have not been able to talk her out of. It goes like this: "Would you like to (fill in here a description of almost any household chore you can imagine)?"

No household chore that I like to do comes quickly to mind. I hasten to add that I'm not saying I dislike these chores, but I do them because they are necessary, not because I like them. That, at least, is my feeling about a good many of the chores to which my attention is directed by a "Would you like to …?" from Marian.

I haven't been able to convince Marian that I could give her a more honest answer if she would simply ask "Would you please …?" or simply "Would you …?"

— January 14, 2001

English or Journalism?

Now a couple of lighter University of Nebraska-Lincoln-connected notes:

Interim Chancellor Harvey Perlman gave this anecdotal example of the quality of UNL faculty: A young Nebraskan enrolled in Harvard Law School, apprehensive about the competition from graduates of elite Eastern schools. He discovered two of the Harvard Law School textbooks that he and his elite Eastern-school-educated fellow students would be studying had been written by UNL College of Law faculty members.

Thirteen of the employers interviewing UNL graduates in 1999 or 2000 were interested in English majors. I was pleased to see The World-Herald among the 13, in view of my longtime association with the newspaper and the fact that I majored in English and history while a student at UNL, with a minor in journalism. (Marian has remarked on occasion – facetiously, I'd like to think – that I might have gone farther had I majored in journalism.)

— January 21, 2001

Blood and Gore

Marian and I and the rest of the audience were informed on the big screen the other evening that the preview we were about to watch had been approved for a general audience by the Motion Picture Association of America.

There followed a couple of minutes of depiction of absolute mayhem – shootings, bombings, explosions and vehicle crashes. Then came this punch line: "THE KILLING DOESN'T STOP UNTIL YOU STOP WATCHING." So ended the preview approved for a general audience by the Motion Picture Association of America.

Another example, it seems to me, of the utter hypocrisy of the motion picture industry in attempting to justify a continued orgy of violence-filled films by saying the industry has devised a rating system that parents can use in an effort to protect younger children from exposure to excessive cinematic blood and gore.

— February 8, 2001

When the Market Slides

The Associated Press picked an odd example to illustrate the fact that "the stock market's slide will become painfully clear to many ordinary investors when they get a look at their end-of-the-year retirement-account statements."

AP quoted a software tester in Sioux Falls, S.D., who said she is "anxiously waiting" for the statement, which she expects will show a 15 percent drop in her 401(k) account.

I would say that software tester Mary Enright should stop any serious worrying, unless, of course, she plans to retire at age 42. Mary, you see, is 41 years old, and if she works to age 65 or even age 60, the traditional workings of the stock market should have more than made up for last year's drop in various investment portfolios, including 401(k) accounts.

It's human nature, of course, to deplore a drop in your investment portfolio with little or no attention to where your various investments started out.

My roommate is much more a day-to-day market watcher than I am and frequently expresses concern when this or that stock is down, say, 10 points to, say, $40 a share. It does little or nothing to ease Marian's disappointment when I point out that she bought the stock at $20 a share.

— **February 11, 2001**

Days Not All the Same

It came during a three-day stopover in Omaha during a two-week period in which I traveled to Boone County in north central Nebraska, then to Kansas, then to New York City, then to Georgia, with Marian accompanying me on the New York City leg of my two-week itinerary. (Pre-departure, I had written four columns for publication while I traveled.)

A nurse in an Omaha hospital was taking a blood sample in connection with my annual physical exam. She said she thoroughly enjoys her job, partly because "every day seems to bring something new." Then she added:

"I suppose every day's pretty much the same for you, since you're retired."

— **February 13, 2001**

A Shrink for Sarah?

Dr. Marian Andersen was particularly busy one recent morning, arranging appointments for me with two doctors who actually have medical degrees. Nothing serious; more in the nature of preventive medicine.

By the time the third telephone call had come my way at the office, confirming the second appointment, I told my energetic roommate that after that second appointment, "Please arrange for me to see a psychiatrist, because you are driving me nuts this morning."

Marian laughed and said that perhaps both of us should visit the psychiatrist and take along one of our cocker spaniels, 5-year-old Sarah, who still has a tendency to beat a timid retreat, barking all the way, when we are visited by someone Sarah doesn't know.

— March 4, 2001

Canines Display Vim, Even Valor

My friend and most loyal correspondent, Elmer Pinkerton of Elmwood, Neb., wrote recently that "we haven't heard about the bionic roommate for a long time." He also asked about "the fuzzy-eared kids." And another friend, William Houck of Decatur, Neb. (he's a friend now, after having once given me a "Harold, Harold, Harold" scolding), wrote to say he agrees with my view that the "superrich" are among the least qualified of Americans to tell Congress what to do about the estate tax, signing his letter, "Bill, Bill, Bill" and adding this postscript: "How are the doggies?"

Four-year-old Peaches continues to be the "class clown" or "prom queen," depending on the particular exuberant performance she is putting on.

My "bionic roommate" is considering becoming more bionic through an operation replacing her left-shoulder joint. Marian's outlook is typically positive – no complaints but rather an attitude that she is glad her ailment is something that could be addressed with medical techniques that repair nature's damage.

Elmer Pinkerton asked about Marian's record of seeing a ballgame in every major league ballpark currently in play. She is short four parks now. Being immobilized part of last summer with hip surgery put her behind schedule.

There are new ballparks in Houston, Detroit, Milwaukee and Pittsburgh. Marian is still considering how she might address this situation. One option would be to rest on her laurels, adding another ballpark or two to her life list but content with the fact that at one time she had seen a game in all of the 28 major league ballparks then in play. (We call it "Marian's Grand Slam.")

As to the "little doggies," a.k.a. "the fuzzy-eared kids":

Little Sugar, who just turned 11, is virtually blind and deaf and is as thin as the proverbial rail from an intestinal ailment. But she is still very much a part of our happy Prairie Avenue family group. Sugar gets around, for example, on the basis of her memory of where the stairs are, bumping her way along until she finds them.

I don't know what it is that alerts her, but when our other cocker spaniels, Peaches and Sarah, come bounding up the stairs to get a treat from a candy jar on the desk in my workroom, Sugar almost invariably follows, slowly but unerringly, to join the tail-wagging group at my feet, even though her lack of vision sometimes has her pointing in the wrong direction.

You'll understand when I say Sugar gets special attention these days, occasionally being carried into the back yard when she can't bump her way there through the laundry room doorway herself, and never failing to get a good deal of petting when she finds her way to Marian's or my feet or lap.

Five-year-old Sarah continues to be the perfect lady when she is around people she knows, waiting her turn when treats are distributed, following Marian around the house as though she feels most secure in the presence of the one who gives her so much attention and affection.

Four-year-old Peaches continues to be the "class clown" or "prom queen," depending on the particular exuberant performance she is putting on. She continues to have a vertical leap that a Husker cornerback would envy, still demonstrating this by pulling down food placed too close to the edge of the kitchen counter. She also seems to have a bottomless reservoir of energy, bouncing on our bed in the morning, for example, then exploding in an all-out run through the sitting room and hall and down the stairs.

— April 15, 2001

... and Grant Andersen Karger

A few months ago I gave you a report on the arrival of our fifth grand-child — Katherine Roe Andersen, third child of our son David and the former Leslie Roe. It's only fair to give equal time — or, in this case, equal space — to Katie's new cousin, Grant Andersen Karger, the third son of our daughter, Nancy, of Denver.

(I know, I know. Many of you, too, are proud grandparents. It's just that I have the advantage over you when it comes to public expressions of pride.)

Grant Andersen Karger weighed in at 8 pounds, 1 ounce and was 20½ inches long (or tall, I guess you would say, if he could stand up). His two brothers, 8-year-old Jack and 5-year-old James or "Jaymo," are fascinated with their little brother. Jack, for example, held Grant at the hospital shortly after his birth and assured him, "When you get home, we'll take good care of you."

Jack Karger, incidentally, is the beneficiary of a much-appreciated act of kindness by a friend and regular reader, Maxine Christensen of Exira, Iowa. When she read that Jack had been making deals with the tooth fairy, negotiating an agreement not only to be paid a dollar but also to get his tooth back, good friend Maxine sent me a "tooth fairy pillow" for young Mr. Karger.

Maxine wrote that her four boys and her 19 grandchildren and now some of her 17 great-grandchildren have all enjoyed having a special pillow by their bedside for leaving the tooth in anticipation of the tooth fairy's visit.

My Iowa friend added: "I still maintain the last paragraphs of your articles are the best part of it all," a sentiment that has been implied by a number of other readers who say they read the last item in my column first.

Five-year-old Jaymo Karger, incidentally, continues to come up with some quotes that have daughter Nancy laughing as she relates them to Marian and me. For example:

After being told to stop bouncing his basketball in the house, Jaymo told his mother: "It's going to be a whole different story in my house when I'm a father."

Jaymo's kindergarten class had been discussing matters of national origin as Hispanic classmates and their families prepared to observe the Mexican Cinco de Mayo holiday. Jaymo told his family that his nationality is "Irish and German and Nebraska" – Irish and German for his father and Nebraska for his mother.

— May 6, 2001

Sports Start Early

In keeping with family tradition (Marian attended her first Cornhusker football game when she was 3 years old), we started new grandson Grant Andersen Karger off on the right athletic foot. At 3 weeks old, he was part of the family group attending the Denver-Golden State basketball game. (He declined comment on the game, explaining that he had slept through it all.)

— May 17, 2001

With Clinton & Co. on the Links

Let's spend a couple of columns in Great Britain, always a fascinating place to visit, made especially interesting for Marian and me and special friend and host Vin Gupta this past spring because we were there at the same time as former President Bill Clinton and could follow the enthusiastic reception he received both at the official and crowd-on-the-street levels.

The president's trip ended with 2$\frac{1}{2}$ days of golf with Vin and me, with Marian and Vin's assistant, Shelly Holcomb, joining us when we weren't on the links. But let's start at the beginning, at Belfast in Northern Ireland.

Vin, a friend and generous supporter of Clinton, had made many of the transportation and lodging arrangements for Clinton's days in Great Britain. He gave this description of the former president's reception in Belfast, where he received an honorary doctorate from Queens University: At a dinner in his honor, Clinton received a five-minute standing ovation. Several thousand people were waiting outside the banquet hall to cheer Clinton and seek handshakes and autographs when the dinner ended at 1:30 a.m.

Clinton's next stop was at Oxford University where, as one Oxford official noted with a politely worded touch of humor, Clinton had studied as a Rhodes Scholar but had not completed his academic studies so did not receive a degree.

After working his way through a large crowd "wishing to shake his hand and capture him on video," according to The London Times, Clinton gave a 20-minute address dedicating Oxford's new Rothermere American Institute.

From Oxford to Hay-on-Wye, a Welsh border town where – for a

Vin Gupta, Marian, Bill Clinton and Andy.

fee reported as $145,000 – Clinton addressed a literary festival sponsored by The London Sunday Times. A thousand people paid $145 each to hear him, and a crowd estimated at 3,000 to 4,000 was waiting outside the hall when a post-speech dinner ended at around midnight.

As to the $2\frac{1}{2}$ days of golf and relaxation: It started at Loch Lomond Golf Club north of Glasgow, where our foursome included Clinton, Vin, Vin's close friend A. D. Sharma, son of the former president of India, and me. (The Sharmas and their three daughters were delightful participants in the Loch Lomond proceedings.)

The former president lived up to his reputation as an enthusiastic golfer who takes the game very seriously but has a good time in the process. He hits a long ball – sometimes a long way off the fairway – and offers tips that he said he's picked up in golfing with pros. (On the 307-yard ninth hole on the Old Course at St. Andrews, with a favoring wind and firm fairways, Clinton drove the green.)

His advice to me, offered in a way that certainly was not offensive, was to keep my wrists firm as I hit short chip shots. He said Greg Norman had so coached him.

Clinton's advice for improving the Gupta game was to take the club head back low and slow – pretty fundamental, but something we amateur golfers tend to forget. Vin started doing this and quickly began to drive the ball better.

In his own game, Clinton is quickly self-analytical when a shot goes awry. Not too many of them did in the two days we played together. I wasn't keeping score for myself or anybody else, but after we moved from Loch Lomond to St. Andrews, The London Times reported that Clinton shot a round of 86 on the Old Course, 14 over par – two over after allowing for a 12 handicap.

From St. Andrews, we flew to Skibo Castle, the baronial residence that Andrew Carnegie built in the land of his birth after making a fortune in the steel business in America. Located just a few miles from Royal Dornoch, one of the world's great golf courses, the Carnegie Club at Skibo Castle has a highly rated 18-hole course of its own plus a nine-hole three-par course.

Clinton lived up to his reputation as an enthusiastic golfer who takes the game seriously but has a good time in the process.

In an example of his enthusiasm for the game, the former president and Vin played nine late-evening holes after our flight from St. Andrews and were on the Carnegie links again early the next morning before Clinton's late-morning departure to make connections for a flight back to the United States. In view of the raw wind and the fact that I had played the course before, I skipped the Carnegie Club golf. We regretted that we didn't have time to play Royal Dornoch, a course that I had the pleasure of playing several years ago.

Any special challenges in playing golf with Secret Service men following and, at St. Andrews, a crowd of more than a thousand spectators lining the fence along the 17th and 18th holes?

Not really. The conversation between golfers and caddies was light-hearted, the usual putts were conceded, the play slowed a bit as Clinton responded to requests for autographs, but the pace of play moved along reasonably well.

I suppose I might feel differently if, with all those people watching, I hadn't played the 17th (the famous or infamous Road Hole) and the 18th reasonably well. I bogeyed each of them after hitting good drives and good bump-and-run approaches, links-golf style, on both holes, finishing with a breaking downhill two-foot putt – to mild applause – on No. 18. (Since my lower-handicap days are only a fond memory, I consider a solid bogey on a difficult par 4 a satisfying achievement for me these days.)

Relaxing over dinner in Loch Lomond and Skibo Castle, Marian and Vin and I talked with Clinton about subjects ranging from the AIDS epidemic in Africa to daughter Chelsea's interest in studying for an advanced degree at Oxford.

The dinner at Skibo was interrupted with the sad news that the daughter of a lifelong Little Rock friend of Clinton's had died in an auto accident. Clinton quickly changed his travel plans so that he could attend the funeral, canceling three presumably lucrative speaking engagements in Japan.

Marian said she found Clinton a charming companion. She told my secretary, Jackie Wrieth, that after it became known that she had suffered a digestive upset, Clinton on three different occasions asked her how she was feeling.

"Andy never asked me once," Marian reported to Jackie.

A final thought: In addition to the Secret Service agents following us and the crowd lining the 17th and 18th fairways, my St. Andrews golfing experience with former President Clinton included another unusual element. I had played the Old Course and visited the club-

Former President Bill Clinton and Andy finish a round of golf at St. Andrews.

house of the Royal & Ancient Golf Club of St. Andrews several times before, but this was the first time that a crowd watched as I arrived and left by helicopter using a field adjacent to the course.

— June 10, 2001

Titanium for the Shoulder

What was I doing TV surfing in a hotel room?

It was part of another chapter in the long story of Marian's continuing involvement with osteoarthritis.

This time it was her left shoulder joint that had worn out, and I was in a hotel room in Seattle between visits to Marian in her room at the University of Washington Medical Center.

Marian and I, of course, had talked with Dr. Kevin Garvin, chairman of the Department of Orthopaedic Surgery at the University of Nebraska Medical Center, who has been so helpful to Marian and a good many other patients with hip and knee problems. We asked Kevin for help in compiling a list of surgeons, local as well as those in other cities, who specialize in dealing with shoulder problems.

Marian and I decided on Dr. Frederick A. Matsen III, chairman of the Department of Orthopaedics and Sports Medicine at the University of Washington School of Medicine, who had come highly recommended to us by friends in North Carolina.

Marian is recovering nicely, thank you. And yes, with her new titanium shoulder joint implant added to others in both hips and her right knee, my room-mate did set off the metal detectors at Sea-Tac Airport on our return home.

Postscript on Marian's Seattle hospital experience: After lunch one day, Marian commented: "I think they did something to my brain during surgery. The hospital food seems to be starting to taste good to me."

— July 8, 2001

A Real Bonus

John Andrew (Jack) Karger, the 8-year-old Denver-resident son of daughter Nancy, the other day outlined a career plan that included a praise-worthy intent to share his hoped-for good fortune with others.

Jack said he wants to become a professional baseball player, earn a million dollars a year "and give half of it to charity."

Marian and I are, of course, pleased both with Jack's enthusiasm for sports (he is a bit unhappy because his coach says he should choose between concentrating on soccer or on baseball), although we will not be disappointed if he doesn't turn out to be a professional baseball player. But we hope his youthful attitude toward sharing with others lasts a lifetime.

— August 19, 2001

Days That End in Y

Some of the best humor Marian and I encounter appears on those pillows you see when you're a guest in other people's homes. We laughed over a new one on a recent visit to friends in North Carolina: "I never repeat gossip, so listen carefully."

Then there's the one hanging in our bathroom, words that both Marian and I consider particularly appropriate for me: "If God had intended us to see the sunrise, he would have made it later in the day."

My always-helpful secretary, Jackie Wrieth, volunteers this offering from one of her pillows: "I only play golf on days that end in Y."

— October 11, 2001

Dr. Marian's Prescriptions

It will not surprise you to know that Marian very quickly called my attention to this World-Herald headline: "Nagging Wife May Keep Husband Healthy." The story reported on a study led by University of Chicago sociology professor Ross Stolzenberg. Among the conclusions:

When a wife is too busy to nag her husband about wearing sun block, eating right and other healthful practices, his health may suffer. So when a wife works more than 40 hours per week, she tends to pay less attention to her husband's health needs.

The sociology professor said there is a whole set of gender attitudes and expectations that we learn from the time we are children, with men "taught that it is not masculine to worry about health issues, while women take on a nurturing role." So nagging becomes nurturing, and it's good for your health.

Candor compels me to report that the Andersen household may offer anecdotal evidence in support of Professor Stolzenberg's reasoning. Consider:

Marian doesn't work more than 40 hours a week. (Heaven knows she is very busy more than 40 hours a week, but she doesn't hold a job that takes her away from home more than 40 hours weekly.)

So I take eight pills every morning, three prescribed by my medical doctors and five (a mixture of vitamins and zinc and iron and stuff like that) prescribed by Dr. Marian. Dr. Marian reminds me to walk on our treadmill with statements like: "I'll fix your dinner after you've finished on the treadmill." Then there are the less subtle health hints like, "Have you kept off the pounds you lost while I was in the hospital and you were fixing your own meals?"

I think good genes have something to do with it, but I'm glad to give Marian a share of the credit for the fact that, for example, son Dave and I last year enjoyed a hunting safari together in South Africa, where I observed my 77th birthday. (No, I didn't shoot a giraffe.)

So thanks for the nagging, Dr. Marian. I think I should add that I have in mind the medical nagging, not any other variety.

— **October 28, 2001**

Friendly Fans at World Series

Marian and I had the good fortune of being in the stands for the first two World Series games in Phoenix. We can offer personal testimony in support of a New York Times reporter's observations about Arizona Diamondback fans.

The headline on the reporter's story read: "Good Heavens, They're Nice." The story offered some examples of contrast with the behavior of New York City fans.

Typical of the quick camaraderie you find in baseball parks (especially if you're all rooting for the same team), Marian and I struck up conversations with fans sitting

Fellow baseball fanatic, M. J. Kratina, son of Mark and Janet Kratina.

nearby. Returning to my seat with hot dogs and Pepsis (sorry, Warren, they don't sell Coke in the Phoenix ballpark), I spilled one Pepsi, fortunately in the direction of two seats that were temporarily empty.

Within 10 minutes, without a word to either Marian or me, a fresh Pepsi was delivered to me by a Diamondbacks fan sitting several seats to my right, followed by a fresh Pepsi delivered to me by a Diamondbacks fan sitting on my left. (The fan on my left decided, quite understandably, to keep the Pepsi when she discovered that the fan on my right had already replaced my spilled Pepsi.)

How's that for friendly?

— November 4, 2001

All in the Cards

Let's end today with an item about one of those three grandchildren in Denver, 6-year-old James Karger.

James went to the Denver Bronco-Washington Redskins football game in the snow in Denver last Sunday with $10 which he had earned. James believes in keeping money in circulation, and he spotted a set of football players cards – one of his favorite collection items – for sale for six dollars. He dug into his pocket for the money.

"Gosh, I wish I had six dollars," said the card vendor.

"You do now," responded James as he handed over his payment for the cards.

— November 21, 2001

Getting Jumpy

Marian's voice carrying up the stairs: "Peaches! You never do that." Then: "Thank you, Peaches."

It turns out that what Peaches (our effervescent 5-year-old cocker spaniel) "never does" – but which she had just done – was to jump up on Marian in an effort to speed up the food delivery process in which Marian was engaged at the kitchen counter.

I suggested that since Peaches does this from time to time, Marian might change her admonition to something like: "Peaches! You know better than that."

— November 25, 2001

The Birth of 'Dear God'

Exercising once again a grandparent's prerogative, let me end today's column on a note I think is appropriate for the season:

Daughter Nancy Karger looked out a window of her Evergreen, Colorado, home and saw what appeared to be a note on the front porch railing in early December. Possibly a message to Santa Claus from one of her two sons?

Not quite.

The fold-over note was addressed to "Dear God." The message inside from an $8\frac{1}{2}$-year-old: "I love you, God! Jack Karger."

An appropriate note on which to take leave of you on this Sunday two days before a great many people across the world will be celebrating the birth of the son of "Dear God."

— **December 23, 2001**

Celebrating a 79th Birthday

Books for Christmas; readers enjoy Marian & the dogs; half-and-half on the Cream of Wheat; cardinals return; 'Chere Amie' builds a home; 'Bopa looks 60; Muzzy looks 53;' a charming Clinton companion in Scotland; back surgery; Sugar's blindness; Lindsey, 12, Robby, 9, Katie, 1, grandpa's birthday party; Michael Douglas; goodbye Peaches; Marian, UNL's Doctor of Humane Letters.

A 'Print-Rich' Home Environment

Twice during the holiday season, a good friend said she hoped I would report in my column what Christmas presents I had given our grandchildren.

A good many readers, especially people who know Marian and me, have said they enjoy my occasional reports on Marian and our dogs and our grandchildren. But Christmas presents to grandchildren had not previously been indicated as a topic of interest, even to very good friends.

It finally dawned on me that my friend perhaps was testing whether I practice what I preach, in this case my "sermon" urging my readers to include books among the Christmas gifts to children or grandchildren. I cited expert opinion that a "print-rich" home environment is a critically important promoter of success in the school classroom.

I'm happy to report that late in the afternoon of Dec. 24, I was at a local bookstore searching for children's books that I selected from a list that John Mackiel, Omaha Public Schools superintendent, had called to my attention.

Two of the books – one a volume featuring "The Legend of Sleepy Hollow" and other Washington Irving stories, the other a collection of poems that children enjoy – went to Omaha grandchildren Lindsey and Robby Andersen. Two others – a Guinness Book of World Records and a volume of poems titled "If You're Not Here, Please Raise Your Hand" – were purchased for Denver grandchildren Jack and James Karger.

One of the highlights of the holiday season for me came when Robby Andersen opened his Christmas-present book, settled himself on my lap and suggested that we read the book together.

— January 20, 2002

Of Sugar, Sarah and Peaches

A heartwarming call came the other day from an Omahan who said he resides in an assisted-living facility and once a month two ladies bring several dogs around for an evening call on him and other residents. "It peps up my day," he said.

I don't need much of an invitation to write about Marian and our dogs, so today a report that I hope will "pep up the day" for my caller and for numerous other readers who have said they enjoy reading about Marian, Sugar, Sarah and Peaches.

Sleeping pals, Sarah and Sugar.

Peaches continues to be the effervescent, "never met anybody I didn't like" ringleader. It's invariably Peaches who leaps up and pulls food down from the kitchen counter. I've told Marian that it's not Peaches' fault but hers when she leaves food too close to the edge of our counter.

My lecture came back to haunt me on a recent morning when Marian was traveling and I got an unopened loaf of bread from the freezer, preparatory to making my breakfast. (Believe me, my breakfasts are always simple when Marian is away. I think I had planned on peanut butter on toast that morning.) You can see what's coming: My attention temporarily diverted by going into the dining room, I returned to find the three dogs halfway through consuming the loaf of bread. I didn't mention this to Marian, but of course she noticed the loaf was missing and assumed, correctly, that I hadn't eaten it but that the dogs had.

I thought her comments were quite restrained, probably because she figured she wouldn't hear any more lectures from me about leaving food too close to the edge of the kitchen counter.

Sarah continues to be the restrained, more ladylike member of the trio. She is adjusting better – a bit better – to strangers.

And dear little 12-year-old blind and deaf Sugar still seems to enjoy life. Partly from memory, partly from bumping against doors and furniture, she finds her way remarkably well, whether it's up the stairs to my workroom at M&M-dispensing time, to Marian's or my lap in the family room or to a warm spot in front of the fireplace. She has become increasingly adept at sensing where I am, stretching out at my feet and insistently pawing at one of my shoes until I respond by petting her.

Sugar continues to wolf down (cocker spaniel down?) all the food we allow her but also continues to be thin as a bone.

We don't know how long Sugar can continue to go on, of course, but if love and tender care have anything to do with it, she should live a very long time indeed.

— January 27, 2002

Winter Hospitality

As far as Marian and I are concerned, that was no ill wind that brought last Thursday's snowstorm.

With the wind and snow came the return of a flock of cardinals to the evergreens and bird (and squirrel) feeder in our back yard.

We counted seven cardinals at one time, fewer than the 10 to 12 we have seen in past winters but a welcome sight after no more than one or two cardinals earlier this winter.

We don't know where the cardinals had been keeping themselves, but we were delighted to have them enjoying our hospitality again.

— March 7, 2002

Half the Half-and-Half?

Dr. Marian Andersen's role as my "health nazi" (her description) sometimes produces surprising but attention-getting advice, direct or implied.

The other morning, the attention-getting advice took this form when Marian observed me preparing to eat breakfast:

"Doctors all over the world are shaking their heads over the fact that you use half-and-half on your Cream of Wheat."

I continued to pour the half-and-half, but, admittedly, I poured a little less than I might otherwise have used. And I was pleased to know that Marian had, figuratively, enlisted the help of doctors all over the world in advising me as to a healthful lifestyle.

"Doctors all over the world are shaking their heads over the fact that you use half-and-half on your Cream of Wheat."

— March 17, 2002

Bootlegging Better

I was deep in the Sunday newspapers when Marian came into the family room and said, "I'm back." I asked her where she had been.

"I went to the grocery store," she replied. "I told you where I was going before I left, but you were reading your Sunday papers. I think I could run a bootlegging operation or a house of prostitution here and you wouldn't notice if you were reading your newspapers."

I told Marian that I thought a bootlegging operation would be the better option.

— March 31, 2002

Welcome Chere Amie

I won't say it's in response to popular demand, but enough of you have consistently told Marian and me how much you enjoy reading about Marian and our dogs and other aspects of our life on Prairie Avenue that I venture to tell you about the latest addition to what might loosely be described as the Andersen family circle.

The addition is a sparrow – we have chosen to assume the sparrow is a female and have named her Chere Amie, which, in French, means "dear friend."

This was the name of the carrier pigeon that delivered a message that led to the rescue of the valiant fabled "lost battalion" of American troops in France in the closing months of World War I. (The pigeon was a male, so its name was spelled Cher Ami.)

Chere Amie has taken up residence in a rather elaborate three-bulb light fixture that illuminates our side yard. One of the light bulbs has been broken for some time. (It's entirely too difficult to get up and replace one bulb when two other bulbs are still operative, in my judgment.)

One evening about six weeks ago, we turned on the lights (two lights, that is) and looked up to see a sparrow looking back at us from a perch atop the socket with the broken light bulb. The bird seemed not at all startled at our presence and looked down alertly when we addressed some welcoming words to her. The next morning, the bird was gone.

That evening, when we turned on the lights and looked up, there was Chere Amie. We have not seen her either enter or leave the light fixture, but this has been going on with only occasional interruption for six weeks now. Marian speculates that Chere Amie is attending some sort of neighborhood avian school during the day.

We are glad to have Chere Amie as our overnight guest and welcome her each evening. In my case, I'm particularly pleased, since I believe this is the best reason to date for installing that elaborate three-candle-simulating light bulb fixture several years ago.

You'll have to ask Marian why that fixture was installed just above our garbage cans. I can only say that little Chere Amie has given me an additional reason – a reason of which Marian approves – for not going through the torturous task of trying to wriggle my hand inside the elaborate fixture to replace that third bulb.

— May 12, 2002

From a Grand Grandson

Members of the Denver branch of the family were watching a television program dealing with facelift operations, including one that cost $25,000.

Jack, 9, and James, 6, asked their mother, our daughter Nancy Karger, why anyone would pay $25,000 for a facelift. Nancy replied that people get facelifts to make themselves look younger but that most people don't do facelifts. She mentioned Muzzy (Marian) and Bopa (me) as examples.

"Yeah," Jack responded. "Bopa looks about 60, and Muzzy looks 53."

"Yeah," Jack responded. "Bopa looks about 60, and Muzzy looks 53." What a grand grandson.

—May 19, 2002

When Daddy's Gone

Overheard on a recent morning as I approached our kitchen:

Marian summoning our three cocker spaniels to breakfast: "Come on, lovies. You are my best boon companions."

Then, with hardly a pause, as Marian became aware of my approach: "My best boon companions when Daddy's gone."

— May 26, 2002

Clinton a Sincere 'People Person'

Again this year, through our friendship with fellow Omahan Vin Gupta, who is a close friend and generous supporter of former President Bill Clinton, Marian and I had dinner with Clinton. He was in Scotland for a two-day visit, which included a round at one of the world's great golf courses, Royal Dornoch.

Marian and I again found Clinton to be a charming companion, very bright and articulate, showing all the signs of a sincere "people person." He called Vin the other day to ask how Marian was doing following her recent back surgery. (Marian is doing very well, thank you, recuperating at home for three weeks or so.)

When we were with Clinton and Vin in Scotland last year, the former president said he had been reading "Seabiscuit," the story of the remarkable horse that captured the hearts of the nation's racing fans in the late 1930s. Marian and I both read "Seabiscuit" and thoroughly enjoyed the story of that stout-hearted horse.

When we saw Clinton in Scotland this month, I asked him what books he has been reading. He reeled off four titles, the names of the authors and a quick summary of the books' themes. I decided to pursue "Wide as the Waters," a story of the evolution of the English-language Bible, and a Benjamin Franklin biography, "The First American." I told Clinton I was reading "Founding Brothers," a new look at the remarkable men who founded this great republic.

Clinton and Marian at the White House.

(A few days after we arrived home, the mail brought a copy of the "Wide as the Waters" book and a handwritten note from Clinton with a list – and a brief summary of the theme – of the 10 books he said he had most enjoyed reading since the first of the year. Incidentally, all are non-fiction.)

Clinton was equally quick and concise in responding to my question about how the Israeli settlements issue would have been resolved under the Israeli-Palestinian proposed peace accord that had been negotiated with his encouragement.

The former president said the contentious settlements issue would have been addressed by requiring Israel to pull out of all but a relatively small slice of the West Bank – a small slice, but one containing a large majority of the Israeli settlers. This was part of the deal which PLO chairman Yasser Arafat rejected.

— June 23, 2002

Hold the Water

Herewith a brief case for artificial plants as against the real thing:

Reporting to Marian on my exemplary "househusband" performance during her recent stay in the hospital, I said I had watered the plants in the garden room and various other rooms in the house but had just noticed that I had missed the large orchid plant sitting in the middle of the dining room table.

Marian's response: "Oh, don't water that. It's artificial. Water would run all over the dining room table."

Now I submit that if an artificial plant looks so realistic that you have to feel the leaves to see whether it's real or artificial, you have a pretty strong argument for making life easier for all hands – including temporary house-husbands – by substituting artificial plants for nature's own. Among other things, it would protect furniture surfaces like our dining room table.

I realize I'm not going to come close to winning this argument. I just thought I'd raise the question.

— July 1, 2002

Canine Members of Andersen Clan Have Fans Aplenty

Today a report on the dogs – and their mistress.

Twelve-year-old Sugar continues to do remarkably well despite being blind and deaf. She spends a good deal of time sleeping, her thin little body curled in a circle, snoozing quietly on a pillow in the back hall. But she also finds her way around the house – partly from memory, partly from simply bumping off walls and furniture, looking for our laps, into which she is promptly lifted as soon as she appears.

Sugar also has a way of sensing when Peaches and Sarah head up the stairs to my workroom and stand looking up at the M&M jar.

Almost without exception, Sugar comes pitty-patting along behind them (which has led to one of her current nicknames, Aunt Pitty Pat).

Five-year-old Peaches is still "the Prom Queen" or "Alpha Dog," ... She continues to merit the description I have used before: A bundle of ears-flying, tail-wagging canine energy who has never encountered a situation she didn't think she could improve by inserting herself smack into the middle of it.

Five-year-old Peaches is still "the Prom Queen" or "Alpha Dog," clearly the exuberant ringleader. She continues to merit the description I have used before: A bundle of ears-flying, tail-wagging canine energy who has never encountered a situation she didn't think she could improve by inserting herself smack into the middle of it.

And 6-year-old Sarah, shyest of the dogs, is slowly getting better about not barking at any strange face. Somewhere in her puppyhood, we believe, Sarah was really frightened by someone new to her and has never gotten over it.

We think this helps account for the fact that Sarah is Marian's shadow, which was being demonstrated as I dictated this on a Sunday afternoon sitting in our family room. Marian was sunning herself in the back yard, clearly visible through the breakfast-room picture window, and Sarah was looking out the window, barking her head off. I opened the garden-room door and allowed Sarah, with Peaches as her figurative wingman, to fly up the backyard steps and assume her customary position at Marian's side.

The human members of the Andersen family get some nice attention, too, from some readers. For example, my good friend in Exira, Iowa, Maxine Christensen, wished us a happy 50th wedding anniversary and included some "if we had it to do over" philosophy including: "I'd do all the things that I wish I had done but was afraid of what people would say or think."

From a reader in Naponee in south-central Nebraska comes reaction to a report on some of our grandchildren.

"Aren't kids fun and especially your own grandkids?," my Naponee reader wrote. Oh, yes: She also said she hopes I continue writing "for many more years."

A letter from a Fremont reader responded to my column emphasizing that the great majority of people living in this country think of themselves as Americans rather than Germans or Italians or Vietnamese or whatever else their ancestors might be. My Fremont reader recalled overhearing a conversation between two youngsters some years ago. A 14-year-old said to a 6-year-old that he is "part German, some Irish and even some Scottish. What are you?" The 6-year-old replied: "I don't know about all that stuff, but I do know I'm a whole bunch American."

The Fremont reader added this postscript: "I admire Marian. In spite of her arthritis, she does all she does. Go for it, girl!"

Elmer M. Pinkerton, the sage of Elmwood, Neb., took note of my report on Marian's latest surgical procedure – this time an operation to ease the pressure between spinal vertebrae. Elmer knows that Marian takes pride in her record of seeing a game in every major league baseball park, although she is currently one short, not having seen a game in the new Pittsburgh Pirates park. Elmer wrote:

"I hope the Bionic Lady is not sitting in a stadium these days. Can you make a small stadium and place it in front of the TV for her?"

Very thoughtful of you, friend Elmer, but Marian would never settle for that. Instead, she is making plans for a visit to the Pirates' new PNC Park late this summer.

— July 28, 2002

SUV Stuff

I figured I'd better think about cleaning out my Jeep when Marian remarked, "You've got enough stuff in your Jeep to hold a garage sale."

I decided to inventory the contents, with this result: Half a box of king-size Kleenex, four glasses cases (three of them empty), a set of tools for the family farm (saw, hammer, kitchen scissors), four golf clubs, a pair of rain pants, a golf glove and a golf towel, a plastic bag of tees and an umbrella, one of those roadside lanterns that will flash yellow or red or white, a first-aid kit, a portable cassette player (the old-fashioned kind that weighs about five pounds) and a canvas tote bag full of outdated electronic equipment. (Anybody out there want a used Motorola cellular phone?)

Marian may not understand that some of these things have accumulated in my SUV because she wanted me to get them out of either Nancy's bedroom (we still call it Nancy's bedroom) or my second-floor workroom.

I'm still thinking about cleaning out the Jeep. (Go back to the start of this portion of the column, Marian. You'll note that I suggested only that I'd think about it.)

— July 25, 2002

Surprise 79th

It was a nice surprise party, and I think everyone had a good time. I know I did.

I'm talking about my birthday party (No. 79) last Sunday. Marian had said that son David and daughter-in-law Leslie and their three children – Lindsey, 12, Robby, 9, and Katie, approaching 2 – were coming over for lunch and

Andy, Marian and grandchildren, Lindsey and Robby Andersen.

a swim. It turned out that it was a surprise party for me, made all the more enjoyable for all hands – including me – when slender Lindsey quickly put up a poolside umbrella with which I had struggled unsuccessfully for 10 minutes the day before.

Then there was more laughter when Katie, being coached to refer to Marian as "Muzzy," as the other grandchildren do, kept referring to her as "Money." Not an inappropriate nickname for a generous grandmother, come to think of it.

A gift from the Dave Andersen family and daughter Nancy Karger's Evergreen, Colo., family was a new DVD/VCR player. I accepted it on the condition that Dave would not leave the house until he had connected it to our family-room television set. The alternative, I pointed out, would be for me to still be struggling to connect it by the time my 80th birthday rolls around.

With the DVD/VCR player came a DVD disc of the movie "The Ghost and the Darkness," which my children considered appropriate, since Marian and I know Michael Douglas and both Dave and I thoroughly enjoyed our hunting safari in South Africa two summers ago. (No, I'm not suggesting that we hunted anything like those man-eating lions in the movie.)

I settled down that Sunday evening with a bowl of popcorn and a martini and watched again "The Ghost and the Darkness." I

Marian with Michael Douglas who visited Omaha to appear at a Red Cross fundraising event.

may do more of this sort of thing. After all, you can't take your own popcorn – and martini – into one of those multi-screen cinema complexes.

— August 1, 2002

The Good Old Days?

As one reaches a more mature age, there is, of course, a tendency to recall ever more fondly "the good old days." That truism came to mind the other day as I was writing a column that involved recalling my college days. My mind turned to the time when son Dave and daughter Nancy were school children, home for a day because snowy weather had once again closed Western Hills or Lewis

David, all grown up, and Marian.

Grown-up Nancy with Mom.

& Clark or wherever Nancy and Dave might have been enrolled at the time.

I recall trying to turn the conversation to something along these lines: "Let me tell you about the days when I was attending Florence Grade

School or North High School, and our schools rarely if ever shut down because of bad weather." I quickly learned that the children were less interested in hearing about the good old days than in talking about their plans for their day off from school.

— August 29, 2002

'Go Back'

Somehow the Biblical "Oh, ye of little faith" came to mind as I settled behind the steering wheel of my Jeep the other morning and noticed the following note from Marian leaning against the dashboard: "Now go back and get your lunch out of the fridge."

As I read the note, my lunch was resting alongside my briefcase in the backseat of my vehicle.

Now in the interest of full disclosure, I feel constrained to report that after I had backed out of the garage, I did have to get out of my SUV and go back to close the door between the breezeway and the garage. Which, of course, raises the prospect that Marian's next dashboard note will read: "Now go back and close the breezeway door."

— September 15, 2002

'Prom Queen' Gave and Got Much Love

First, an explanation: With the election results still being tallied as I write this, I must include post-election comments in this coming Sunday's column.

Next, a hope that the frequent expressions of reader interest in Marian and the Andersen family's three cocker spaniels justifies my devoting today's column to a tribute to Peaches, our 6-year-old "Prom Queen" or "Alpha Dog," who died last week.

Marian says she will find comfort in the thought that in our memory, Peaches will always be young, as full of life and joy and love as she was when she went to the veterinarian's clinic to have her teeth cleaned. (She didn't suffer long, dying within hours when one of her lungs filled after she was placed under anesthesia for the teeth-cleaning.)

Marian and I find comfort, too, in thinking that Peaches brought a bit of pleasure into the lives of those many readers who over the years have told Marian and me how much they enjoyed reading about Peaches and our other dogs.

Peaches has been the dog most often mentioned by readers, perhaps because I have written about her in such words as these:

"Peaches is clearly the exuberant ringleader ... a bundle of ears-flying, tail-wagging canine energy who has never encountered a situation she didn't think she could improve by inserting herself smack into the middle of it."

And then there is considerable comfort in the fact that Peaches should be – and, we hope, will be – remembered as the inspiration for the city-ordinance amendment that raised from two to three the number of adult dogs that can legally reside in an Omaha residence.

We had two cocker spaniels (Sarah and Sugar, who still live with us) when a Minnesota dog-breeder friend told Marian she had another cocker spaniel that was just right for Marian. I told Marian there was a legal limit of two dogs per household. She was disappointed – for about 15 minutes. Then she said, "I'm going to try to get the law changed."

Marian went to work con-tacting members of the City Planning Board, the late Ron Hemingsen of the Nebraska Humane Society, then-Mayor Hal Daub and members of the Omaha City Council. On the day the City Council was to vote on the three-dog-

Peaches takes charge. Any questions?

limit ordinance change approved by the Planning Board, council members indicated general approval, but there was talk of delaying the vote to work on amendments.

City Clerk Mary Cornett stepped to the microphone and said she thought council members knew her yellow Lab named Gabriel and her female mixed-breed named Ginger. But now, she said, a third dog had entered her life – Itty Bear. "Please make me legal," Mary Cornett asked the City Council.

The ordinance was promptly passed, making law-abiding citizens out of Omahans who had three dogs living with them and opening the door for others who would like to add a third dog to the family circle, as we added Peaches.

Among the words of consolation that friends have offered following Peaches' death was this comment from a longtime friend in California: "She probably had the best six years any dog ever had," which prompted this response from Marian: "I told Peaches every day what a great dog she was and how much I loved her."

We will scatter Peaches' ashes in Memorial Park, where Peaches enjoyed making friends of strangers on her frequent walks with Marian.

Peaches' death brought to mind something I wrote 6¹/₂ years ago when another of our cockers, 11-year-old Sister, had to be put to sleep because of widespread cancer:

"We believe that loving much and being much loved contribute in large measure to the living of a good life. By that standard, Sister lived a good life indeed."

And by that standard, our beloved Peaches also lived a good life indeed.

Dear little blind and deaf Sugar, 12, and shy but devoted Sarah, nearly 7, will be joined by another cocker spaniel as soon as Marian is successful in her search for a puppy, a search that started the evening of the day Peaches died.

We can think of no better way to honor and remember Peaches than to continue to be a three-dog family. After all, Peaches inspired the city-ordinance amendment that allows us to have three dogs to love and be loved by, as we loved and were loved by Peaches.

— **November 7, 2002**

Let the Birds Decide

Marian bought a new brand of bird seed this autumn. On opening the package, she didn't like the looks of the seed and said she was going to use it up, then find some of the kind that we used last year.

I observed that the cardinals and other birds seemed to be enjoying this new brand of seed very much, and Marian agreed. I then suggested that perhaps the important thing is that the birds, rather than Marian, like the new seed.

Again, Marian agreed and said she would continue to buy the new brand of bird seed.

She usually doesn't give up that easily.

— **December 22, 2002**

A Doctor in the House

Our Prairie Avenue home is aglow with pride this week. Marian Battey Andersen's title of "Doctor" is now official.

I had given Marian the unofficial title of Doctor Marian, based on her prescription of six daily vitamin and nutrition pills and various other encouragements to maintain my good health, including such not-so-subtleties as "I'll fix dinner as soon as you've finished on the treadmill."

Marian is now a Doctor of Humane Letters, a degree conferred last Saturday at mid-term commencement ceremonies at her alma mater, the

University of Nebraska-Lincoln. She was recognized for dedicating her adult life "to the service of others" through leadership roles involving the university (she was the first woman and first Omahan to chair the University of Nebraska Foundation, for example) and numerous civic and cultural organizations at the local, state and national levels.

As Marian turned away from the podium with her red-and-white doctoral collar over her shoulders, I kissed her on the cheek. (I was the commencement speaker and sitting next to her on the platform.)

I started my commencement address by observing that I couldn't remember the name of the commencement speaker or anything he said when I graduated in 1945. But one thing I was quite sure of, I said, was the fact that the commencement speaker hadn't kissed any honorary degree recipient.

Among many honors came the Perry Branch Award of the University of Nebraska Foundation.

So far, Doctor Andersen continues to be her easy-to-live-with self. No suggestion yet that I address her as Doctor Andersen, as in, for example, "Is breakfast ready yet, Doctor Andersen?"

— **December 25, 2002**

CHAPTER 12 – 2003

Claire Joins the Clan

Positives on peanut butter; spoonable vs. drinkable Cream of Wheat; grandson's income goals; 7 miles to empty; Sarah & Sugar meet Claire; Coumadin; taste tests; dislocated hip; winning Claire's heart; Reds' new ball park; cheerful caregiver; Marian's remarkable memory.

Naggee vs. Nagger

In Marital Relations I, as taught by Dr. Marian Andersen, total responsibility for the ending of wifely nagging rests not with the nagger but with the naggee.

This was explained by Dr. Andersen as she urged me – several times urged me – to perform three specific household tasks during the weekend between Christmas and New Year's Day.

After I told her I intended to perform the three specific tasks on my timetable, Marian replied: "You say that I sometimes continue to nag you. But if you would just do what I ask you to, I wouldn't nag you."

— January 1, 2003

Moderation With Peanut Butter

You can bet that Marian, who reads The World-Herald very thoroughly, didn't call my attention to a recent news item that started with these words: "If you like peanut butter, you now have a solid, guilt-free reason for enjoying it."

The story quoted Harvard School of Public Health researchers as saying that the fats of most nuts "are good for insulin sensitivity and cholesterol levels."

OK, so the story did also say that "peanuts are not a cure-all for diabetes. Moderation is the key. Too many nuts can lead to gaining fat."

Next round in my discussions with my self-described "health nazi" will probably revolve around the definition of "moderation" when the issue is peanut butter consumption.

— January 9, 2003

Preparing for Claire

At hand is a letter from yet another reader who expresses special enjoyment of the final item in each of my columns and, again like a number of other readers, wants to read more about Marian's doings.

Marian is happily preparing to welcome another cocker spaniel into the family circle — a 1-year-old female raised by a breeder in Alabama. She will bring our number of cockers again to the legal limit of three.

Note that I did not say that the new dog will replace the irrepressible Peaches, who died several months ago at the age of 6 while in the care of a local veterinary clinic. Peaches is irreplaceable. But Marian and I are sure that our new dog, to be named Claire, will carve her own place in our hearts.

Marian is preparing for Claire's arrival by, coincidentally, her first birthday, Valentine's Day. Marian can't understand why I would prefer to be hunting rather than on hand to welcome Claire.

It's a guy's thing, Marian. I'm sure Claire won't notice, but I promise to make it up to her with some special attention after my hunting trip. Special attention which must be tempered, of course, by the knowledge that we must be sure not to slight 7-year-old Sarah and 13-year-old Sugar as we make Claire feel at home.

Sugar, blind and deaf, probably won't know quite what is going on, but the sensitive Sarah certainly will.

— February 6, 2003

Spoonability

"I want you to write in your column that my Cream of Wheat is getting better," Marian said to me the other morning.

Yes, ma'am. The consistency of the Cream of Wheat that Marian serves me from time to time is getting better, and I do appreciate her successful efforts to address a problem that I mentioned in this space a few weeks ago.

Regular readers may recall that when I told Marian her Cream of Wheat was more drinkable than "spoonable," she replied: "Cooking's not an exact science, you know."

— February 13, 2003

Just Look at the House

Please indulge me in telling another grandchild story, this one involving James Wheaton Karger, 7, son of daughter Nancy Karger.

James confided to his mother that he wants to make $250,000 a year. Nancy replied that this would be nice and he could have a nice house with that kind of annual income. James said he doesn't care about the house. Look at Warren Buffett, James said.

I hasten to add that James and his brother Jack, 10, don't think Warren Buffett lives in shabby surroundings. It's just that both James and Jack were very favorably impressed when, on a visit to Omaha some months ago, Marian drove them by the Buffett residence and said that our friend Warren has lived in that house for many years, long after he had become a multibillionaire.

— **February 16, 2003**

Little Reminders

Personal item No. 2: Marian doesn't think it's particularly funny — in fact, she suggested that it's a little stupid — when I tell her that "I had an illustrated dashboard in the Jeep again today." She knows that means a little chime has sounded and the image of a gasoline pump has appeared, warning me that the tank is nearly empty.

When the chime rings and the gas tank image appears, I immediately punch my way to the overhead electronic message which tells me how many "MILES TO EMPTY," then I calculate whether I can carry out a mission like delivering Marian to the airport and still make it back to a filling station.

The other day I delivered Marian to the airport and drove back across town to my office in Ralston, where the display panel said, "7 MILES TO EMPTY," obviously more than an ample safety margin for my trip to a nearby filling station on my way home from work.

Now I don't carry this (Jackie calls it "a macho thing") to extremes. When the message panel said "7 MILES TO EMPTY" the other day, I asked Jackie to place a "GET GAS!" note where I would be sure to see it as I left the office.

I'm not totally confident that even "GET GAS!" reminders — or any other kind of reminder — will consistently work. The other day I boarded the office elevator and punched the button, continued to think about something else and finally realized that the elevator wasn't moving. My first suspicion was, of course, that there was something wrong with the elevator. But you guessed it; the problem was that I had punched the button for the same floor from which I had entered the elevator.

It's not that I'm having senior moments, you understand. It's just that we columnists are so consistently absorbed thinking about, for example, such weighty subjects as the loony legislative proposal to pay salaries to Cornhusker football players. (Pass that bill, senators, and be prepared for the barrage of complaints from feminist activists who for years have been saying that universities already spend far too much on their football programs.)

— February 23, 2003

Canine Newcomer Isn't Sure What to Make of Her New Owner

Today please indulge me as I turn to rather personal subjects, leaving for another day further attention to such serious matters as Iraq's continued defiance of a 12-year-old United Nations mandate ordering Iraq to rid itself of all weapons of mass destruction.

Personal item No. 1 deals, as regular readers might expect, with the arrival of a new dog and her impact on the Andersen household. Several readers have been kind enough to send greetings to the new dog through letters to me. One reader, perhaps noting my remark that we must be sure not to neglect veteran Andersen dogs Sugar and Sarah as we welcome newcomer Claire, sent her good wishes to all three dogs in a letter addressed to them.

Claire is a very pretty (beautiful might not be an overstatement) – a very light buff-colored cocker spaniel whose first birthday was properly celebrated on Valentine's Day, the day after her arrival from her former home with a breeder in Mobile, Ala. She immediately bonded with Marian and my dog-loving secretary, Jackie Wrieth.

It's hard to say this without a touch of envy, but I must report that Claire has bonded much better with Marian and Jackie and Sugar and Sarah than she has with me.

The disappointing reality that she has not yet bonded with me is not due to lack of effort on my part. I felt a bit better about the non-bonding when the breeder pointed out that she is unmarried and lives alone and thus Claire has had no opportunity to become acquainted with men.

I have tried a variety of tactics, including making sure that I don't have a hunting cap on when I approach Claire, that I don't talk loudly around her, that I hold out my hand to her with fingers closed into a fist, supposedly a non-threatening approach the reason for which, I must add, no one has ever satisfactorily explained to me.

So far I have been willing to go no lower than one bended knee in efforts to avoid the image of a threatening male towering over a small dog. My bended-knee approach to Claire is accepted if I keep my voice lowered, extend my hand very slowly with perhaps a snack in it and – this is the most important condition of all – Claire is on Marian's lap, which is approximately 50 percent of the time.

I've joked about buying a wig and talking in a falsetto voice, but I'm considering a less demeaning approach. I'm skeptical about the possibility that I could find a way to make Claire understand that I'm the one who writes the checks that pay for her dog biscuits, but how about my being the only one who puts her morning and evening bowls of dog food before her?

It's not that I resent the attention that is being showered on Claire, including bags full of goodies delivered by some of Marian's special pals (and mine) like Kim Lauritzen, Janet Kratina and Sally Barton. I just want her to stop running from the room or hurrying to stand behind Marian every time her meal ticket approaches.

— February 23, 2003

Progress

Claire, the cocker spaniel who joined our family six weeks ago, now has a man in her life: me.

Claire came to us as a 1-year-old, and her breeder explained that she had not been around men. The breeder suggested that I feed Claire liver soaked in garlic and that I be the only one offering this particular treat. A couple of readers, bless their hearts, offered their advice as to how to win Claire over. (For example, ignore Claire while lavishing attention on our two other cockers, Sugar and Sarah.)

I decided to let my inherent charm and lovability do the job. The charm/lovability approach was enhanced by the fact that I was careful never to raise my voice around Claire and to buddy up to her while she was not too far from the love of her life (it's mutual), my roommate.

The result has been that Claire now comes running to greet me at the back door with the other dogs, comes upstairs to my workroom to get M&Ms along with Sugar and Sarah and approaches me to be petted and pampered along with her siblings. (They're really not related, but you know what I mean.)

I'm not taking anything for granted. Perhaps it's best for me to consider that my relationship with Claire is still a work in progress. Females — some of them — can be fickle creatures, you know.

— March 30, 2003

Golf 'After Four Weeks'

A recent four-day stay in the hospital turned out to be for diagnostic purposes only, thank goodness. All vital signs are in good working order, but a medication change was made for moderately high blood pressure, and it was decided that I should stay on a blood thinner, Coumadin, for the rest of my days because of deep-vein thrombosis in my right leg, dating back perhaps to surgery removing my cancerous prostate gland in 1994.

Because of the deep-vein thrombosis and the necessity of stabilizing the Coumadin dosage, I was directed to take it easy for two weeks and was told "you can play golf after four weeks."

The word that I can "play golf after four weeks" was a happy prognosis indeed, considering that some, including me, might say that I really haven't been playing golf (but trying to) for the past 10 years or so.

— April 6, 2003

Pups Who 'Read'

Some of my more mature readers may recall a song popular some decades ago titled "I Had the Craziest Dream." That song came to mind recently during a period when we were looking for a new dog to bring our cocker spaniel complement back up to three following the death of our "alpha dog, Peaches, a.k.a. "the Prom Queen." The dream went like this:

I told Marian that I would like to take her downstairs and introduce her to two cocker spaniel puppies who were prepared to demonstrate that they could read newspapers.

Marian indicated she wasn't particularly interested, so I left in something of a snit, presumably to look for someone who would like to own a couple of cocker spaniel pups who were smart enough to read newspapers.

Then I woke up.

I was telling a friend and fellow dog lover, Jim Abel of Lincoln, the story of my dream. Jim's response: "I think I'll stick to dogs you can teach to shake hands."

— April 13, 2003

Passing Both Tests

Marian put me to two taste tests the other evening. I'm pleased – "greatly relieved" might be a better description – that I passed both tests.

Marian had frequently questioned whether I could really tell the difference between certain kinds of liquids. She looked askance when I turned down a certain cola drink when my favorite brand was not available on, say, an airline flight. And she thought I was perhaps being needlessly elitist when I said that I preferred a certain single-malt scotch better than a less aged – and less expensive – version.

With some trepidation, I agreed to a taste test in both cases. Out of my view, Marian poured a sample of one of the cola drinks in one glass and one in another. She asked me to sample each and see whether I could tell the difference. With only brief hesitation, I picked the cola drink I prefer.

Then we moved on to the single-malt scotch test. Same ground rules. Without hesitation, I picked the longer-aged variety that I prefer.

Marian has been a good sport about this so far. But she has a persistent way about her, so I wouldn't be surprised if I'm asked to revisit the subject. If that happens, I'm simply going to take the position that further tests would constitute "double jeopardy" and any one of a number of my attorney friends would gladly take my case against another trial.

— April 27, 2003

Go Ahead: Make My Day

From time to time, people, bless their friendly hearts, tell me how well they think I'm doing, physically as well as mentally, in my advancing maturity. (I'll be 80 in July.) Then there are times like the recent day in which a 40ish friend described me as "elderly." Accurate, of course, but he might have chosen another word. ("Elder statesman" is OK, however).

In the Phoenix airport, a young attendant, who had just finished assisting another passenger and had an empty wheelchair in hand, looked my way and invited me to be wheeled to our departure gate. I declined, of course.

When we reached home, waiting in our mail were not one but two invitations – both directed to me, not to my partner in maturity – offering to provide advice about "long-term care."

I'm certainly not putting down the importance of wheelchair assistance when needed or the importance of long-term care facilities, which have made life much more comfortable for great numbers of senior citizens.

It was just that the four-way "grand slam" impact – "elderly," an offer of a wheel chair ride, two offers of "long-term care" advice – didn't exactly make my day.

— May 4, 2003

A Dislocation

Sometimes referred to by friends as "the bionic woman" because of a number of titanium artificial bone joints in her body, Marian has experienced another example of what might be described as temporary titanium failure. In other words, her ball-and-socket artificial right hip joint dislocated the other day. This sent Marian to the emergency room, where she was placed under heavy sedation while doctors manually corrected the dislocation.

My roommate was put temporarily on crutches and is being especially careful about the way she bends over.

Those who know her will not be surprised to be told that Marian is in her usual good spirits.

— May 18, 2003

M&Ms Out & Out

Thanks to various readers who have kindly cautioned me that chocolate is bad for dogs and that a regular dispensing of M&M treats to Sugar, Sarah and Claire is not a good idea.

After confirming this with a good friend and expert veterinarian, Dr. Kent Forney of Lincoln, I have changed my "treat" menu for our three cocker spaniels. Since I happened to have most of a bag of "Goldfish" snacks left over from cocktail hour on a recent golf outing, I switched to Goldfish. This certainly did nothing to diminish the enthusiasm with which our cocker spaniels follow me upstairs to my workroom, where they stand expectantly below the snack shelf.

I hope that I won't learn that there's something toxic to dogs in those cheesy little Goldfish snacks. (I know, I know, I could get some little snacks especially for dogs. I may make the switch after I run out of Goldfish, but that was an expensive golf outing I was on.)

— May 25, 2003

Strong Bloodlines

An Omaha reader who had followed my story of our search for a new dog to keep our family complement at three cocker spaniels said she was delighted that we had found another cocker. But, she wrote, she was "disappointed that you did not adopt the animal from a humane society or rescue group." (We had purchased our new cocker, Claire, from a breeder in Alabama.)

I think that humane societies and rescue groups do a splendid job. And like my Omaha reader, I deplore "puppy mills." But I know a number of breeders with high principles, and I recognize the importance of their work in maintaining strong bloodlines that extend down through generations of well-bred dogs.

Another Omaha reader wrote a letter of sympathy in regard to our beloved Peaches, whose death created the opening Claire has filled. (Yes, Claire and I are getting along better all the time, in those brief interludes when she can be lured from Marian's side or lap.)

At 78, my reader wrote, "My pet from the Humane Society is my reason for living."

— June 22, 2003

North Platte Chips?

Another "I Had the Craziest Dream" contribution, this one from Marian:

It seems that daughter Nancy was here from Denver, discussing plans for a party that Nancy was arranging in Marian's honor.

I had agreed to play a part, by providing potato chips. Not just any potato chips, you understand, but potato chips from North Platte.

Marian woke up.

OK, Dr. Shrink, explain that one to us. I have always liked North Platte, but I have never commended that fine city to Marian or Nancy as a special place for buying potato chips.

— July 3, 2003

A Man in Claire's Life

In answer to a question which I still encounter: I'm continuing to get along very well – getting along even better, in fact – with Claire, the 1-year-old newest addition to the Andersen household. (You may recall my original report that Claire at first backed away, usually running to stand behind Marian, every time she saw me.)

My campaign to win Claire's heart has been increasingly successful. Obsequious behavior (don't wear a cap around Claire, speak in a low voice, don't move toward Claire, let her come to you) is no longer necessary. Claire, for example,

"Can we go, too?"

will now come and stretch up to my lap and beg for attention rather than heading automatically for Marian's lap. Marian's appraisal: "You are now the man in Claire's life."

Seven-year-old Sarah is, as always, the perfect lady around the family but suspicious – in a very noisy way – about most visitors. Claire doesn't automatically bark at visitors but joins in when Sarah starts the racket.

Observing how much attention Claire gets when she comes leaping onto laps or otherwise seeking attention, Sarah almost automatically tags along seeking the same kind of ear-scratching, back-scratching treatment that Claire is getting.

Dear little 13-year-old Sugar is thinner than ever. She still has a sweet face but she is so thin that her ribcage shows clearly through her furry sides. On veterinarian's advice, we have started feeding her a more nutritious diet.

Yes, I have stopped giving M&Ms as treats, thanks to reader advice that chocolate is bad for dogs. The treats now are very small Milk Bones.

My grandson Robby Andersen, who just turned 10, and I are taking care of the leftover M&Ms.

— July 27, 2003

Back to 30 ... Again

Marian has caught up again with her particular version of the Holy Grail.

Last week, she saw an extra-inning victory by the Cincinnati Reds over the Colorado Rockies in the Great American Ball Park, the Reds' new stadium. (She loved the game but wasn't too impressed with the new ballpark.)

This meant that Marian has again updated her record of having seen a game in every currently-in-use major league ballpark. That's 30 major league parks, in case you haven't been keeping count.

— August 10, 2003

Quiet, Please

Marian's concern for our furry housemates involves a good deal more than their creature comforts.

It extends, for example, to policing the language I use when Sarah greets visitors with a barrage of barking in which Claire, our newest cocker spaniel, almost invariably joins.

I have been informed that it is acceptable, if delivered in a tone that implies affectionate chiding, to say "be quiet" but not to use stronger language.

— August 31, 2003

Caregiving With Cheer, Almost

The bad news is that I didn't make the cut after the first round in the competition for Cheerful Caregiver of the Year Award, Domestic Division.

It was that "cheerful" part that did me in.

The good news is that the object of my caregiving, Marian, is recovering nicely at home, using a hospital bed, crutches, wheelchair and a walker after the latest of her more than 10 operations to repair the effects of chronic osteoarthritis. This time the problem was with her left foot. Marian has to be careful during a bone-mending period that will extend for a few months. The schedule calls for her to change from a heavy cast to a lighter cast to one of those "ski boots."

Friends, of course, have joined in the caregiving in a variety of ways, including providing some delicious soups, casseroles, cookies and the like and lending help in some on-site visits.

A fringe benefit of my caregiving role has been a weight loss. The exercise and irregular eating pattern (gin and tonic and a bowl of popcorn for dinner one evening, for example) have my weight down five pounds. (Please be polite enough not to ask me "down from what?") Not as scientific as the currently popular South Beach Diet, but my South Fairacres Caregivers' Diet is working, at least in the short term.

Speakers Marian Andersen and Coach Bobby Bowden. Bowden came to speak at a Cornhusker athletic event.

Among the more contentious issues in the caregiver/patient relationship have been suggestions from the patient, frequently starting with, "If I were doing it …," and frequently dealing with matters which any non-mentally challenged husband could handle efficiently without the need for coaching. I have been modestly successful (from my point of view) in cutting off debate of some of these suggestions by quickly responding, "But you're not doing it." (I suppose some of you out there might say you can understand why I was knocked out of the "cheerful caregiver" competition after the first round.)

— **October 20, 2003**

Umpteen Catalogs

"How many catalogs do you think I got in the mail today?" my roommate asked. "Seventeen," I replied.

Marian's incredulous response: "How did you know that's exactly how many I got?"

No, I didn't go through Marian's mail and count the catalogs, nor am I clairvoyant. "Seventeen" was just what was meant to be an exaggeration, indicating to Marian that I realize how many catalogs come to people like her – and me – who are occasional catalog-shoppers.

— **December 11, 2003**

CHAPTER 13

Andersen Family Photo Gallery

The following pages offer pictures that capture the flavor of family life, philan-
thropy and travel … all part of life with Marian.

In Norway … Nancy, David, Andy and Marian. Family travels included trips to Olympic Games in Munich and
Montreal.

Marian's mother, Freda Battey, with granddaughter Nancy.

Grandfather Wheaton Battey with Dave and Nancy Andersen.

From left, David and wife, Leslie, Andy, Marian and Nancy before the dinner at which Marian and Andy received the Distinguished Nebraskalander Award – the first couple so honored.

Andy escorts Nancy at the Omaha Symphony Debutantes' ball.

David Andersen flew as radar intercept officer in F-14s.

Marian and Andy enjoy a few minutes with two of their canine pals.

Dogs have always been a part of the Andersen household, including a collie named Holly.

But cocker spaniels like Sarah and Sugar have dominated the pet population.

David, left, and Andy share a hunting outing.

Andy and Nebraska State Game and Parks Director Eugene Mahoney with a turkey shot in the Sow Belly Canyon near Harrison, Nebraska.

The Andersens' support of Nebraska parks yielded a naming honor. The 272-acre Andersen Wildlife Management Area is on the Middle Loup River north of Dannebrog, Nebraska.

Grandkids James, Jack and Grant (in Jack's arms) visit "Crane Meadow" in the Lee G. Simmons Conservation Park and Wildlife Safari. A gift from the Andersens helped pay for Crane Meadow.

Granddaughter Lindsey Andersen and her "Muzzy."

Poolside birthday party with grandchildren Lindsey and Robby Andersen.

Andy golfed regularly with non-golfer Marian's blessing. Here he joined singer Gordon McRae, entertainer Bob Hope and Governor Jim Exon in a charity-promotion golf event.

The Phillie Phanatic helps Marian celebrate her completed tour of major league ballparks.

Marian was the first woman and the first non-Lincoln resident to head the University of Nebraska Foundation. On this evening, she was inducted into the Ak-Sar-Ben Court of Honor.

The Midlands Chapter honors the Andersens. Marian was the first woman to head the Red Cross – Midlands Chapter. As American Red Cross board vice chairman, she recruited Elizabeth Dole to head the Red Cross.

Marian's service to the American Red Cross included many addresses.

President George H. W. Bush greets national Red Cross Vice Chairman Marian Andersen.

Neither rain nor snow nor surgeries kept Marian from the speaker's rostrum. Here she receives the Nebraskalander Award. At right is Gov. Kay Orr.

Entertainer Bill Cosby shares a laugh with the Andersens after his performance in the Aksarben Coliseum. Andy was king of Ak-Sar-Ben in 1983.

Pied Piperette from Omaha visits Tibet with Andy and other Associated Press board members and their spouses.

Andy's travels took him and Marian to more than 60 countries. Here he talks with the editor of The Times of India in New Delhi on a visit to India with close friend Vin Gupta.

Friends helped Marian celebrate a birthday with a surprise early morning visit. Marian was in a hospital-type bed in the room behind the window, recovering from another operation.

Good friends and neighbors Mike and Joan Walsh and family. (See column starting on page 23)

We Lose Sugar; Charlotte Arrives

Café Cardinale for flying friends; Sugar dies at age 14; the hole-in-one; Grant's broken finger; Padres welcome an extraordinary fan; family room becomes mini-hospital; Charlotte joins the cockers; political polling – but not you; smaller glasses; when Santa isn't jolly.

Un-bored

Pre-breakfast message from Marian: "If you're bored, why don't you bring me the turkey from the family room 'fridge?"

I assured Marian that I was not bored and had other things to do but that I would be happy to bring her the smoked turkey from the family room 'fridge, since she was going to cut off a few slices to make my desk-at-the-office lunch.

— January 18, 2004

Now Serving: Café Cardinale

We call it Café Cardinale, and it has been heavily patronized these recent snowy and cold winter days.

The feeder outside our kitchen and garden room windows the other afternoon had attracted seven brilliant-red male cardinals, Marian reported. Some of them sat on nearby branches, waiting their turn for a sunflower-seed meal.

Cardinals are definitely the predominant class of patrons, but we also serve chickadees, juncos, finches, an occasional woodpecker and an occasional blue jay. And, of course, sparrows are always very welcome, as are the squirrels which, baffled by the metal shield that prevents them from climbing the pole, still find plenty of feed scattered on the ground to make them additional patrons of Café Cardinale. (The squirrels are welcomed by Marian only so long as they don't find a way to climb the pole.)

— January 25, 2004

Sugar at 14

Now as to the Andersen family's dogs:

Dear little Sugar, deaf and blind for three years, had a 14th birthday party March 16. She and her two siblings (they are not actually blood relatives, but we like to think of them as sisters) each quickly devoured a cupcake-sized birthday cake.

Suggie enjoys her meals, of course, especially since our veterinarian suggested supplementing her dog food with rice and canned chicken. She also enjoys sitting on my lap or sleeping by the gas-log fireplace. And she continues to do remarkably well in finding her way about the house, including the path up the stairs to my work room.

Shy Sarah – shy until a stranger appears – and our latest alpha dog, Claire, continue to be Marian's constant companions as she moves about the house.

Claire, whose breeder said she comes from a line of cockers trained for agility trials, the type you see at some dog shows, continues to live up to her lineage, occasionally leaping over one of our sofas, for example. And she never lets one of her canine sisters slow her down in the rush for chow time in the kitchen. She simply leaps over them.

— April 1, 2004

Life with Marian Included Andy's Golf

A few friends, along with offering congratulations, have asked a question about my making a hole-in-one on the 16th hole at Augusta National Golf Club. They asked what club I used.

For the 150-yard over-water carry the hole required, I used my driver. (The pin was perhaps 20 yards back on the green.)

I used to use irons on No. 16 as well as Augusta's No. 12, where I had a hole-in-one with a 3-iron in 1997. As my age has gone up, my choice of clubs of necessity has changed accordingly.

Andy and Vin Gupta at Augusta National Golf Club.

I might add that as I watched other members of my foursome put half a dozen balls in the water on the ninth hole on the "short course" at Augusta, I was pleased to use my driver to hit the ball up the bank behind the green, then chip down the slope for a "gimme" par.

Any other questions?

— May 31, 2004

Happy Father's Day

Our daughter, Nancy Karger, had 3-year-old Grant with her last Sunday while a doctor was putting a splint on 11-year-old Jack's finger, which had been broken in a baseball game.

Little brother Grant, of course, was keenly aware that big brother Jack had a problem. Looking for some way to express sympathy and support for big brother, little brother came up with this:

"Happy Father's Day, Jack."

— June 24, 2004

Looks Deceiving?

At a recent large dinner party, I was talking to a friend when a silver-haired lady standing close by looked at me and said, "What's your name?"

"Harold Andersen," I replied.

"You don't look like you used to," said the silver-haired lady.

I resisted the temptation to tell her that she, too, didn't look like she used to and settled instead for agreeing with her appraisal of my current appearance.

— July 1, 2004

Worst Fears Confirmed

It happened that our 14-year-old, blind and deaf cocker spaniel, Sugar, died while daughter Nancy Karger and her three boys were visiting Marian and me for five days that included my birthday.

Before returning to Denver, the Kargers shared firsthand in the sorrow that followed Sugar's drowning in our backyard swimming pool. They heard me say that I cried when I recovered Sugar's skinny little body from the pool.

James Karger, 8, tried to cheer us up. "Maybe Sugar will meet Peaches in heaven," said James, who remembered that nearly two years ago, Peaches, 6, died in a veterinarian's clinic. We all appreciated James' efforts to put a happier face on our loss of Sugar.

Sugar had been deaf and blind for about three years, and we had tried hard to be careful about keeping her away from the swimming pool.

But one evening, she slipped out the door, unbeknownst to us, when our two other cockers, 2-year-old Claire and 8-year-old Sarah, were let out to "be good girls."

An hour or two later, we couldn't find Sugar in the house. I headed for the pool, where my fears were confirmed.

The lesson for us and for other dog owners who have in-the-ground swimming pools: You can't be too careful.

I was about to dictate "a final thought about Sugar," then realized that in years to come there will be many more thoughts about Sugar in the form of happy memories of the time she spent with us.

So here's a non-final thought about Sugar: It has been said that one measure of a good life is to have given much love and to have been much loved in return. By that standard, dear little Sugar had a very good life indeed.

— August 8, 2004

Keeping up With New Ballparks

There it was, in bright lights on the message display board in right field in the San Diego Padres' new home, Petco Park: "The Padres welcome an extraordinary fan – Marian Andersen, completing her tour of major league ballparks."

I had arranged for the Padres to display this message recognizing that

Marian holding "I've done all 26" sweatshirt.

Marian had again caught up with her version of the Holy Grail – her quest to have seen a game in every one of the current major league ballparks.

Marian first reached that goal in September 1991, when we visited Veterans Stadium in Philadelphia. The Phillies, incidentally, gave Marian more attention than did the Padres. The Phillies mascot, the Phillie Phanatic, came down to our field-side box seats, kissed Marian, danced with her and sat on her lap while the message board welcomed her on the completion of her several-year tour of the 26 parks in which major league baseball was being played in 1991.

In the 13 years since our visit to Veterans Stadium (since replaced), Marian has several times caught up with her goal as new major league franchises are added or new ballparks replace old ones.

In addition to the 26 ballparks in play in 1991, Marian has seen a game in 19 ballparks that have been put into play since then.

Her opinion of the Padres' new park? So-so. It was a clever idea to leave standing a well-preserved old warehouse building as sort of a left-field corner anchor of the new park, with bleacher seat extensions built out from top floors of the building. But the result is to leave the left-field corner at ground level, completely out of the view of a good many fans down the left-field foul line.

When will Marian stop striving to keep current? Never, so far as she's concerned, "if I have to go in a wheelchair."

— August 22, 2004

Salute to Caregivers

My very capable assistant, Jackie Wrieth, and I know our roles when another Caregiving 101 assignment comes our way.

Jackie calls American Homepatient Homecare. (She has been in frequent enough contact that she is on a first-name basis with the always cheerful and helpful Vickie there.) Jackie orders a hospital bed and wheelchair to be delivered to our home.

I head for the attic in search of crutches, the bedside commode, fold-up walker and "walking boot" that we keep on hand.

Andy and Marian visit with University of Nebraska President Ronald Roskens and British ambassador.

Regular readers will know I am about to tell you that Marian is again in a home-care situation after undergoing yet another orthopedic surgical procedure, this one on the same foot – the left one – that was operated on last year. That led to a week of in-bed healing in our family room.

This week marks the fourth time in recent years that we have turned the family room into a mini-hospital pavilion. Marian's longest previous stay was for a month. This time, she expects to be up and about in a week or so.

Our supercharged alpha dog, Claire, is enjoying Marian's immobilization. It makes it easier for constant companion Claire to be on Marian's lap or jump across her lap onto the bedside window seat. Our more ladylike cocker spaniel, Sarah, also stays close at hand but at carpet level.

I share this information with you because so many of you have said you enjoy keeping up with Marian, our dogs and other facets of life on Prairie Avenue.

Marian and I agreed, however, that it also would be appropriate for me to pay tribute to those home caregivers whose responsibilities are much heavier and longer-lasting than mine.

Countless temporarily or permanently disabled persons, from infants to the elderly, are able to live at home only because of the devoted attention of other family members. Marian and I salute these truly praiseworthy, devoted caregivers.

— September 2, 2004

First Time's a Charm

Marian says she doesn't nag, but she will concede that she can be persistent in repeating advice and requests directed my way.

The other day, she said there's an easy way to take repetition out of our relationship: "I'd never mention anything a second time if you would just do it the first time."

— September 9, 2004

Welcome, Charlotte

The vacancy on the Andersen team roster – a vacancy created two months ago by the death of our sweet little cocker spaniel Sugar – has been filled. Filled almost to overflowing, one might say.

Within 24 hours of arriving at our Prairie Avenue home, 7-month-old Charlotte had fallen into the swimming pool, dog-paddled her way to the steps and climbed out by herself, fallen off our rock wall into the hosta, discovered that I serve "goldfish" snacks in my upstairs workroom, chewed up two or three newspaper pages and joined our two older cockers – Sarah, 8, and Claire, 2 – on sleeping pads in the breakfast room without those plaintive howls that newly arrived dogs sometimes emit.

Marian, Andy and friends.

We had been assured by Charlotte's breeder, Kristi Ahiquist of Hutchinson, Minn., that Charlotte was both people-oriented and other-dog-oriented. But Claire has been such a dominant alpha dog that we wondered if any new arrival would be somewhat cowed by her.

I can report that Claire is still the alpha dog, but Charlotte is definitely a beta-plus new member of the family. As usual, ladylike Sarah goes along with the gang.

As to her chewing up papers, so far I have picked up the shreds without complaint. After all, we are a newspaper family. We can always rationalize that Charlotte is just digesting the news.

Charlotte is receiving visitors from other dog lovers, and we are proud to show her off – assuming we can lure her down from the back yard, where she spends a good deal of time sniffing the flowers and running through the evergreens.

When Marian was preparing to welcome some fellow dog lovers and good friends who were stopping by, she had to comb Charlotte out a bit because our beta-plus dog had been rolling around in the hosta.

One of Charlotte's littermates has been sold to a resident of Finland, where he already has won a prize in the show ring. Another littermate is scheduled to be sold to an owner in Australia, perhaps also for a show-ring role.

Kristi, who has become a very good friend since we have acquired four dogs either from her or with her advice, says that Charlotte would have been a good candidate for the show ring, too, if her tail had turned up instead of down.

Marian and I are agreed that if Charlotte's tail ever shows signs of turning up, we're not going to tell Kristi.

— **October 3, 2004**

Clear Case of Age Discrimination

I'm not sure where to take this complaint, but I think I have a strong case for filing a charge of age discrimination. Let me explain.

A few days before the election, a woman with a pleasant voice said she was conducting a political poll and would like to talk to the youngest member of voting age in our home.

I replied that the youngest member was out of the city. The pollster asked me if I would like to participate in the pole. I replied that I surely would. The pollster then asked my age. "Eighty-one," I replied.

The pollster asked me to pardon her a few moments, then came back on the line to say: "Thank you very much, but I discovered that we already have our necessary quota of respondents in your area."

A few days later, another pollster called, this time a man who seemed a little bored by it all. He asked me which age bracket I fit in, moving upward through a number of brackets until he came to "Over 75."

I replied: "That's me." The pollster's response: "Thank you, and have a nice evening."

— **November 14, 2004**

On the Stump

I don't know whether grandson Grant Karger of Denver would have voted for Colorado Republican U.S. Senate candidate Peter Coors if he had been old enough. But our daughter, Nancy, reports that he seems to have been impressed by a Coors campaign commercial.

When Nancy stepped from the shower one day shortly before the election, 3-year-old Grant greeted her thus: "I'm Pete Coors, and I approve of this ad."

Coors, who over the years has appeared in many television commercials promoting the family's popular beer, lost the Colorado senatorial contest to Democrat Ken Salazar.

— November 18, 2004

Seeing is Believing

Marian and I the other day had a spirited discussion (that's one way to describe it) about which pair of glasses I should wear to meetings that day.

Marian, you see, has an intense interest (it might also be called an obsessive interest) in advising me that my smaller-size glasses (Ben Franklin presumably would have been comfortable with them) make me look "10 years younger" than the bifocals I wear most of the time. (I'm not sure how much I benefit from looking like a 71-year-old rather than an 81-year-old.)

I explained to Marian – not for the first time – that I can't read very well, if at all, with the smaller glasses. And since I was headed for a meeting that would involve looking at long columns of numbers, I left the house wearing my bifocals.

The spirited discussion ended in a good-natured truce. "I'll pick you up this afternoon after your class in Anger Management," Marian said. I replied: "You can swing by after your class in Nagging Suppression."

— December 2, 2004

Ho-Ho-Ho Test Failed

Another grandchild story, again involving 3-year-old Grant Karger, our daughter Nancy's quick study in what goes on around him:

Nancy took Grant for a visit to one of those department-store Santas in Denver. Once out of Santa's hearing, Grant said to Nancy: "He isn't jolly."

Nancy, not wishing to leave Grant with a bad impression of Santa, said she was sure that Santa was happy in his work. Grant's response: "But, Mom, he isn't jolly."

That Santa obviously didn't pass the "ho-ho-ho" test so far as Grant Karger was concerned.

— **December 23, 2004**

'Charlotte the Scamp'

My assistant, Jackie Wrieth, does a superb job of figuring out my sometimes less-than-clear language spoken into my portable dictating machine and my handwritten editing and re-editing of first drafts of some of my columns.

She usually does so without comment, but there are exceptions, as when she left a blank in her transcription of one of my pieces of dictation. After the blank, she typed in "chomp, chomp, chomp," to indicate that eating while dictating doesn't make for clarity.

After the gentle scolding, I confirmed to Jackie that "chomp, chomp, chomp" was not the sound I was trying to convey.

I might add that "chomp, chomp, chomp" sounds more like the sound that our newest cocker spaniel, 10-month-old Charlotte, makes as she chews on just about anything she can get her teeth into.

We love her dearly, but her passion for chewing, which leads her to leap onto beds and make off with anything that is remotely chewable, has helped persuade us to add a descriptive nickname, as in "Charlotte the Scamp."

— **December 27, 2004**

Nine Cocker Spaniels – One Little Princess

Brown bags add 120 hours; Jackie's upscale bird feeder; my fully utilized work-room; list of cockers reaches 9; Sports Babe strikes again; canine update; happy birthday, little princess; when pets take charge.

Brown-bag Saves Time

Any number of you over the years have said you enjoy reading vignettes about our Prairie Avenue family life. So let me share with you that, with very few exceptions, Marian prepares a brown-bag lunch for me each day when we are both in town and I'm planning to work at my desk through the lunch hour.

I estimate this allows me to work at my desk a minimum of 120 hours a year that I otherwise would spend going elsewhere for lunch. That, you could calculate for yourself, is equivalent to three weeks at work for people who have 40-hour work weeks.

It does not diminish my appreciation for Marian's lunch preparation when I report that in the past 10 days or so, she left out on one occasion the customary cookie for dessert, on another the sweet pickles that customarily come with my sandwich and on another a small bag of potato chips, which also regularly accompanies the sandwich.

But I'll not register a complaint of any kind unless one day she leaves out the sandwich.

— January 2, 2005

◆

Expanded Offerings at Café Cardinale

My valued associate, Jackie Wrieth, gave Marian and me a very upscale bird feeder for Christmas. It was placed perhaps 10 yards from our older feeder (which looked a bit weather-worn by comparison).

If you are into bird-watching, the results have been spectacular. The number of avian guests has increased substantially.

On one recent sunny afternoon, I counted eight cardinals waiting their turn in one tree while three or four cardinals lunched at the two feeders.

Eight squirrels ate sunflower seeds that had fallen to the ground as the birds worked away at the eight feeding troughs. There was also the usual scattering of sparrows, chickadees and other smaller birds.

As a result, Café Cardinale not only expanded its dining facilities but also created another squirrel dining room on the lower level.

Marian especially appreciates the two dining levels. She had been unhappy with the squirrels' occasional invasion of the bird feeders. I rather admired the squirrels' acrobatic success.

But now, with so many more seeds scattered to the ground, we have a two-level segregation of which I would hope even People for the Ethical Treatment of Animals would not disapprove.

— January 23, 2005

'Fully Utilized' or 'Messy?'

Andy's Personalized Clipping Service – a.k.a. Marian Battey Andersen – is frequently a more thorough reader than I am when it comes to the five daily papers delivered to our home. (I have to set aside considerable time for careful perusal of the catalogs – mostly hunting equipment catalogs – that come my way in very substantial volume.)

A good many items in my column result from news stories Marian has called to my attention. On a recent brief trip to New York City, Marian broadened her field of research by buying a copy of the New York Post. From that paper she passed along – honest clipping provider that she is – a story with this headline: "Messy desks are a mark of $uccess."

> *"Marian reminds me, with some frequency, that all the considerable desk space in my Prairie Avenue workspace is what I prefer to call "fully utilized" but Marian would call "messy."*

Marian reminds me, with some frequency, that all the considerable desk space in my Prairie Avenue workroom is what I prefer to call "fully utilized" but Marian would call "messy." (My desk and surrounding cabinets and bookcases in my office would qualify for the same description.)

So special thanks to anti-messy Marian for supplying me with a clipping saying, among other things, that a survey by a human resources consulting firm found that about two-thirds of lower-paid employees, making $35,000 a year or less, "like to call themselves neat freaks. But among people making $75,000 or more, the vast majority prefer messy workspaces."

A senior vice president of the survey firm observed: "Basically, when you go up the ladder to the corporate suite, you don't really care what people think anymore. Clutter could be a sign of position."

— February 3, 2005

Nine Cocker Spaniels

The cast of characters changes from time to time, but the tradition is unchangeable. Our cocker spaniels have breakfast with me every morning.

Morning after morning, Sarah, Claire and Charlotte the Scamp sit within arm's reach at my side – always the right side and, in the case of the current cast of characters, Charlotte and Claire always in the front row with ladylike Sarah waiting patiently close behind.

There they sit, looking soulfully (hungrily is perhaps the more appropriate word) up at me, waiting for the small scrap of food (usually a bit of toast) that I dispense near the end of my breakfast. You would think I'm serving a five-course meal, considering the patience with which they wait for the small scraps of food, one scrap to each dog.

And so it has gone through a succession of nine cockers – Sassy, Daphne, Sugar I, Sister, Sugar II, Sarah, Peaches, Claire and Charlotte.

A family walk in the park.

Like dog lovers everywhere, Marian and I figure a few small treats a day are the least we can do in return for the unquestioning affection that our dogs shower on us every day.

— February 27, 2005

The Sports Babe Strikes Again!

I should have known better than to risk a shootout on sports memories with my roommate, whom one friend admiringly calls "The Sports Babe" because of her remarkable knowledge of sports and equally remarkable recall of athletes and sporting events from the past.

Marian and I were exchanging baseball memories with good friend Charlie Wright, a Scottsbluff native who was a Cornhusker baseball player and law student before embarking on a distinguished career as a lawyer in Lincoln.

We were recalling the days a half-century or more ago when Lincoln had a crowd-pulling Class A professional baseball team, probably best remembered for two players who went on up to "The Show" – Nellie Fox as a second baseman for the Chicago White Sox and Bobby Shantz as a pitcher for the Philadelphia Phillies and later for the New York Yankees.

I said little Bobby Shantz (5 feet, 6 inches and 139 pounds) had the misfortune to be pitching for the Yankees when Bill Mazeroski, the Pittsburgh Pirates shortstop, hit one of the legendary home runs in World Series history – a homer in the bottom of the ninth inning in the seventh game, giving the Pirates a 10-9 victory and the 1960 World Series championship.

Not so, said The Sports Babe. I went to my Baseball Encyclopedia and confirmed that The Sports Babe was right. Bobby Shantz wasn't on the mound. Then who was? We left the question unanswered.

The next day, I was headed up the stairs to my workroom, and Marian walked by on her way to the kitchen. "Ralph Terry," Marian said over her shoulder without pausing or further comment.

I took a more thorough look into all the information available in the Baseball Encyclopedia. Marian was right. Ralph Terry was on the mound for the Yankees when Bill Mazeroski made World Series history 45 seasons ago.

The Sports Babe had scored again.

— April 10, 2005

◆

Household Canine Update

For dog lovers out there, a report on canine traffic patterns in the Andersen household:

The morning path invariably leads to positions sitting at my side (Charlotte and Claire side by side, with ladylike Sarah sitting behind them) waiting patiently for the scrap of toast or pancake or whatever that I toss to each of them. Occasionally, Marian calls from the kitchen, "Come outside with me and be good girls." None of the dogs moves. We haven't finished our breakfast, you see.

Another traffic pattern: Whenever I turn to go upstairs, the dogs invariably race ahead of

Our three cockers and a guest share in a treat.

me, knowing that they will surely be rewarded with a goldfish wafer treat from the bowl in my workroom.

And if I proceed from the kitchen past the stairs to the family room where Marian is reading and watching TV (probably a baseball game), my three furry cocker spaniel friends trot ahead of me, as if escorting me on my trip to join Marian.

— June 19, 2005

Moving Up in the Charts

I don't win many verbal skirmishes with Marian, so let me tell you about one such occasion.

The other evening, she said it was approaching 10 p.m. and "we can see the fireworks" (from Commercial Federal's annual bash in Memorial Park). I responded with something less than enthusiasm: "Fireworks aren't my thing."

To which Marian responded: "Oh, then what is your thing?" To which I responded: "I have a lot of things. Reading. Writing. History. You." Marian quickly – and understandably – surrendered.

— July 14, 2005

… And From Plattsmouth

Perhaps the lack of a "brightener" at the end of today's column will satisfy a Plattsmouth, Neb., reader who said that last Sunday's column on less serious subjects "was about as interesting as watching paint dry."

My reader from Plattsmouth wants me to talk about how voters registered as independent can't vote in the primary election. Or about abolishing the Electoral College since "it is a foregone conclusion that the Republican is the one that will get all the votes."

The letter from Plattsmouth underscores the difficulty – a challenge I welcome – of writing a column that appeals both to readers who like serious issues and to those who prefer lighter subjects, such as life on Prairie Avenue with Marian and our dogs.

I will continue to write from time to time on the lighter subjects. If this offends my Plattsmouth reader, on those lighter subject days he can skip my column and go find some paint to watch dry.

— July 21, 2005

Why Now, Not Then?

Another birthday (No. 82) has passed, which prompts me to tell you of a conversation with Marian sometime or another during the past year.

Marian repeatedly has advised me to wear small glasses. After I resisted with an argument like "But I can't read with them," Marian countered, "But they make you look 10 years younger."

So, I responded, they make me look like I'm 71? Big deal. (Yes, I now regularly wear small glasses on social occasions.)

— July 31, 2005

Happy Birthday, Little Princess

The occasion was granddaughter Katherine Roe Andersen's fifth birthday party.

Marian asked daughter-in-law Leslie, wife of our son Dave, what effervescent little Katie wanted for her birthday that hadn't yet been purchased by others, including the other proud grandparents, Jerry and Mimi Roe of the Bennington banking family.

The response was a princess crown and a tool chest.

— September 15, 2005

When Pets Take Charge

It's been too long since I shared with you some of the views of Elmer Pinkerton, the Sage of Elmwood, Neb., who writes me a letter of reaction to every column I write.

One of Elmer's recent contributions included this reaction to the debate on whether an "intelligent designer" (generally interpreted as a Supreme Being or God) is responsible for the development of life on this planet: "There had to be a God or a very smart engineer at the helm."

Elmer's relatively new wife, Juanita, is a cat lover, and her cat started out sleeping on the bed until she (the cat, not Juanita) tired of being thrown off by Elmer. While Elmer and Juanita were gone for a week, the cat was in charge. She again now sleeps on the bed. Marian and I know all about pets taking charge of things.

Elmer reports being in Kearney at a World War II veterans' convention and hearing Gov. Heineman speak. Elmer reports: "I was impressed. No notes. No stuttering. … My problem is to know if he is an intelligent man to vote for or if he is an intelligent politician who tells us what we want to hear."

— November 6, 2005

'Let Me In!'

I told you the other day about Marian's latest surgery and hospitalization. Here, as radio personality Paul Harvey says, is the rest of the story.

It started at about 4 p.m., when I visited Marian in her hospital room after she was recovering from the effects of the anesthesia.

I hurried home from the hospital to change into coat, shirt and tie and turned up 20 minutes late for a haircut appointment with Tom Squires. Then I headed for a holiday cocktail buffet at the home of dear friend Mrs. John (Libby) Lauritzen on Underwood Avenue.

In the gloom of a rainy evening, I was looking for a circular driveway on Underwood Avenue east of 69th Street. I found a circular driveway with a car parked in it (perhaps indicative of a party).

I parked near the front door and rang the doorbell. Repeatedly rang the doorbell. Pounded on the door. Repeatedly pounded on the door. No response. Maybe they're having such a joyous good time that they can't hear the doorbell or the pounding, I speculated.

As I turned to leave, I glanced to the east and there – you're probably way ahead of me now – was another circular driveway, filled with cars. I drove to the other circular driveway and was welcomed by valet parkers, went inside and had Libby's staff in stitches as I told my story.

I was informed that the owner of the adjacent house with a circular drive-way is Dr. Clarke Stevens, and – the level of laughter increased here – Dr. Stevens was in Libby's dining room with other guests, enjoying the buffet.

I introduced myself to Dr. Stevens and told him something like this: "No hard feelings. I accept your explanation of why you didn't respond to my doorbell-ringing and door thumping."

We had a good laugh and agreed that my experience would be a likely candidate for one of my column-ending items. (I received a Christmas card from Dr. Stevens with this gracious message: "I enjoyed our conversation and promise to be hospitable next time you knock at my door.")

— **December 25, 2005**

Huskers, Green Jackets and Random Kindness

R.E.S.P.E.C.T.; bluebird of my eye; Florina and the lunch bag; I've got a bone to pick with you; stocking before storms = catsup time with old friends; a salute to our magnificent country; Brownville Fine Arts Association; the green jacket; talking to a policeman; Mrs. Snodgrass; what she meant.

Longhorns vs. Huskers

At about 11:30 on Wednesday evening, shortly after the sensational finish of the national championship game in the Rose Bowl, our phone rang.

Usually, such post-telecast calls come from Marian's brother, Chuck Battey – a Kansas City resident who wants to share his observations about the Cornhusker game he has just watched on television. This time, grandson James Karger, 10, one of daughter Nancy's three sons, was calling – very excitedly calling – from his home in Denver.

James asked if we had been watching. I told him that Marian and I, like him, had been cheering for the Longhorns. (We later learned from his mother that he had told her that we had been pulling for Texas "because they knew I was." Marian and I have no objection at all to that explanation.)

I don't know where James picked up his affection for the Longhorns. But he is allowed to wear his Texas ball cap on his Omaha visits, with this stipulation: On days when Nebraska and Texas are competing in any sport, he will wear his red ball cap with the big white "N" and cheer for the Huskers. James has graciously agreed to these terms.

— **January 8, 2006**

Enjoy!

Marian was preparing one of my favorite breakfasts – waffles, one-half waffle at a time. (I like them that way. It ensures two halves of warm waffles.)

Her attention was diverted as the first half was in the waffle iron. The burned result was tossed in the garbage, and Marian went back to work and served up a nicely done half-waffle. She pointed out that this was all the waffle I was going to get that morning.

"So eat slowly," she advised.

— January 15, 2006

The Bluebird of my Eye

As I have reported in this space before, Marian wakes up like a bluebird. I'm definitely more owly.

Marian doesn't intend it, but a sure-fire way to jog me from early-morning blahs is to listen to her remarks directed to our three beloved cocker spaniels. In the kitchen, as the dogs scampered around wildly after being awakened one recent morning, Marian herded them toward the garden-room door with this language: "Come on, wild women of the prairie."

I asked her how she came up with that description of her darlings. "It just came to me," Marian replied. "But when I called them back in, I switched to calling them 'baby cakes.' That just came to me, too."

— January 29, 2006

Florina and the Lunch Bag

Florina, a cheerful and efficient lady who helps Marian with the housecleaning (a charitable characterization of Marian's role in the process), came up with a better idea for reminding me not to forget the sack lunch that Marian prepares for me to take to the office each morning.

Andy,
Now go back and get your lunch.

After hearing Marian's customary "Don't forget your lunch; it's sitting on the stove," Florina the other morning took the sack lunch from the stove and hung it on the knob of the door that I must open on my way to the garage.

Florina's approach to dealing with an absent minded husband is pretty clearly more efficient than the technique Marian has tried on me, like sticking a note on my SUV's dashboard that says, "Now go back and get your lunch."

— February 5, 2006

Dream Weaver

As we were changing from our nightclothes the other morning, Marian and I were comparing dreams. Hers was a lot more disturbing than mine.

Marian said she dreamt that a male acquaintance – certainly not a close friend in real life and certainly far from a friend in her dream – began to argue violently with her and actually threw a punch at her. Marian, who in real life might have had more difficulty as she recovers from another hip surgery, eluded the punch and woke up.

My dream was less exciting. I rode my motorcycle – when I'm awake I don't have a motorcycle – through hills northwest of Omaha where I knew a new golf course was being built. It looked like yet another upscale course from the size of the half-finished clubhouse. But there wasn't a tree or any sign of vegetation anywhere on the terrain on which the course would be built.

As I rode away on my motorcycle, I reflected that a desert course can be made attractive in its proper setting. But I didn't think I was interested in one located north of Omaha.

— February 9, 2006

I've Got a Bone to Pick with You

It seems to me – Marian and our three dogs would agree, I'm sure – that Gretna can add to its reputation as something of a role model

for enlightened, growing suburban communities by raising its dogs-per-family limit from two to three.

A recent news story brought to light the fact of Gretna's two-dog limit. The City Council made a compassionate decision in favor of letting three-dog families continue the status quo and license all their pets

Dressed-up cockers take a nap.

for the life of the animals. Why not go the next step and join Omaha, Council Bluffs, Bellevue, Papillion and Elkhorn by allowing at least three dogs per family?

Three-dog families will demonstrate, I'm confident, that they can keep their pets from becoming neighborhood nuisances and – this is important –

help humane societies to find more happy homes for dogs that have come to the animal shelters through no fault of their own.

Give dog lovers and dogs a break. I think you'll be glad you did.

— February 23, 2006

We Salute NU Foundation

If I owned one (I believe as a graduating senior I rented one), I would tip my tasseled mortarboard in salute to the University of Nebraska Foundation.

This salute is well-deserved for the way the foundation has raised and managed funds to help finance a level of excellence so important to Marian's and my alma mater, the University of Nebraska-Lincoln, and the rest of the University of Nebraska system.

Significant evidence of the foundation's performance was included in a recent Associated Press story, which ran under this headline: "More colleges join elite ranks."

The story read: "The number of North American colleges with endowments topping $1 billion has jumped to 56, according to a new study. Among the universities passing the $1 billion endowment mark, according to the study, was the University of Nebraska Foundation."

Marian and I are both past chairmen of the NU Foundation. But I think I still can be reasonably objective when I offer a sincere "Thank you!" to the foundation's chief executive, Terry Fairfield, his excellent staff and the thousands of contributors who have moved the University of Nebraska steadily upward in terms of endowed funds, which are so important to the quality of a university.

— March 16, 2006

Weather Conspiracy?

Before the repetitively predicted snowfall – 12 inches, 17 inches, 21 inches – finally began to fall last Sunday, Marian had said facetiously that she suspected a conspiracy between supermarkets and weather forecasters.

One positive side effect of the snowfall, Marian said, was that it allowed her to see some friends she hadn't seen for some time. They met on food-stocking supermarket visits Saturday afternoon.

— March 26, 2006

Stand Up for America

It was a scene that I thoroughly enjoyed having described to me.

In the family room of daughter Nancy's home in Denver, there were Marian, 10-year-old grandson Jack and 5-year-old grandson Grant, standing with their right hands over their hearts while the television set delivered a playing of "The Star-Spangled Banner" before the start of the National Basketball Association All-Star Game.

It was 5-year-old Grant who called the little family group to attention. He said he had learned that this is what you're supposed to do when our national anthem is played.

— April 9, 2006

Brownville Concerts 'Magnifique'

I refer to the concerts that have been sponsored for 16 annual seasons by the Brownville Fine Arts Association in a former church building converted into a concert hall in historic Brownville, Neb., on the banks of the Missouri River some 70 miles south of Omaha.

The brainchild of Jim and Ruth Keene of Omaha, who for more than 25 years have owned a restored historic house in Brownville, the annual Brownville concert series has presented a variety of outstanding musical performers.

This year's series, for example, includes the upcoming performance of cabaret stars Mark Nadler and K. T. Sullivan.

The Nadler/Sullivan presentation of this program received a highly favorable review in the New York Times when they performed last September at the opening of the 25th fall cabaret season at the famed Oak Room in the Algonquin Hotel in New York City. A more recent Nadler and Sullivan performance last month in the Oak Room, featuring the music of Cole Porter, drew a Times review that described the performance in these words: "C'est magnifique!"

I must disclose that Marian and I are sponsoring the Brownville appearance of Sullivan and Nadler, but I call attention to their upcoming performance with a clear journalistic conscience. I believe they are representative of the kind of talent that the Brownville Concert Series has been bringing for the past 15 years to a unique venue in historic Brownville, which is within relatively easy reach of a good many eastern Nebraskans and western Iowans, including residents of Omaha and Lincoln.

— April 13, 2006

The Green Jacket

As someone who is fortunate enough to be a member of Augusta National Golf Club, I continue to be somewhat surprised – and very pleased, of course – at the reaction of people who play the course for the first time or have the opportunity to be one of the tens of thousands who visit Augusta National during Masters week.

For example, a friend from Omaha who had tickets this year to the three days of practice rounds, not to the tournament itself, described the experience as "simply magical … they sure do make visitors feel welcome." Over the years, I've had similar comments from any number of people.

When I hear such comments, I sincerely reply that members are happy when they have opportunities to share the club with guests or with "patrons" during Masters week.

My most surprising example of the attention that a green jacket attracts – I'm talking about a jacket on one of the members, not on a Masters champion – came during this year's tournament, when Marian and I were sitting out in patio chairs on the lawn in the sunshine in front of the cabin built for the late President Dwight D. Eisenhower, who was a club member.

We had been sitting in front of the Eisenhower cabin for only a few minutes when I looked up and noticed a crowd of 50 or so people assembled on the sidewalk looking at us, cameras at the ready.

An older lady stepped forward and confided to Marian that "I wanted Mr. Nelson to know I once played in a foursome that included Sam Snead." Marian informed the lady that I am not the legendary Byron Nelson.

I announced that I am Harold Andersen from Omaha, Neb. Members of the crowd continued to come forward, one at a time, to ask if they could have their picture taken with me. I know, of course, that the Eisenhower cabin in the background was a major factor in this scenario, and I believe the green jacket helped.

I didn't keep count, but Marian and I agreed that there must have been 50 to 75 people who came forward and asked if they could have their picture taken with me. I, of course, agreed. Before the photo-op ended, I had been photographed with Masters week patrons from 15 states, Canada and Ireland.

I had a delightful time greeting some very nice people and thanking them for their support of the Masters tournament.

— April 16, 2006

Gun Control ... Out of Season?

A recent Public Pulse critic of opponents of the concealed weapons legislation said it was predictable that such opponents are also in favor of more "gun control" whether the weapons are concealed or not.

Speaking only for myself, I'm against legalizing concealed weapons, but I'm certainly not a "gun-control" extremist. I own an extensive collection of shotguns and rifles, the exact number of which will not be revealed here since Marian is a regular reader of this column.

— **April 20, 2006**

Cubbies Win One for Marian

After a chorus of comment and criticism, which included the astonishing charge that the University of Nebraska at Omaha administration is intentionally diminishing UNO's athletic department with the ultimate goal of dismantling it, a UNO athletic booster finally put the situation in better perspective.

Pat Lemmers, president of the Blue Line Club, UNO's hockey booster group, said in a July 15 news story that he is looking forward to putting financial difficulties in the past. "I think they just need to redirect some fundraising from the top down and connect with people in the community who have the money and the ideas about how to put some marketing plans together," Lemmers said.

In other words, university administrators and athletic staff and booster club members should look to the future and work together to return the university's athletic program to the position of relative financial stability through the school's own efforts (which are already heavily subsidized to the extent of $3.5 million in state funds and student fees).

(Chancellor Nancy) Belck has moved to assure that the annual Diet Pepsi Women's Walk for Women's Athletics will continue to be a major funding source for the athletic department by naming a new leadership team for the event. The team is Rose Shires, recently named as senior woman administrator and head volleyball coach; Marian Andersen as chairman of the walk; and Maggie Lehning, a veteran of having led five women's walks.

As regular readers of my column will know, Marian is my wife.

*   *   *

Word from the home front: Marian is recovering nicely from her 13th major orthopedic surgical procedure to deal with the effects of osteoarthritis – this time, an operation to give her an artificial right shoulder.

A more enjoyable addition to Marian's list of all-time records involved our June 3 visit to the new Busch Stadium in St. Louis, bringing up-to-date Marian's record of having seen a game in every major league ballpark currently in play. (There are 30 such at present.)

I was rooting for the Cardinals, but I didn't begrudge Marian's enjoyment of the Cubs' 14-inning victory. A victory of any kind is so exceptional for the poor Cubbies, recently the victims of a rare phenomenon in baseball, whether Little League or major league – two grand slam home runs hit by the opposition (in this case, the New York Mets) in the same inning.

— July 23, 2006

'Mrs. Andersen's Secretary'

I've written before about answering the telephone at home in Marian's absence. Lately, I've taken to answering with these words: "Mrs. Andersen's secretary." And, of course, about nine times out of 10, the call is indeed for Mrs. Andersen.

Also newly adopted is this technique when the call is for Marian and I'm asked to relay a message: I reply that I don't want to be charged with forgetting to pass the message along, so I suggest that the caller call back immediately. I let the phone ring five times, after which Marian's "Please leave a message" voice-mail recording kicks in.

I assure callers that Marian checks her voice mail about every 15 minutes. I confess that this is what is known as hyperbole – intentional exaggeration for the sake of effect – as I learned in English class at Omaha North High School. But she does check messages very regularly.

The caller is pleased to use this means to see that the message is delivered directly to Marian without the chance that her "secretary" will somehow drop the message ball.

— July 30, 2006

While Talking to a Policeman

Marian was on her cell phone, calling me at the office with a brief message about something or the other (possibly something like "the Cubs are playing the Cardinals on Channel 26"). She finished abruptly with these words: "I'm talking to the policeman. Bye."

(Such intriguing, puzzling messages from Marian are not all that unusual. Another example comes to mind: "The men came today, but they couldn't fix it.")

I was left to wonder why Marian was talking to a policeman. Had she been pulled over for speeding? Was she, cell phone in hand, talking in our driveway to a policeman who had come in response to one of the periodic false burglar alarms set off by one or the other of us? Was it a matter of greater import? Might the next call be to come post bond for Marian's release? (Only kidding. I really didn't spend any time speculating on that possibility.)

Arriving home, I asked Marian about her conversation with a policeman. She replied: "Oh, that. I was parked at the curb at Eppley Airfield after letting Nancy and the grandchildren out. I just told the officer that I thought he was a very nice policeman because he let me stay at the curb briefly to make sure the flight to Denver was on time."

— August 17, 2006

It Just Seems Longer

Occasionally, I tell Marian she is giving me more advice than I need in regard to what I eat and drink – and how much I eat and drink. To one of my recent suggestions along these lines, Marian replied:

"Don't you know that statistics prove that married men live longer?"

My reply: "It just seems longer."

— August 27, 2006

Breakfast and a Show

I'm still trying to wake up, wondering why I stayed up so late (reading, you should understand) the night before. I hear Marian in the kitchen, cheerily preparing breakfast for our three cocker spaniels. She is singing.

"Sarah makes the world go 'round, the world go 'round, the world go 'round. It's Sarah who makes the world go 'round."

Then a version with "Claire" substituted for "Sarah." Then another repetition, except that it's Charlotte who is now making the world go 'round.

> *"Sarah makes the world go 'round, the world go 'round, the world go 'round. It's Sarah who makes the world go 'round."*

Marian explains that this is her way of greeting the dogs some mornings and that the batting order never changes. Sarah is first, because she is the oldest. Claire comes next, because she is the next oldest. Finally, the newest kid on our Prairie Avenue block, Charlotte.

I believe that the dogs are more interested in breakfast than in the singing. But Marian enjoys these returns of affection (sometimes she assures the dogs that she and they are "co-dependents"), and so do I.

— September 3, 2006

The Kids?

I like Jim Rose and his style of radio reporting of the University of Nebraska football games. But for friend Jim, I have some advice (NU Coach Bill Callahan also might be interested):

Stop repeatedly referring to the Cornhusker football players as "kids."

"The kids" this and "the kids" that doesn't seem to me to apply to young men ranging in age into the 20s and in size to 6-foot-3 or so and upward of 300 pounds.

When I mentioned this to Marian, she said, "Well, what would you call them?"

Good question. How about "the guys" or "our players" or, whenever referring to the team en masse, simply "the team"?

— September 14, 2006

Baseball Faculty?

A friend invited Marian and me to take part in a daylong "Baseball 101" session in Lincoln under the direction of Nebraska baseball coach Mike Anderson. We declined with thanks.

I said I might benefit as a student in such a class, but if Marian were to be involved, she clearly should be on the faculty.

Marian could lecture on the suicide squeeze, the hit-and-run, a manager's occasional decision to have a relief pitcher face only one batter – all that sort of stuff.

We don't call her "the Sports Babe" for nothing.

— January 25, 2007

The Chair

The mail recently brought a letter inviting me to become a member of the "Chair's Leadership Circle," a part of a conservation organization in whose work I strongly believe.

I wrote to decline, saying I would continue to support the conservation organization but I'm not looking for any additional public-service roles. And I couldn't resist adding this advice:

Think of a better name for that leadership circle instead of bowing to what I suppose is political correctness (or gender correctness) by referring to your organization's leader as its "chair." If he is a man, call him a chairman. If the leader is a woman, call her a chairwoman if she prefers. (Marian has headed a number of civic organizations, and she has never asked for any title other than chairman.)

If you really think that the time-honored title of chairman, which is defined in the dictionary as non-sex-specific, is offensive to feminists, you could always cop out by settling on "chairperson," unattractive as that name sounds to a good many people.

But avoid "chair." A chair, after all, is something to sit on.

— February 1, 2007

The Pied Piperette of Omaha

We exchanged Christmas greetings with longtime dear friend Helen Silha, widow of Otto Silha, widely respected publisher of the Minneapolis Star Tribune. Helen is as charming and perky as ever and demonstrated that she has a remarkable memory as she recalled two incidents from our Associated Press directors' and wives' visit to China 27 years ago.

One incident involved Marian's attracting a following of delightful Tibetan children (see photo page 182), some scarcely past the toddler stage, as members of our party walked the streets of Lhasa, the Tibetan capital.

Obviously fascinated by this smiling representative of a race previously unknown to them, the children followed Marian and showed their willingness to repeat, in English, two or three words spoken by the Pied Piperette from Omaha.

I had lagged behind, taking pictures. By the time I caught up with the party, the other members were standing by our tour bus. Gathered around Marian was her crowd of new little friends. She had prepared them, willing mimics as they were, to repeat with her on my arrival, "Hi, Andy!" This was followed by "Go Big Red!"

Friend Helen also recalled the morning when, at breakfast in Lhasa, Marian, who had figured we might need a bit of American food somewhere along the route of our two weeks in China, appeared at breakfast with a jar of Jif crunchy peanut butter. Marian – and the peanut butter – were, of course, greeted with cheers and applause. The only complaint was that she didn't bring two jars.

— **February 25, 2007**

Fun Time of Year

Speaking with Marian on my car cell phone while coming home from the office the other evening, I was informed that Kansas State was beating somebody (I don't remember who) in the National Invitation Tournament on ESPNU and, as best I recall, Syracuse was having a tough time with somebody (I don't remember who) in the NIT.

Later that evening, we tuned in to the Phoenix Suns' dramatic double-overtime win over the Dallas Mavericks in a professional NBA game.

"This is such a fun time of the year," my roommate enthused.

Friends impressed by Marian's enthusiasm for sports – and voluminous knowledge of sports and athletes, past and present – call her "the Sports Babe" with good reason.

— **March 25, 2007**

55 Great Years

Marian and I recently celebrated our 55th wedding anniversary.

I thanked her for more than half a century of great years together and for simply being the finest thing that has ever happened to me – except for what happened on July 30, 1923.

That was my birthday, you see.

— May 3, 2007

Mrs. Snodgrass

Marian continues to amaze and amuse me with the variety of names she gives to the world's three most appealing cocker spaniels, which we are fortunate enough to have living with us.

This past week, our youngest dog, formally named Charlotte (age 3), had been referred to as Mrs. Snodgrass. (Marian said she doesn't know why she chose Mrs. Snodgrass. It just occurred to her, she said.)

Claire, age 5, this past week was known as Mrs. Jorge Posada. Posada is the catcher for the New York Yankees whose batting average has been leading the American League. Marian said she just considers Claire an outstanding dog and worthy of having a nickname linked to an outstanding baseball player. Very logical, don't you think?

As for Sarah, age 12, there were no special names this past week, just the usual "dear lady" or "sweet Sarah," voiced loudly enough for an aging family member to be able to hear.

— May 27, 2007

Junk on the Shelves

Marian: "Why don't you get rid of that junk on the shelves in the garage?"

Andy: "Why? We're about the only ones who see it, and sometimes I use some of what you call 'junk.'"

Marian: "Some people really fix up their garages – paint the floors and sometimes even have a sofa and an easy chair."

Andy: "Have you ever been in a garage like that?"

Marian: "No, but I've seen pictures of that sort of thing in magazines."

I made a mental note that if we ever put a sofa and an easy chair in our garage, I'll clean the "junk" off the shelves.

— June 3, 2007

A Good Shortstop

Year after year, it's the same positive story going out to the nation over ESPN and other press outlets: Omaha and the College World Series are partners again. And isn't that a happy combination for the benefit of the baseball world?

The ESPN broadcast on opening day of this 58th annual CWS in Omaha included commentators' words like these: "So many memories, so much tradition here. I can't imagine a city doing more" to host such an event. And these words: "The goal isn't to get to the College World Series. It's to get to Omaha."

One of the ESPN commentators, Barry Larkin, said he came to the CWS in Omaha twice while playing for Michigan. "When I was a senior in high school," Larkin said, "I knew about Omaha."

Larkin's remarks indicated that he had gone from the CWS to the major leagues. I confess I had not heard of Larkin.

While dictating this, I asked Marian: "Have you ever heard of Barry Larkin? He's one of the ESPN commentators." Marian's instant reply: "Oh, sure. He played for Cincinnati. He was a good shortstop."

Another consistently reliable source of baseball information, The Baseball Encyclopedia, lists Larkin as a shortstop for Cincinnati from 1986 to 2004. His career batting average: .295. His fielding percentage: .975. He was the National League's most valuable player in 1995 and a 12-time All-Star.

As Marian said, "A good shortstop."

— June 21, 2007

Cells and Big Purses

Marian (talking to me on her cell phone from her car): "No, Andy. I don't have your cell phone. I'm talking to you on my cell phone."

Andy: "Why don't you look in your purse? All I know is, I put my cell phone in the charger last night, and this morning it's gone."

Marian: "Well, I don't have it."

Fifteen minutes later, the phone rings at our residence. It's Marian. (You're probably already ahead of me on this.) "Mea culpa, mea culpa. Your cell phone was in my purse."

Marian carries purses about the size of one of the duffel bags I take on hunting trips. She throws in a great variety of things, somewhat at random. It's easy to lose things in there, things usually discovered after several assertions like, "Nope, it's not in here. I thought I put it in here. I must have left it on the dining room table."

— June 28, 2007

For Cat Lovers

Marian and I are dog owners and lovers. (Isn't that about the same thing?) Cat-loving readers have been very tolerant. I can recall only two comments – friendly – from cat lovers over the years.

All of which is a prelude to today's report on the spring/summer issue of "Tail's Tales," a publication of the Nebraska Humane Society. There were some letters telling about very successful "adoptions" of dogs and letters telling similar success stories in regard to cat adoptions. (I wonder if that's the right description. It seems to me that the owners of dogs or cats are the ones "adopted.")

Of the "we love our adopted cat" letters, my favorite was this: "My brother, Casey, was just out of college and undertaking his first job teaching sixth grade. This 6-foot-7-inch guy decided he needed a feline friend and fell in love with Felix (a. k. a. Ernie). Felix began ruling the house, hanging from shower curtains, hunting bugs and stealing jewelry!

"As the two began to bond, Casey found out he had cancer. Felix became his 'cancer cat.' When Casey was too tired to get off the couch after chemo, Felix was always at his side.

"This kitty is so special that we don't think Casey would be cancer-free today without Felix!"

— July 19, 2007

Andy Gets a Promotion

My duties as my roommate's phone-answering and message-taking executive assistant (Marian says she is promoting me from secretary) reached a new peak of activity one recent morning – with Marian out of the house and me answering five phone calls in 15 minutes. (Two calls were from Marian on her car phone. She had left the house in her customary rush less than 10 minutes earlier.)

I've encountered flurries of calls for or from Marian before, but I can't recall any previous occasion when the calls came at an average of one every three minutes.

As I may have told you, I have on occasion simply answered the phone with, "This is Mrs. Andersen's secretary." That proves to be appropriate about nine times out of 10.

I'm pleased that, with my promotion, I'll now be able to answer, "This is Mrs. Andersen's executive assistant."

— July 22, 2007

A Witty Invitation

(This anecdote came at the end of a column on the life and death of Paula Varner, widow of the late University of Nebraska President Woody Varner – editor.)

In a long friendship with Woody Varner, I had frequent occasion to observe that a good part of Woody's charm was his quick wit, his grand sense of humor. For example:

Marian and I were among the guests one evening at the university president's home in south Lincoln. After a post-dinner musical performance, plus an appropriate interval for chatting with fellow guests, Woody rose to say that guests were free to enjoy the post-dinner conversation and refreshments as long as they wished, "but as for me, I'm going to put on my jammies and go to bed."

This witty invitation to hit the road resulted in laughter and, of course, prompt departures.

— July 26, 2007

What She Meant

Two good friends, banker Chris Murphy and barber Tom Squires, and I have been joking about publishing a book titled "What She Meant."

The idea would be to interpret what a wife really means when she puts certain questions or comments to her husband.

My first offering for our book would go like this: We are dressing to go out for the evening. Marian asks: "Are you going to wear that tie?" The temptation is to reply: "Yes, that's why I put it on."

But the peace-in-the-family response would go like this: "I just put it on to see if you think it goes with this shirt and jacket. Please tell me if you think I could do better. Let's go to my tie rack, where you can pick out something that we like."

— July 29, 2007

It's Alarming!

For some years now we have had an electric alarm clock that offers the usual range of options, plus an additional option that Marian hasn't yet been able to master: a second alarm setting.

Thus it was the other day that Marian said something like, "The alarm clock keeps going off at a time I haven't set it for." I quickly confirmed that Marian had inadvertently activated the second alarm.

I explained to Marian what had happened and said something to the effect that after years of practice, she still didn't know how to control the various options.

Her reply: "Well, I don't have any problem 350 days of the year."

I pointed out that this meant she isn't in control of the alarm clock 15 days a year – 16 days in leap years.

"That's about right," my roommate cheerfully replied.

— August 9, 2007

The Mix Includes
Controversial Columns, Too

The anecdotes recounted in the preceding chapters were, of course, only part – but an important part – of the more than 1,300 columns which I have written since my retirement as publisher of The World-Herald in 1989. Those columns included a much larger proportion of "non-Marian" comment, some of it lighthearted but most of it more serious.

My editor, Jim Fogarty, suggested that readers might be interested in examples of those more serious comments.

Incidentally but importantly, in the great majority of the columns, "life with Marian" included Marian's review of the column before it went to press, a review which frequently helped me from making a mistake of fact or changed the language to better express my comments. (Occasionally Marian simply told me to "lighten up" after a series of serious comments on serious subjects.)

This chapter offers a sampling to give readers a taste of the many columns which did not comment on "Life with Marian." Segments that follow are mostly recent, and there are many others of an earlier vintage that would fit nicely here, but space does not permit.

— Andy

Boys Town Management Dispute

Parts of Memo Refute Archbishop's Account of Boys Town Dispute

Today, a chance for you to read pertinent portions of the wording of that controversial two-page memo Archbishop Elden Curtiss sent to fellow members of the board that makes policy for Girls and Boys Town. (Curtiss has refused to release a copy of the memo.)

The wording reveals that despite statements to the contrary, Curtiss had quite clearly delivered an ultimatum in, for example, his demand for veto power over any proposed change in the bylaws of the board. Consider the final sentence of Curtiss' two-page memo sent June 13 to fellow board members:

"If the majority of the members do not support the changes in the bylaws which I consider necessary to maintain the proper relationship between the archdiocese and Boys Town, then either these members will have to resign from the board because they are unwilling to support my special role as chairman of the board or I will be forced to resign from the board, which I will do at the September 4th meeting."

This language – and other portions of the two-page message made public for the first time in this column today – flatly contradict the archbishop's post-resignation statement indicating that he had simply "called for dialogue about some changes to the board's bylaws." They contradict, also, a statement of the Rev. Gregory Baxter, chancellor of the archdiocese, that the changes that the archbishop wanted were presented in a spirit of "let's discuss this." ("Flatly contradict" may not be explicit enough wording. "Simply untrue" might be a better way to describe those post-resignation statements.)

In his explanation of why the board should give the archbishop as chairman authority to veto any proposed bylaw change even if approved by a majority of the board, Curtiss wrote:

"As Chairman I am not just one voting member of the Board of Trustees. As Archbishop I represent the Archdiocese of Omaha and the long relationship which has existed between the Archdiocese and Boys Town beginning with Father Flanagan. Consequently, no change in the bylaws can take place without the agreement of the Chairman of the Board of Trustees."

It has been reported that the board, in addition to looking at local possibilities, is considering a national search for a priest to become executive director when the Rev. Val Peter steps down. Archbishop Curtiss wrote that it would require a change in the bylaws for the board to conduct a national search for priest candidates "at the same time the archbishop presents priest candidates from the Archdiocese of Omaha." He wrote he thinks he might not support such a change in the bylaws.

Archbishop Curtiss' sensitivity about anything he perceives as diminishing his status appears to be behind one of his proposed bylaw changes. The bylaw now reads that the board of trustees "shall appoint as its presiding officer and chairman … the Archbishop of the Catholic Archdiocese of Omaha." Curtiss wrote: "I am not willing to serve as Chairman of the Board at the pleasure of the members of the board. The Bylaws need to state that the Archbishop serves as Chairman of the Board ex-officio as Archbishop of the Catholic Archdiocese of Omaha."

The clearly stated requirement that the board of trustees "shall appoint" the archbishop as board chairman is not enough for Curtiss. He insists that the archbishop serves as chairman "ex-officio" without the board taking its already mandated action of appointing him as chairman.

To this layman, there wouldn't appear to be much difference. The archbishop would wind up as board chairman in either case. I understand, of course, that the approach preferred by Curtiss would keep laymen from being involved in the process of his ascension to the chairmanship.

There has been a tendency to report the controversy in terms of a power struggle between Curtiss and Peter.

But former Omahan John J. Gillin, now a resident of Atlanta and retired senior vice president of the Coca-Cola Co., elected to succeed Curtiss as board chairman, emphasized to me that Peter was kept out of the board's discussions on how to respond to Curtiss' demands. For example, Gillin said, Peter did not participate in a previously unpublicized special board meeting in Dallas in August.

In his post-resignation statement depicting his memo to the board as only a call for dialogue, Curtiss said: "It is unfair, and a discredit to all that Girls and Boys Town stands for, to depict my resignation from the board of trustees as a power struggle between Father Peter and myself." (The Rev. Val Peter is president of the board and executive director of Girls and Boys Town.)

In regard to a potential conflict between the archbishop as board chairman and the board president (now Father Peter), Curtiss' memo said:

"If the President decides to distance himself from me as Chairman of the Board, and as a priest of the archdiocese decides to distance himself from me as Archbishop, then either he must resign as president or I will resign from the board and sever all relationships between the Archdiocese and Father Flanagan's Boys' Home." (This is still the corporate name of what has become known as "Girls and Boys Town.")

The archbishop's memo then proposed this new bylaw: "If unresolved conflicts develop between the president and the chairman of the board of trustees or with a majority of the members of the board of trustees, the incumbency of the president shall be terminated."

The current bylaws provide that the board appoints the president "to serve in such position until the board of trustees shall terminate such incumbency."

The archdiocese released a post-resignation statement saying that the archdiocese "will not assume the responsibility in the future of providing one of its priests for the traditional role of executive director, the pastor of Immaculate Conception Parish on campus or any other ministry on the campus."

This raised the yet-unanswered question of whether the archbishop would order Father Peter, who as a priest in the Omaha Archdiocese is subject to Curtiss' authority, to withdraw from his role as executive director of Boys Town.

(One man's opinion: If Archbishop Curtiss, who has shown a continuing tendency to put his public relations foot in his mouth, tries to pull Father Peter off the Girls and Boys Town job, his already shaky standing in the community will be further damaged. Such action, of course, would also receive national news coverage because Girls and Boys Town and its programs – now serving 38,000 children in 14 states – are so widely known.)

It is worth noting that of the 13 board members, eight are non-Omahans. (Two of them were previously Omaha residents.) Worth noting, too, that among the 16 members are a nurse, a nun, two women described as community volunteers, retired business executives and active business executives, including two executives well known to Omahans – Ken Stinson, chairman and CEO of Peter Kiewit Sons', Inc. and Ronald J. Burns, former CEO of the Union Pacific Railroad, now a resident of Phoenix, Ariz., and chairman of management firms that he founded.

At bottom, the real issue involves a showdown between a power-seeking archbishop and a board of trustees with backbone. The trustees recognize that Girls and Boys Town best fulfills its nationwide mission of serving children of various religious faiths when, while maintaining its Omaha roots and the traditional and cherished special relationship with the Catholic Church, the board looks at the larger national picture and rejects domination by the archbishop of Omaha.

— September 28, 2003

Readers Respond to Curtiss Column

You might be interested in reader reaction directed my way following last Sunday's column in which I detailed the expanded powers Catholic Archbishop Elden Curtiss sought as chairman of the Girls and Boys Town board.

I wrote that Curtiss and his chancellor, the Rev. Gregory Baxter, misrepresented the archbishop's two-page memo to the board as simply an effort to start a dialogue. The memo was clearly an ultimatum to adopt Curtiss' proposals or the result would be resignation of a majority of the board or resignation of the archbishop. The board unanimously rejected Curtiss' proposed bylaw changes, one of which would have given him veto power over any bylaw change even if all other board members favored it. Curtiss resigned.

Nine letters or phone calls came my way from Catholics who expressed approval of what I wrote. Some of the approval included strongly worded criticism of Curtiss. One letter spoke of "double-talking babble" in Curtiss' statements.

The tone of a few of the letters was reflected in statements such as, "Thanks for being objective in your perception. I believe that the truth has been told," or, "You're helping in many ways. Hopefully things will get better in our church."

Favorable comments also came from three Protestant readers. Dissent expressed to me by two Catholics included these comments:

"The archbishop is not seeking personal power but is merely taking care (as it is his duty to do) that if the Boys Town board elects to be completely independent, it should be just that and not continue under apparent auspices of a church which in fact does not have control over it."

And this brief message: "If that's all you have to do, I feel sorry for you."

Department of Full Disclosure: In a post-resignation statement, Curtiss said he has never indicated disagreement with the bylaw giving each board member "an equal vote" in selecting the executive director of Boys Town. He failed to mention the fact that one of the bylaw changes he had proposed as, in effect, his price for his continuing on the board was the following:

"If unresolved conflicts develop between the president and the chairman of the board of trustees or with a majority of the members of the board of trustees, the incumbency of the president shall be terminated."

The president of the corporation is also the executive director of Girls and Boys Town, currently the Rev. Val Peter. The current bylaws provide that the board of trustees appoints the president and executive director, who can serve "until the board of trustees removes him."

— October 5, 2003

Senator Chuck Hagel

Hagel's Critical Comments on Iraq Might Not Play Well Back Home

It was a surprising coincidence – one that suggested more care if you want to help, not hurt, your party's presidential candidate. And Nebraska's voluble U.S. Sen. Chuck Hagel was squarely in the middle of it.

The day before The World-Herald published an interview in which Hagel said he has been "trying to help," the Democratic National Committee (DNC) ran a full-page ad in the New York Times including Hagel's picture and two widely publicized Hagel quotes implying sharp criticism of the Bush administration's policy in Iraq.

The clear implication was that, in the view of the DNC, Hagel by his continuing outspoken criticism has been helping Democratic presidential candidate John Kerry by hurting the Republican candidate, President Bush.

Hagel's remarks in his interview with Jake Thompson of The World-Herald Washington Bureau indicated that Hagel can now strongly support Bush's re-election because the administration has decided to move in Iraq in the direction Hagel has been advocating – including bringing other nations and the United Nations and NATO into the peacemaking process.

A headline published Sept. 28 with The World-Herald story read: "Hagel: White House may be heeding him on Iraq."

The Hagel quotes most prominently displayed in the Democratic National Committee ad came from remarks Hagel made to reporters Sept. 16: "The worst thing we can do is hold ourselves hostage to some grand illusion that we're winning. Right now, we are not winning. Things are getting worse."

The other Hagel quote used by the DNC in its full-page ad was voiced during one of Hagel's periodic stops on the Washington Sunday-morning political talk-show circuit, this time on CBS's "Face the Nation." The quote: "We're in deep trouble in Iraq."

The DNC ad quotes two other Republican senators, John McCain of Arizona and Richard Luger of Indiana, with remarks that the DNC obviously felt to be critical of the Bush administration and therefore helpful to Kerry.

Also quoted were two Democratic senators, Bob Graham of Florida and Joseph Biden of Delaware. But the space devoted to a Hagel picture and quotes took up nearly one-third of the page.

Incidentally, the Democratic National Committee isn't the only anti-Bush voice that welcomed Hagel's critical remarks. New York Times columnist Bob Herbert approvingly quoted Hagel's "Face the Nation" remark (Sept. 25 More Commentary). And Sen. Kerry praised Hagel on "The Late Show with David Letterman."

All in all, not a performance likely to win back for Hagel some of the stature he has lost in the eyes of more than a few folks back home – Nebraskans who have supported him in the past but are increasingly skeptical, if not sharply critical, of his attention-attracting performance on the national news-media stage in recent years.

— October 3, 2004

Reply to Hagel's Rebuttal

Regular readers of this page may wonder if I intended to reply to U.S. Sen. Chuck Hagel's 23-paragraph response published three days after my 11-paragraph report and comments on Hagel's criticism of the way the Bush administration has been trying to bring peace to Iraq.

When Hagel's rebuttal (Oct. 6 Midlands Voices) came to my attention, I already had written a column for last Sunday's paper. It was about baseball. I could have scrapped the baseball column and responded promptly and in detail to Hagel's criticism.

I decided to go with the baseball column. Pointless, I concluded, to try to respond in detail to a critic whose 23-paragraph article didn't directly address either of the two main points in my column:

(1) Some of Hagel's remarks were used by the Democratic National Committee as the dominating feature of a full-page, Bush-policy-bashing ad in the Sunday New York Times.

(2) Hagel's continuing performance on the national news-media stage has cost him stature among some folks back home, including more than a few Nebraskans who have supported him in the past.

A final thought: In the 17th paragraph of his essay, Hagel said: "If people disagree with me, I understand and respect that." Ten paragraphs earlier, Hagel had said: "With all due respect, Harold Andersen does not know what he is talking about."

Perhaps it's just that Hagel has what some would consider an unorthodox way of showing understanding and respect when someone says something that he disagrees with.

— October 14, 2004

President Bush's Intellectual Depth

A Single Sentence

I fell to thinking the other day about something I wrote in November 2002. It was a single sentence that provoked a good deal of criticism from readers.

The words came to mind again last week as I reflected on President Bush's performance in vetoing additional federal funding for embryonic stem-cell research ....

My column on Nov. 10, 2002, included this brief sentence near the end of the column: "I'm still not impressed with the president's intellectual depth." (Note: That column also gave Bush full credit "as a gutsy, energetic and effective campaigner in support of his generally conservative political agenda" and described the Nov. 5 election results as "a significant victory for the Republican Party and especially for President Bush.")

Now, the president may be strong-willed and quick to make what he thinks are the right judgments – he has described himself as a "decider." A quick mind certainly can be an invaluable asset, capable of looking at the broad picture and weighing options without unduly delaying important decisions. But to be a consistently effective "decider," that mind had best be not only quick but also reasonably deep, in my opinion.

My bottom line, I say again: "I'm still not impressed with the president's intellectual depth."

— August 13, 2006

A Former Republican Named Andersen

Republicans Have Way to Protest Party Takeover by Religious Right

The "let Terri live" voices are by far the loudest, but three national polls have indicated that the majority of Americans, relatively silent as the controversy continues, feel that the most compassionate treatment for Terri Schiavo – as well as the proper legal course of action – is to let her vegetative existence end, as advocated by her legal guardian, her husband.

The majority of Americans are simply outgunned when it comes to anything like "equal time" in the debate and legal maneuvering.

Representing the minority viewpoint are people with their hands on the levers of power: President Bush, House Speaker Dennis Hastert, House Majority Leader Tom DeLay (and isn't he a fine one to be lecturing on the "moral" way to handle the Schiavo case) and Senate Majority Leader William Frist, holders of the most powerful positions in the U.S. Congress and all members of the Republican Party. What do members of the relatively silent majority do? How do they speak out? For Republicans who consider their party a captive of the religious right on matters like medical research and right-to-die legislation and now legislative intrusion into the judicial system, there is a way to at least feel more comfortable with their political consciences.

That way is to leave a party whose leadership is currently attempting to leave behind in the dust of American constitutional history the principle of separation of powers that has served this country well for more than 200 years.

Republican-mandated congressional action last week attempting to intrude into areas traditionally reserved to the courts was tragic, yet not without almost comic opera overtones. For example:

CNN's live coverage of proceedings in the House of Representatives included repeated references to the "save Terri Schiavo" bill as having been "passed unanimously" by the Senate earlier that day.

But only three senators were present when the bill was rushed through what has sometimes been referred to as the world's greatest deliberative body. (Under rules in the House of Representatives, there did have to be a quorum present, that is, at least 218 of the 435 members – when the

House voted on the measure "unanimously" passed by three senators.)

The press, in my opinion, have generally done an inadequate job of coverage. For one thing, the fact that the Senate's "unanimous" vote involved only three senators has received too little attention.

And I've been reading story after story and listening to broadcasts on the Schiavo case and it wasn't until two days ago that I read that Terri's husband, Michael, was not alone in recalling that his wife had said she didn't want to be kept alive by extraordinary means if her case appeared hopeless.

In one of the many judicial proceedings – more than 20 in all – Michael Schiavo's brother and sister-in-law testified that Terri had said "I don't want to be kept alive on a machine" and made several similar statements.

And there has been too little public discussion of two other factors that seem to me to be of considerable relevance:

Presumably, the religious conservatives deeply involved in the case believe in an afterlife – eternal life in circumstances considerably more appealing than lying in a hospital bed in a vegetative state for 15 years, being kept alive by food and liquids fed into your body through a hole in your abdomen.

Wouldn't the more compassionate course be to release Terri from a vegetative existence in the belief you are sending her on to a better life after death?

Also scarcely mentioned is the great irony in this fact:

Conservatives who excoriate judges for intruding onto legislative turf by "legislating" in some of their decisions are now applauding legislators for intruding onto judicial turf by telling the courts they must yet again review the Schiavo case.

Incidentally, I wonder if those fighting to continue to allow Terri to exist believe that those televised hospital room scenes are helpful to their cause in that they show Terri with mouth and eyes open, from time to time turning her head and seeming to smile.

But I believe those pictures including the shot of nurses' hands inserting feeding tubes into Terri's abdomen – can be interpreted as tending to confirm medical experts' testimony as to Terri's vegetative state.

Whatever the motivation, the pictures seem to me a cruel invasion of what should be the privacy of pathetic Terri Schiavo's hospital room.

*   *   *

I would think that I'm not the only Republican who feels the party's leadership has engaged in an irresponsible and perhaps unprecedented effort to subvert the traditional separation of government powers. How to express our disapproval?

I'm going to the Douglas County Election Commissioner's office on Monday to change my political registration from Republican to Independent, while continuing to feel sympathy for Terri Schiavo and her parents and believing that the most compassionate course is to free her from her sad existence, Republican Party politicians to the contrary notwithstanding.

— March 27, 2005

More Political Commentary

'Mrs. Clinton's Words Ring False in Nebraska Hospital'

This past week I had occasion to spend some hours at the University of Nebraska Medical Center, where my wife underwent hip surgery. (Marian is recovering nicely, prepared to accept invitations for tennis dates later this summer – although her doctor may have something to say about the timing of her return to the courts.)

The University Medical Center and the people who work there came to mind when I read a news story dealing with a speech that Hillary Rodham Clinton made to members of a union representing hospital and nursing-home employees. The reporter described the speech as a preview of "the bare-knuckles political strategy she will use in seeking a revolution in American health care."

Her health care system, Mrs. Clinton indicated, will be designed to care for people, "not to enhance the profits of those who are providing the services."

Mrs. Clinton urged her audience of hospital and nursing-home employees: "Talk to your friends and neighbors about what you see every day in terms of price gouging, cost shifting and unconscionable profiteering."

I thought of those staff members whom I had observed at the University of Nebraska Medical Center, including the cheerful and competent people who were caring for Marian and other patients on the sixth floor of University Hospital.

It is preposterous to suggest that these dedicated health care providers and others like them across America are involved in a system that puts profits ahead of patients – a system in which they daily see "price gouging, cost shifting and unconscionable profiteering."

Mrs. Clinton's speech may be what the reporter called the start of a "bare-knuckles" campaign. It was also, in my opinion, a false and irresponsible depiction of the way the American health care system operates every day in hospitals and nursing homes across this country.

Surely a case can be made for improving our health care system – moderating costs, expanding services to those not adequately covered – without resorting to such demagogic rhetorical overkill as Mrs. Clinton stooped to in her speech last week.

— May 30, 1993

Stem-cell Research

Religious Objections Shouldn't Keep UNMC Research From Saving Lives

A recent item on The World-Herald's More Commentary page underscored the importance – in this case, the international importance – of research being conducted at the University of Nebraska Medical Center.

Also underscored, in my mind, was the importance of keeping that Med Center research unfettered by the kinds of restrictions that some people might seek to impose.

The life-saving potential of medical research – such as that involving the use of stem cells from fertility-clinic embryonic fetuses that otherwise simply would be destroyed – cannot justifiably be restricted no matter how conscientiously held are the religious beliefs of the minority who seek to impose their views on medical researchers.

The commentary in The World-Herald quoted the chief executive officer of Medicines for Malaria Venture in Geneva, Switzerland, and the director of the Malaria Vaccine Initiative in Bethesda, Md., as reporting that Nebraska is playing an important role in waging the fight against the widespread scourge of malaria, which is estimated to kill at least 2 million people a year.

The commentary reported that Jonathan Vennerstrom, a University of Nebraska Medical Center researcher, led a team of scientists in the discovery of a potentially powerful and affordable drug for combating malaria. The drug is being tested in clinical trials in patients in Thailand.

But, some research-limiting advocates might argue, we certainly aren't opposed to anti-malaria research. The University of Nebraska Medical Center's research is of international importance.

What they may not understand is that if you saddle the Medical Center with a reputation for research restrictions imposed in response to the religious beliefs of certain pressure groups, you run the very real risk of losing researchers in fields all across the board.

— April 28, 2005

Stem-cell Research – Reader Reaction

Critics of Embryonic Stem-cell Research Miss Point

Predictably, I received both praise and criticism in response to my column criticizing President Bush for his veto of federal funding for the use of excess fertility clinic embryos for stem-cell research designed to prevent or cure debilitating or life-threatening physical ailments.

Criticism from a reader in Bloomfield, Neb., demonstrated once again that critics just don't get it. In other words, they simply don't understand – or are unwilling to acknowledge – the simple fact that unneeded frozen embryos, which are the result of excessive production of embryos by couples seeking help in fertility clinics, will simply be discarded in nearly all cases unless they are used for stem-cell research.

How many times does this truism have to be pointed out before critics will stop writing with criticism like this: "Is it right for society to destroy life to try and improve life for others?"

The obvious response – as it has been time and again to such questions – is this: Is it right for society to destroy embryos that aren't needed by their owners simply for the purpose of getting them out of fertility clinic freezers rather than using some of them "to try and improve life for others?"

The disposal of the embryos can be done in a way that extracts the stem cells for medical research. From a moral and sensible religious perspective – I stress sensible – isn't this a better end for the embryo than simply to destroy it by discarding it, without any societal benefit at all?

And we shouldn't let the discussion be led down the misleading detour of suggestions of the supposedly great promise that lies in encouraging couples – perhaps childless couples – to adopt one of these thousands of frozen embryos by having it implanted in a woman on the way to producing the birth of a child.

In the first place, to make a significant reduction in the thousands of frozen embryos, you would have to find a great many couples who want to become adoptive parents under such circumstances. This should prove especially difficult in the case of Catholic couples, since their Church strictly defines the only acceptable form of birth as resulting from sexual intercourse between husband and wife.

Such "adoptions" also would require approval of the couple who used the services of the fertility clinic, services that resulted in production of excess embryos. It could be a hard sell to convince very many such couples to allow what could turn out to be literally their child, their offspring bearing their genes, to be turned over to another couple.

Incidentally but importantly, embryonic stem-cell research is reported to be booming in Singapore laboratories, which are attracting researchers from other countries. And a recent policy decision by the European Union will broaden the funding of stem-cell research in Europe, predictably attracting researchers from other countries, including the United States.

Also incidentally but importantly (importantly at least from the standpoint of a columnist's ego), I have received more letters and phone calls endorsing what I wrote in support of embryonic stem-cell research than I did in communications criticizing my views.

A friend whose opinion I value very highly – incidentally, he's Catholic –

called to say how much he appreciated what I wrote. A doctor in Norfolk said he agrees with my remarks "1,000 percent." Another reader said my column had done a good job of explaining the issue and "cutting through all the politics."

A Lincoln reader wrote that the stem-cell issue "is not the only one on which this administration is using theocratic reasoning to make decisions." This country, he wrote, was not established as a theocracy, "and it is ironic that the president uses his personal theocratic ideas to appeal to his right-wing base on this and other issues while attempting to shove democracy down the throats of other truly theocratic countries."

The Lincoln writer noted that all five Nebraska members of Congress opposed federal funding for expanding embryonic stem-cell research.

— **August 6, 2006**

Intelligent Design

Intelligent-design Theory Holds More Questions Than Answers

Some thoughts today on the current hot-button topic of whether the tremendous complexity of living things on this planet resulted not from a process of natural evolution (the Darwinian theory) but from intelligent design, which implicitly presupposes the existence of a designer like the all-powerful God of the Bible.

It's clear that some intelligent people on the religious right realize that the mountains of scientific evidence disproving the biblical six-days-and-He-rested version of creation require the replacement or modification of the biblical version with a theory that still embraces the notion of an all-powerful supreme being – a God Almighty, if you will.

So we are asked to consider the theory of intelligent design – which concedes that the complex pattern of life on this planet wasn't created in six days (or 6,000 years) but contends that the very complexity of the developed life-forms suggests that there must have been an intelligent design to produce that complexity.

Now, if there was an intelligent design, the theory suggests, there must have been a powerful intelligent designer, a powerful deity like the one described in the Bible.

It seems to me that all of this raises some questions: If an all-powerful intelligent designer was at work, why did he take so long to bring living things – mankind, especially – to their present state of development?

Why require man's ancestors to develop from common ancestry with apes – the evidence of such development is irrefutable – and go about on all fours for multiple generations before finally becoming Homo erectus walking upright and then Homo sapiens with a well-developed brain?

And why did the intelligent designer include so many crippling or killing diseases in his design?

And assuming there was an intelligent designer, he must have been very busy indeed. Consider the staggering variety of life-forms on our planet today.

As I thought about today's comments, my eye fell on "The Guide to North American Birds," which Marian and I keep close at hand in our breakfast room. The nearly 400 pages include, for just one example, 50 separate varieties of woodpeckers. This suggests the staggering variety of life-forms that the intelligent designer would have had to provide for in his design.

> *"The Darwinian theory does not say there isn't such a supreme being. It simply establishes that the world was created by natural evolution, not the way the Bible says it was."*

The answer of the intelligent-design theorists, I suppose, would be that the designer was and is all-powerful, so this incredibly complex job would have been easy for him.

A bottom-line question, it seems to me, is this: Why are some religious conservatives going to such lengths in an attempt to discredit the Darwinian theory of natural development of species? There are countless people across the globe today who not only accept the reality of Charles Darwin's theory of evolution but also believe in the existence of a supreme being.

The Darwinian theory does not say there isn't such a supreme being. It simply establishes that the world was created by natural evolution, not the way the Bible says it was.

So why teach the intelligent-design theory as a scientific competitor to the Darwinian theory of evolution, as is being considered by state school authorities in Kansas and Ohio and in a number of school districts across America? You can defend belief in a supreme being without trying to make science out of a religious theory.

It seems to me that Eugene Selk, a Creighton University philosophy professor who teaches a course on science and religion, summed up the situation very well: "It's not science. It's as simple as that. It's a religious position, which they are trying to get into science courses under the guise of science. It would be perfectly OK if they would say, 'This is a theological position, and we would like to teach this in a religion course.' But that's not what they claim."

— **August 25, 2005**

Genesis Lite

Apparently, some people have not been paying attention to what is being written and said about the hot-button topic of intelligent design as an explanation for the evolution of the many species of living things, including humankind.

There came to my attention recently an assertion that no one has been telling the public that the widely accepted explanation of evolution does not rule out religious belief if an individual chooses to embrace both Darwinism and God.

The truth is that it has been rather widely reported that countless people across the globe, including a great many scientists, accept the reality of Charles Darwin's explanation of evolution but also believe in the existence of a supreme being.

As I wrote in this space six weeks ago, the Darwinian explanation "does not say there isn't such a supreme being." It simply established that species developed as a result of natural selection, not the way the Bible says they were created and not as a result of the work of an all-powerful intelligent designer.

Incidentally, it seems clear to me that intelligent-design advocates are trying to blend some of the Bible's creationism story into their theory of a supreme being who was an intelligent designer; i.e., God. This has led to one description of intelligent design as "Genesis lite."

— October 6, 2005

My Aching Back

Count me among those who are more than willing to accept the Darwinian explanation of mankind's evolution from creatures that went about on all fours.

I realize that some of my lower-back pain results from my walking about upright instead of, with arched spine, going about on what amounted to four legs. But I consider lower-back pain a very modest price to pay for being the beneficiary of mankind's evolution into Homo erectus (and then on into Homo sapiens, of course).

— November 17, 2005

Staunch Allegiance to Israel

Moving Quickly to the Israeli Side

Without going deeply into the merits – or demerits – of Israeli reaction to Hezbollah's incursion into Israel and capture of two Israeli soldiers, a brief comment on one aspect of the violent confrontation that has resulted:

Once again, the United States, through President Bush, moves quickly to the Israeli side of the controversy – in sharp contrast to, for example, the European Union's criticism of Israel for "disproportionate" reaction.

I wonder if there is any real hope for peaceful resolution of the Israeli-Palestinian confrontation. The thought is prompted by this coincidence:

Cleaning out some files this week, I came across a copy of the March 20, 1978, front page of The World-Herald. The major international story, reported on that front page 28 years ago, carried this headline: "Israelis: Troops Along River Line."

The lead paragraph read: "Armor-led Israeli forces, backed up by war-planes and naval bombardment, pushed deeper into southern Lebanon Monday despite a U.N. resolution calling for immediate withdrawal, Lebanese State Radio reported."

— July 20 2006

Standing Alone with Israel Means 'Diplomatic Isolation'

From conversations with a good many Americans over time, especially in recent years, I know I'm not alone in being concerned with this question:

To what extent does our lockstep march by Israel's side in controversy and confrontation in the Middle East do harm to the United States in terms of our relations with the rest of the world, Arab and non-Arab?

That question becomes even more important, it seems to me, in light of the course the United States has been pursuing in the Israeli/Hezbollah/Lebanese crisis.

It took the deaths of an estimated 55 people, most of them children, in the Israeli bombardment of a building in southern Lebanon to awaken the United States to the fact that Israel and America – once again – were standing virtually alone in defense of Israeli policies. A USA Today report described one result of the bombing this way: "The response … increased the two nations' diplomatic isolation at the United Nations and elsewhere."

It also increased the level of hatred for Israel and the United States in the Arab world, making it much harder for the United States to play the role of honest broker in negotiating any kind of settlement in the Middle East.

Finally – finally – the United States agreed to press for a cease-fire, followed by negotiations for a long-term solution and creation of an international military force to support the Lebanese army and keep Hezbollah militia forces out of southern Lebanon. But as of this writing, Israel had refused to yield to worldwide pressure for an immediate cease-fire, and the United States once again went along with the Israelis.

To question President Bush's leadership ("followership" is perhaps the more descriptive word) in the current crisis can result, as I know from experience, in suggestions that the questioner is guilty of promoting anti-Semitism or that he or she has forgotten the horrors of the Holocaust in Europe more than 60 years ago.

Somehow, in the eyes of some Jewish people in the United States and in Israel, Israel is entitled to relative immunity from questions and public criticism of the type that we direct at an ally like France, for example. This immunity stems in large part, I believe, from the influence of some members of the American Jewish community.

Israel is a democracy and an American ally. Israelis – and the Palestinian people –

> *"The fact that Hezbollah is a terrorist group that must be opposed and hopefully somehow neutralized does not justify all-out retaliatory tactics that result in the kind of carnage that Israeli forces have visited on Lebanon."*

certainly deserve to live within the secure borders guaranteed by the United Nations in resolutions passed more than half a century ago.

It does not follow, I believe, that the United States was somehow bound to stand staunchly by Israel's side when Israel turned a Lebanese border incident – several Israeli soldiers were killed and two were captured, hardly Armageddon – into justification for pounding a good deal of Lebanon into rubble.

The fact that Hezbollah is a terrorist group that must be opposed and hopefully somehow neutralized does not justify all-out retaliatory tactics that result in the kind of carnage that Israeli forces have visited on Lebanon.

Neither Israeli bombs nor Hezbollah bombs will bring peace. A negotiated settlement is the only long-term answer. And, most unfortunately, prospects for such a settlement have been damaged by the Israeli/Lebanon/Hezbollah confrontation.

* * *

Apropos of the theme of my column today: After an earlier column in which I had said it was predictable that the United States would quickly stand with Israel in the confrontation with Hezbollah, a reader in Utica, Neb., called to say:

"You really are in favor of Hezbollah, which is just an organization set out to destroy Israel as a nation. Are you being paid by the Arabs?"

No, I'm not being paid by the Arabs, and I'm certainly not "really" in favor of Hezbollah.

Rather, I'm really impressed with the realistic viewpoint expressed by an Israeli newspaper, Haaretz, in the following editorial comment that was cited on the July 19 More Commentary page by New York Times columnist Nicholas D. Kristof. The Israeli newspaper said:

"It is simple to join emotionally in George (W.) Bush's culture war against the axis of evil, but it must be remembered that, at the end of the day, it is the citizens of Israel and not the Americans who have to continue living in the Middle East. Therefore, we have to think of ways that will make it possible for us to coexist, even with those we do not enjoy being with."

I'm really impressed, too, with the opinions voiced by Kristof. The New York Times columnist wrote in that same column, among other things, that while it's easy to sympathize with Israeli outrage, Israel escalated the conflict in a way that has created anger throughout the Arab world and "may make life in Israel far more dangerous for many years to come."

— August 3, 2006

Reflections

Happy 120th, World-Herald

My recent column wishing The World-Herald a happy 120th birthday set me to thinking about my long relationship with this newspaper.

It started about 70 years ago in the mid-1930s, when I helped my two big brothers with their World-Herald routes. I then took time out for eight years to attend high school and college and work a year as a reporter for the Lincoln Star. A job as a World-Herald reporter in 1946 started a continuing relationship that stretches over 59 years.

So many vivid memories. For example, there was the angry reaction of a good many readers when we called on Richard M. Nixon to resign as president. There was also the joyous reaction at World-Herald Square when the late Peter Kiewit persuaded World-Herald owners to sell the paper to the Kiewit construction company to keep the ownership local rather than sell to a newspaper syndicate headquartered in New York.

Vivid memories, too, of walking a World-Herald route during summers in the 1930s when the temperature frequently went above 100 degrees and during winters when the temperatures frequently went below zero.

Before I got a World-Herald route of my own, my oldest brother, Russ, now deceased, occasionally drove the family car while I stood on the running board, jumping off when he stopped and running up to a residence for doorstep delivery.

I suppose our big brother/little brother act could be compared to Tom Sawyer getting his buddies to paint the fence for him. But I never thought of it that way. I was delighted to be out with my big brother, and I thought it was a big deal to be able to ride on the running board as we delivered The World-Herald.

Today, I suppose that what we did in the 1930s would lead to a charge of child abuse. But I had a ball.

— August 25, 2005

Sixty-year World-Herald Career Brings Recollections, Reflections

Yesterday was a 60th anniversary for me – 60 years to the day in 1946 when I went to work as a World-Herald reporter at a salary of $45 a week. (The World-Herald had lured me away from the Lincoln Star, where I had worked for a year as a reporter and acting sports editor for $25 a week after graduating from the University of Nebraska-Lincoln.) You might be interested in my recollection of some of the highlights – some serious, some not so serious – of my 60-year association with The World-Herald.

So, today, a column of very personal recollections. Next Sunday, a report with previously unpublicized details on the way the late Peter Kiewit assured the people of Omaha and Nebraska that The World-Herald will continue to be owned and operated by Omahans, in sharp contrast to the absentee ownership that is the predominant pattern in newspapers across the United States.

First, an explanation of how much I owe to Jim Keogh's appendix. (Keogh died May 10 at age 89. His career had included 13 years as one the best journalists ever to work for The World-Herald. His noteworthy service later in his career was as a senior executive of Time magazine, as head speechwriter in the Nixon White House and as director of the U.S. Information Agency.)

Jim and I kept in touch over the years and often recalled with a laugh the opportunity that came my way when Keogh, the top reporter on The World-Herald staff, with assignments that included City Hall, suffered an attack of appendicitis.

Executive Editor Fred Ware, who over the years took a special interest in me and to whom I owe a great deal, assigned me, the newest reporter on The World-Herald staff, to City Hall for what was assumed to be a very short stay.

Keogh's recuperation stretched into several weeks. And by the time he returned, Fred had decided I could handle the City Hall assignment, Keogh continued to cover politics and the Legislature for a short time before being promoted to city editor.

After a variety of "learning the ropes" reportorial assignments, I was assigned in 1949 to open a World-Herald Lincoln news bureau, which I shared with legendary World-Herald sportswriter Gregg McBride. The assignment in Lincoln was, of course, the most important of all, because it was there that I met and married Marian Louise Battey.

Marian is a UNL journalism graduate who, on more than one public occasion, has pointed out that she is the journalism graduate in the family and wonders how far I might have gone if I, too, had majored in journalism instead of English and history.

I moved to the general management side of the paper in 1960. In 1966, three years after Peter Kiewit Sons' Inc. bought The World-Herald, I was named president at the age of 42.

The World-Herald continued to be "the Newspaper of the Midlands," with circulation across Nebraska and into bordering states, especially western Iowa. But there were changes, including the addition, opposite the editorial page, of a full page of opinions other than those of The World-Herald.

Examples of changing to a more moderate editorial policy included our endorsement of a state corporate income tax (for years, we had opposed all proposals for state sales and income taxes) and our endorsement of then-Gov. Norbert Tiemann when he ran for re-election in 1970 after steering state sales and income tax proposals through the Legislature. (Tiemann lost.)

We continued our emphasis on conservation of natural resources, including a prophetic series of articles in 1980 that we pulled together and published in a pamphlet under the title "Water: Will it Last?"

Also prophetic was a series of stories published in 1984 after I had visited Latin America as a member of the Associated Press board of directors. What I learned about population growth resulted in sending reporters Jim Flanery and Paul Goodsell and photographer Phil Johnson to Latin America. This produced a series titled "The Population Bomb."

The bomb, which our stories said was ticking away, has, of course, exploded, contributing significantly to the estimated 12 million illegal Hispanic immigrants living in the United States today. "The Population Bomb" series reflected our increased emphasis on international news.

By far the biggest impact of anything that The World-Herald did on my 24-year watch resulted from our call in May 1974 for President Richard M. Nixon to resign. The editorial made national news.

Some readers were calling to cancel their subscriptions before they had read the editorial, having heard the news on television or on the radio. In his autobiography, Nixon mentioned our editorial along with one in the Chicago Tribune when he explained why he decided to resign rather than face impeachment.

> "By far the biggest impact of anything The World-Herald did on my 24-year watch resulted from our call in May 1974 for President Richard M. Nixon to resign."

* * *

I spoke earlier of an increased volume and variety of commentary after I became president. For example:

Some liberal columnist or other – I forget his name and his message – wrote what I considered a piece of utter nonsense. And I asked our then-editor, Woody Howe, why we published such drivel.

"We thought it was provocative," Woody replied. My response: "Well, you've achieved your purpose in my case. It provoked the hell out of me." But we continued to print commentary from time to time from the same columnist.

— May 21, 2006

Kiewit Worked Hard to Keep Paper Here

Today, more reminiscing, with some previously unrevealed but significant aspects regarding the lengths to which Peter Kiewit went to ensure that the ownership of his hometown newspaper would remain in his hometown and owned by Omahans rather than owned by a newspaper group headquartered in Chicago, Washington or wherever.

The result was to leave The World-Herald an employee-owned newspaper and one of the very few where ownership is concentrated in the city where the paper is published.

The story begins sometime before 1960, when some of the heirs of Gilbert M. Hitchcock, who founded the paper in 1885, began to disagree. By 1962, representatives of the majority shareholders were willing to sell the paper to the Newhouse newspaper group, headquartered in New York City. The story leaked to the Wall Street Journal, and a number of Omaha business and civic leaders, including Peter Kiewit, were concerned.

Hitchcock's widow, Martha, whom Hitchcock married after his first wife died, owned some 26 percent of the stock. She resisted and delayed the decision on the Newhouse offer.

The delay gave time for intervention by Peter Kiewit, who previously had not expressed interest in corporate ownership beyond Peter Kiewit Sons' Inc., which had become one of America's foremost construction companies under his leadership. A bid of $40.4 million was accepted by The World-Herald board on Oct. 30, 1962, and ownership passed to the Kiewit company on Dec. 31, 1962.

At a civic dinner held in his honor, Peter said, "It surely is wonderful to be honored for making what we hope is a sound investment for our company in Omaha."

But the primary motivation was clearly not monetary. Peter said later: "Having lived here all my life, it was natural for me to have pride in and loyalty to Omaha. It was this pride and loyalty which first prompted our interest. The World-Herald has always had a strong influence in the progress of the area, and the people of our company have always been proud of our strong, constructive hometown newspaper."

This part of the "Peter Kiewit as newspaper owner" story has been published before. But there are additional facts that indicate the lengths to which Peter Kiewit went to ensure continued local ownership of The World-Herald and, in the process, meet another important objective: leaving ownership of the Kiewit construction company in the hands of employee shareholders.

To ensure that ownership of The World-Herald would pass to his estate, Peter struck a deal with the Kiewit corporation: The corporation would sell its World-Herald stock to Peter's estate. In return, he would sell his controlling interest in the Kiewit corporation to the corporation.

There was no previous restriction on how Peter might have disposed of controlling interest in the Kiewit corporation. If he had sold it to outside interests, the return would have been a great deal more than book value – predictably well more than double the $179 million with which the Peter Kiewit Foundation started business in 1980. And if The World-Herald had been sold to a newspaper organization outside of Omaha, there would have been a handsome return in which Peter's estate would have shared.

Other ways in which Peter Kiewit ensured continued local ownership of The World-Herald: The Kiewit Foundation is to continue owning up to 20 percent of the voting stock. The paper cannot be sold without a majority vote of (1) voting stock held by the employees and (2) voting stock held by the foundation. The foundation trustees are instructed not to vote their class of stock in favor of selling the newspaper. The foundation must continue to own stock in The World-Herald and cannot be terminated so long as it holds such stock. This has the effect of continuing indefinitely the "not for sale" power of the foundation trustees.

Ground rules for World-Herald employee stock ownership are patterned closely on those of the Kiewit company: The stock is bought and sold at book value, and employees must sell the stock back to the corporation at the end of active employment. The result has been succeeding generations of World-Herald employees who have a direct share in the financial results to which their efforts contribute.

On various occasions, Peter Kiewit indicated his pleasure and pride in The World-Herald's performance. In remarks to a group of employee shareholders in 1975, he said: "It has been, and I hope will continue to be, one of the more pleasant experiences in my business career."

And in his instructions to his foundation trustees, he included a recommendation that part of his estate be used for scholarships for worthy students to pursue their education, "preferably along engineering and journalism lines."

— May 28, 2006

Kiewit Didn't Meddle in Paper's Coverage

Addendum to my recent Sunday columns reminiscing about my 60 years of association with The World-Herald:

In the 17 years that Peter Kiewit Sons' Inc. owned The World-Herald, I was frequently asked about my relationship with Peter Kiewit. A good many people assumed that a man who ran a construction company with a very firm hand surely must be playing a strong role in management of the newspaper that the construction company had purchased in order to keep the ownership in Omaha.

My reply was that Pete Kiewit didn't envision himself as a newspaper publisher directing management's operating decisions and editorial policies. He recognized that other people had more experience and more competency in newspaper publishing than he did.

I would quickly add that Pete could recognize what he considered effective – or ineffective – performance on the part of those in charge of operating the paper. In my 13 years of chief executive responsibility during the period of Kiewit ownership, I was keenly aware that I didn't have a no-cut contract.

I never called Pete Kiewit to ask him what we should do in the way of editorial decisions or any matters involving news coverage. Occasionally, in matters of special significance, I called to inform him what we were going to do. He never asserted an owner's prerogative to countermand our plans.

An example of giving Pete a "heads up" on a major decision was my call to tell him that we planned to call for then-President Richard M. Nixon's resignation. This was a call to a man who had contributed $100,000 to Nixon's re-election campaign – a fact that had been duly reported on the front page of The World-Herald.

I told Pete that I felt – and our editors agreed – Vice President Gerald Ford could do a better job than the embattled Nixon. "I think damn near anybody could" was Pete's response.

Pete took an active interest in the financial side of our operations, including my recommendations as to operating budgets, capital expenditures, price increases and charitable contributions. His attitude was that we should not hesitate to sacrifice short-term profits to ensure our long-term stature as a good-quality and profitable – and independent – newspaper.

My file of memoranda from the Kiewit years includes this item written after a World-Herald board of directors meeting on April 16, 1969: "Pete Kiewit told the board … that he is willing to spend more to improve the newspaper and build circulation – earnings should not be enhanced at the expense of our product and our circulation."

The best example I can recall of Pete's consistent policy of non-intervention in editorial policies or news coverage followed a complaint by some Kiewit construction company staff member or members that The World-Herald was giving too much attention to criticism from the late Edward Zorinsky (then a member of the Omaha Public Power District board and later mayor of Omaha and a U.S. senator) of the Kiewit company's performance in construction of the Fort Calhoun nuclear plant.

After Pete and I discussed the situation, I wrote this memorandum on June 19, 1969, quoting Pete: "You're running the newspaper. Do the same thing in this case as you would if Hawkins were the contractor."

* * *

Shortly after Pete Kiewit's death, world-renowned investment manager Warren Buffett commented on what Kiewit had accomplished by providing that his interest in the construction company and the newspaper be sold to employees, with the proceeds building the philanthropic resources of the Peter Kiewit Foundation.

Buffett, like Peter Kiewit, built a reputation that stretched far beyond Omaha without ever straying from his hometown roots. Buffett wrote of Kiewit's decision:

"In this manner, the residents of the Midlands and charitable entities elsewhere inherit the current financial worth of Kiewit's interests in his companies. The employees, with whom the responsibilities of the future lie, inherit the right to capitalize on that future. They have organizations with the momentum, tradition and business discipline that almost guarantee great success.

"Peter Kiewit could not have better served his community and his compatriots."

* * *

My son, Dave, a grade-schooler at the time, once asked veteran photographer John Savage what he did at The World-Herald. Savage replied: "I make your daddy look good."

If I looked good at any time during my 24 years in charge, due credit goes to the excellent staff members with whom I had the pleasure and privilege to work – and, of course, to Executive Editor Fred Ware and President and Editor Walter Christenson, who helped open the door to the opportunity that Pete Kiewit gave me.

I believe I can say I was perfectly willing to accept the downside from time to time as well as the more frequent upside of being in the corner office at World-Herald Square. I suppose it could be called one of the downsides, although I couldn't really hold it against our mail room when I found on my desk one morning an envelope addressed thus:

"Chief Idiot, Omaha World-Herald."

— June 11, 2006